BAHÁ'Í WORLD CONGRESS

BAHÁ'Í WORLD CONGRESS • CONGRÈS MONDIAL BAHÁ'Í

BAHÁ'Í WORLD CONGRESS

Second World Congress
Jacob Javitz Center, N.Y.C.
Nov. 1992
30000 Bahá'ís
from around the
World

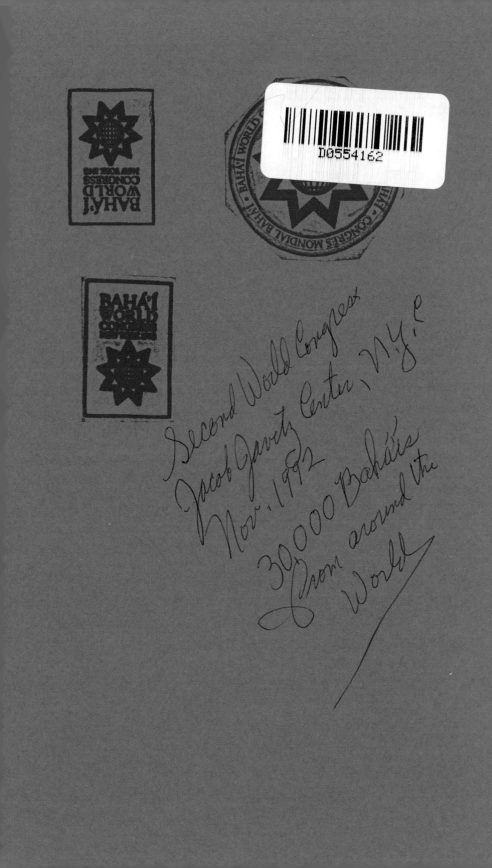

*Published for the Bahá'í World Congress
on the Occasion of the Centenary
of the Ascension of Bahá'u'lláh
and the Inauguration of His Covenant*

1992

Published for the Bahá'í World Congress
on the Occasion of the Centenary
of the Ascension of Bahá'u'lláh
and the Inauguration of His Covenant

1992

Call to Remembrance

Call to Remembrance

Connecting the Heart to Bahá'u'lláh

Compiled by
GEOFFRY W. MARKS

Bahá'í Publishing Trust
WILMETTE, ILLINOIS

Bahá'í Publishing Trust, Wilmette, Illinois 60091

Printed in the United States of America

Library of Congress Cataloging-in-Publication Data

Bahā' Allāh, 1817–1892.
Call to remembrance : connecting the heart to Bahá'u'lláh / compiled by Geoffry W. Marks.
p. cm.
Includes bibliographical references (p.).
ISBN 0-87743-236-8. — ISBN 0-87743-237-6 (pbk.)
1. Bahā' Allāh, 1817–1892. 2. Bahai Faith—Biography. I. Marks, Geoffry W., 1949– . II. Title.
BP392.A3 1992
297' .93'092—dc20 92-33638
CIP

Every receptive soul who hath in this Day
inhaled the fragrance of His garment
and hath, with a pure heart,
set his face towards the all-glorious Horizon
is reckoned among the people of Bahá
in the Crimson Book.
Grasp ye, in My Name,
the chalice of My loving-kindness,
drink then your fill in My glorious
and wondrous remembrance.

—*BAHÁ'U'LLÁH*

CONTENTS

PART 4 / UNFOLDING REVELATION

PREFACE

THE HOLY YEAR, 1992, dedicated to the commemoration of the centenary of the ascension of Bahá'u'lláh and the inauguration of His Covenant, is a time for reflection on the source and purpose of our being and for recommitment to the essentials of Bahá'í belief, a time for revitalizing one's dedication to the promotion of unity and the spiritualization of society.

Call to Remembrance has been prepared to help Bahá'ís in their personal observance of the Holy Year and to introduce the character of Bahá'u'lláh's life and ministry to others whose curiosity has been aroused. The book brings together passages from the wide range of Bahá'u'lláh's writings to relate in His own words many of the events of His life. Taken together, the extracts offer an intimate approach to the life of a figure Who, in the words of Shoghi Effendi, Bahá'u'lláh's great-grandson and Guardian of His Faith, towers forever above us, "preeminent in holiness, awesome in the majesty of His strength and power, unapproachable in the transcendent brightness of His glory."[1]

Call to Remembrance is organized around the four phases of Bahá'u'lláh's life enumerated by Shoghi Effendi. Part 1 concerns Bahá'u'lláh's childhood and youth, which spanned the years 1817 through 1844, a twenty-seven-year period "characterized by the carefree enjoyment of all the advantages con-

1. Shoghi Effendi, *God Passes By,* p. xiv.

ferred by high birth and riches, and by an unfailing solicitude for the interests of the poor, the sick, and the downtrodden."[2] Part 2, from 1844 to 1853, covers a period "of active and exemplary discipleship" in the service of His forerunner, the Báb.[3] Part 3 focuses on Bahá'u'lláh's four-month imprisonment during 1853 in the Síyáh Chál, the Black Pit of Ṭihrán—a period "overshadowed . . . by mortal peril, embittered by agonizing sorrows, and immortalized, as it drew to a close, by the sudden eruption of the forces released by an overpowering, soul-revolutionizing Revelation."[4] Part 4 reviews Bahá'u'lláh's thirty-nine year ministry from 1853 through 1892, during which His afflictions intensified as the orb of His revelation rose to its zenith. Here the devious plottings of jealous clergymen and corrupt officials, the acts of cowardice and betrayal committed by Bahá'u'lláh's half-brother Mírzá Yaḥyá, and the transgressions of well-meaning but misguided followers stand in vivid contrast to the courage, dignity, and uprightness that constantly characterized Bahá'u'lláh's conduct. Part 5 examines Bahá'u'lláh's provision for the extension into the future of divine authority over the affairs of His Faith and reviews the appointment of 'Abdu'l-Bahá as the Center of His Covenant and the events surrounding Bahá'u'lláh's ascension. Part 5 is followed by the Tablet of Visitation to be recited in remembrance of the Báb and Bahá'u'lláh.

The extracts from the writings of Bahá'u'lláh that make up *Call to Remembrance* are drawn from works of His or compilations of His works that have been translated and published in English, including *Epistle to the Son of the Wolf, Gleanings from the Writings of Bahá'u'lláh, The Kitáb-i-Íqán, Prayers and Medi-*

2. Shoghi Effendi, *God Passes By,* p. 107.
3. Shoghi Effendi, *God Passes By,* p. 107.
4. Shoghi Effendi, *God Passes By,* p. 107.

tations, The Proclamation of Bahá'u'lláh to the Kings and Leaders of the World, A Synopsis and Codification of the Kitáb-i-Aqdas, and *Tablets of Bahá'u'lláh revealed after the Kitáb-i-Aqdas.* Some extracts are taken from passages quoted by Shoghi Effendi in such works as *God Passes By, The Promised Day Is Come, Messages to America,* and *The World Order of Bahá'u'lláh.* A few passages of Bahá'u'lláh's writings are taken from H. M. Balyuzi's *Bahá'u'lláh: The King of Glory* and David S. Ruhe's *Door of Hope.* Oral accounts dictated by Bahá'u'lláh and recorded in *The Dawn-Breakers* by Nabíl-i-A'ẓam, Bahá'u'lláh's poet laureate and chronicler, are also included.

Because there is little from Bahá'u'lláh's own pen about His childhood and youth, accounts by 'Abdu'l-Bahá—Bahá'u'lláh's eldest son and Center of His Covenant—are taken from His *Traveler's Narrative* and from *The Promulgation of Universal Peace,* the record of talks He delivered during His visit to the United States in 1912. Accounts by 'Abdu'l-Bahá that are recorded in J. E. Esslemont's *Bahá'u'lláh and the New Era* are also included, as well as a few passages from the writings of Shoghi Effendi and of Nabíl-i-A'ẓam.

Where background information is needed to understand the context of the extracts or to clarify the chronology of events, brief explanatory passages have been added. In addition, a minimal number of footnotes have been added to clarify certain terms and supply other useful information. At the end of the book a glossary provides additional information, and a chronology gives dates of significant events in Bahá'u'lláh's life and shows when many of His major works were revealed.

Call to Remembrance is not a biography, nor is it a history. Rather, it offers a view of Bahá'u'lláh's life told mostly in His own words, a view that draws one closer to His will and purpose and leads to what the Universal House of Justice describes as that "rendezvous of the soul with the Source of its light and guidance," that "retreat to one's innermost being, to the dwelling-place of the Spirit of Bahá, that interior to which He summons us when He says: 'Turn thy sight unto thyself, that thou mayest find Me standing within thee, mighty, powerful, and self-subsisting.'"[5]

The compiler would like to express his gratitude to Dr. Betty J. Fisher, General Editor of the U.S. Bahá'í Publishing Trust, and to editorial assistants Terry J. Cassiday and Amy J. Neeb for their hard work and insightful recommendations.

Geoffry W. Marks

5. The Universal House of Justice, letter dated Riḍván 1992 to the Bahá'ís of the World, p. 6.

Call to Remembrance

Part 1/ NOBLE YOUTH

Chapter 1 / CHILDHOOD

On 12 November 1817 a child named Mírzá Ḥusayn-'Alí was born in Ṭihrán, the capital of Persia. His father was a nobleman and a favored minister of Fatḥ-'Alí Sháh; his mother was Khadíjih Khánum. His family's ancestral home was in the village of Tákur in the district of Núr (Light) in the northern province of Mázindarán, which lies along the shore of the Caspian Sea.

Though Mírzá Ḥusayn-'Alí received little formal education, He showed signs in childhood of innate knowledge and unusual nobility of character—signs that foreshadowed the divinely ordained role He would later assume as Bahá'u'lláh, the Glory of God. His revelation would shake Persia to its depths, revolutionize the fortunes of the world, and usher in a new and glorious age in human history.

THERE WAS BORN A CHILD in an ancient and noble family of Núr, whose father was Mírzá 'Abbás, better known as Mírzá Buzurg, a favoured minister of the Crown. That Child was Bahá'u'lláh. At the hour of dawn, on the second day of Muḥarram, in the year 1233 A.H., the world, unaware of its significance, witnessed the birth of Him who was destined to confer upon it such incalculable blessings.

—*NABÍL 1*

HE DERIVED HIS DESCENT, on the one hand, from Abraham (the Father of the Faithful) through his wife Katurah, and on the other from Zoroaster, as well as from Yazdigird, the last king of the Sásáníyán dynasty. He was moreover a descendant of Jesse, and belonged, through His father, Mírzá 'Abbás, better known as Mírzá Buzurg—a nobleman closely associated with the ministerial circles of the Court of Fatḥ-'Alí Sháh—to one of the most ancient and renowned families of Mázindarán.

—SHOGHI EFFENDI 2

WHEN BAHÁ'U'LLÁH WAS STILL A CHILD, the Vazír, His father, dreamed a dream. Bahá'u'lláh appeared to him swimming in a vast, limitless ocean. His body shone upon the waters with a radiance that illumined the sea. Around His head, which could distinctly be seen above the waters, there radiated, in all directions, His long, jet-black locks, floating in great profusion above the waves. As he dreamed, a multitude of fishes gathered round Him, each holding fast to the extremity of one hair. Fascinated by the effulgence of His face, they followed Him in whatever direction He swam. Great as was their number, and however firmly they clung to His locks, not one single hair seemed to have been detached from His head, nor did the least injury affect His person. Free and unrestrained, He moved above the waters and they all followed Him.

The Vazír, greatly impressed by this dream, summoned a soothsayer, who had achieved fame in that region, and asked him to interpret it for him.

This man, as if inspired by a premonition of the future glory of Bahá'u'lláh, declared: "The limitless ocean that you have seen in your dream, O Vazír, is none other than the world of being. Single-handed and alone, your son will achieve supreme ascendancy over it. Wherever He may please, He will proceed unhindered. No one will resist His march, no one will hinder His progress. The multitude of fishes signifies the turmoil which He will arouse amidst the peoples and kindreds of the earth. Around Him will they gather, and to Him will they cling. Assured of the unfailing protection of the Almighty, this tumult will never harm His person, nor will His loneliness upon the sea of life endanger His safety."

That soothsayer was subsequently taken to see Bahá'u'lláh. He looked intently upon His face, and examined carefully His features. He was charmed by His appearance, and extolled every trait of His countenance. Every expression in that face revealed to his eyes a sign of His concealed glory. So great was his admiration, and so profuse his praise of Bahá'u'lláh, that the Vazír, from that day, became even more passionately devoted to his son. The words spoken by that soothsayer served to fortify his hopes and confidence in Him. Like Jacob, he desired only to ensure the welfare of his beloved Joseph, and to surround Him with his loving protection.

—*NABÍL 3*

FROM CHILDHOOD HE WAS EXTREMELY KIND and generous. He was a great lover of outdoor life, most of His time being spent in the garden or the fields.

He had an extraordinary power of attraction, which was felt by all. People always crowded around Him. Ministers and people of the Court would surround Him, and the children also were devoted to Him. When He was only thirteen or fourteen years old He became renowned for His learning. He would converse on any subject and solve any problem presented to Him. In large gatherings He would discuss matters with the 'Ulamá (leading mullás) and would explain intricate religious questions. All of them used to listen to Him with the greatest interest.

—*'ABDU'L-BAHÁ* 4

Chapter 2 / YOUTH

In His youth Bahá'u'lláh's extraordinary abilities were widely recognized, and it was expected that He would succeed His father and rise to a position of prominence. His lack of interest in pursuing a career as a minister of the Sháh was the cause of much surprise and comment.

At seventeen Bahá'u'lláh married Ásíyih Khánum, described as remarkably intelligent, winsome, vivacious, and exceedingly beautiful. She was the younger sister of the husband of Bahá'u'lláh's older sister and, like Bahá'u'lláh, came from a noble and wealthy family. Her wedding treasures were so extensive that forty mules were needed to carry them to His home.

In the early years of their married life Bahá'u'lláh and Ásíyih Khánum devoted themselves to charitable activities. Their daughter, Bahíyyih Khánum, recounts that they "took part as little as possible in State functions, social ceremonies, and the luxurious habits of ordinary highly-placed and wealthy families in the land of Persia." They "counted these worldly pleasures meaningless, and preferred rather to occupy themselves in caring for the poor, and for all who were unhappy, or in trouble." Their acts of service earned them widespread renown as "The Father of the Poor" and "The Mother of Consolation."

About the time of Bahá'u'lláh's marriage, His father, Mírzá Buzurg, fell upon hard times. A year earlier, Fatḥ-'Alí Sháh had died and been succeeded by his grandson, Muḥammad Sháh. Muḥammad Sháh's prime minister, Ḥájí Mírzá Áqásí, was a vain and vengeful man whose later outrages against the Báb caused

Shoghi Effendi to denounce him as "the Antichrist of the Bábí Revelation." When Ḥájí Mírzá Áqásí learned that Mírzá Buzurg was horrified at the Ḥájí's role in murdering his predecessor, he retaliated by stripping Mírzá Buzurg of his governorships, cutting off his annual allowance, and engineering his divorce from Fatḥ-'Alí Sh̲áh's daughter, whom he had married a few years earlier. Thus, in addition to losing his income, Mírzá Buzurg faced a costly divorce settlement. When his ex-wife sent thugs who beat him daily in an effort to extract the money, he was forced to sell his complex of homes in Ṭihrán and many valuable furnishings hurriedly and at a very low price. A few years later he passed away. Despite Ḥájí Mírzá Áqásí's antagonism toward Mírzá Buzurg, he held Bahá'u'lláh in high regard, extended to Him every consideration, and spoke to Him as if He were his own son.

THERE WAS IN ṬIHRÁN . . . A YOUTH of the family of one of the ministers and of noble lineage, gifted in every way, and adorned with purity and nobility. Although He combined lofty lineage with high connection, and although His ancestors were men of note in Persia and universally sought after, yet He was not of a race of doctors or a family of scholars. Now this Youth was from His earliest adolescence celebrated amongst those of the ministerial class, both relatives and strangers, for single-mindedness, and was from childhood pointed out as remarkable for sagacity, and held in regard in the eyes of the wise. He did not, however, after the fashion of His ancestors, desire elevation to lofty ranks nor seek advancement to splendid but transient positions. His extreme aptitude was nevertheless admitted by all, and His excessive acuteness and intelligence were universally avowed. In the eyes of the common folk He enjoyed a wonderful esteem, and in all gatherings and assemblies He had a marvelous speech and delivery. Notwithstanding lack of instruction and education such was the keenness of His penetration and the readiness of His apprehension that when during His youthful prime He appeared in assemblies where questions of divinity and points of metaphysic were being discussed, and, in presence of a great concourse of doctors and scholars loosed his tongue, all those present were amazed, accounting this as a sort of prodigy beyond the discernment natural to the human race. From His early years He was the hope of His kindred and the unique one of His family and race, nay, their refuge and shelter.

—'ABDU'L-BAHÁ 1

WHEN BAHÁ'U'LLÁH WAS TWENTY-TWO years old, His father died, and the Government wished Him to succeed to His father's position in the Ministry, as was customary in Persia, but Bahá'u'lláh did not accept the offer. Then the Prime Minister said: "Leave him to himself. Such a position is unworthy of him. He has some higher aim in view. I cannot understand him, but I am convinced that he is destined for some lofty career. His thoughts are not like ours. Let him alone."

—'ABDU'L-BAHÁ 2

HE WAS MOST GENEROUS, giving abundantly to the poor. None who came to Him were turned away. The doors of His house were open to all. He always had many guests. This unbounded generosity was conducive to greater astonishment from the fact that He sought neither position nor prominence. In commenting upon this His friends said He would become impoverished, for His expenses were many and His wealth becoming more and more limited. "Why is he not thinking of his own affairs?" they inquired of each other; but some who were wise declared, "This personage is connected with another world; he has something sublime within him that is not evident now; the day is coming when it will be manifested." In truth, the Blessed Perfection was a refuge for every weak one, a shelter for every fearing one, kind to every indigent one, lenient and loving to all creatures.

—*'ABDU'L-BAHÁ* 3

Bahá'u'lláh's reputation as a young man of remarkable ability and the favors extended to Him by Ḥájí Mírzá Áqásí, the prime minister, made Him an object of the jealousy of ministers who feared the high position to which He was expected to rise. It also made inevitable a confrontation with the scheming prime minister, who could be expected sooner or later to seek Bahá'u'lláh's support for one of his intrigues. The uprightness of Bahá'u'lláh's dealings with the prime minister and His skill in handling the confrontation while remaining unscathed are indicative of His uncompromising adherence to principle and the divine protection that encircled Him.

ONE DAY, AS HE [ḤÁJÍ MÍRZÁ ÁQÁSÍ] was passing through the village of Qúch Ḥisár, which belonged to Bahá'u'lláh, he was so impressed by the charm and beauty of that place and the abundance of its water that he conceived the idea of becoming its owner.

Bahá'u'lláh, whom he had summoned to effect the immediate purchase of that village, observed: "Had this property been exclusively mine own, I would willingly have complied with your desire. This transitory life, with all its sordid possessions, is worthy of no attachment in my eyes, how much less this small and insignificant estate. As a number of other people, both rich and poor, some of full age and some still minors, share with me the ownership of this property, I would request you to refer this matter to them, and to seek their consent." Unsatisfied with this reply, Ḥájí Mírzá Áqásí sought, through fraudulent means, to achieve his purpose. So soon as Bahá'u'lláh was informed of his evil designs, He, with the consent of all concerned, immediately transferred the title of the property to the name of the sister of Muḥammad Sháh, who had already repeatedly expressed her desire to become its owner. The Ḥájí, furious at this transaction, ordered that the estate should be forcibly seized, claiming that he already had purchased it from its original possessor. The representatives of Ḥájí Mírzá Áqásí were severely rebuked by the agents of the sister of the Sháh, and were requested to inform their master of the determination of that lady to assert her rights. The Ḥájí referred the case to Muḥammad Sháh, and complained of the unjust treatment to which he had been subjected. That very night, the Sháh's sister had acquainted him with the nature of the transaction. "Many a time," she said to her brother, "your Imperial Majesty has graciously signified your desire that I should dispose of the jewels with which I am wont to adorn myself in your presence, and with the proceeds purchase some property. I have at last succeeded in fulfilling your desire. Ḥájí Mírzá Áqásí, however, is now fully determined to seize it forcibly from me." The Sháh reassured his sister, and commanded the Ḥájí to forgo his claim. The latter, in his despair, summoned Bahá'u'lláh to his presence and, by every artifice, strove to discredit His name. To the charges he brought against Him, Bahá'u'lláh vigorously replied, and succeeded in establishing His innocence. In his impotent rage, the Grand Vazír exclaimed: "What is the purpose of all this feasting and banqueting in which you seem to delight? I, who am the Prime Minister of the Sháhansháh of Persia, never receive the number and variety of guests that crowd around your table every night. Why all this extravagance and vanity? You surely must be meditating a plot against me." "Gracious God!" Bahá'u'lláh replied. "Is the man who, out of the abundance of his heart, shares his bread with his fellow-men, to be accused of harbouring criminal intentions?" Ḥájí Mírzá Áqásí was utterly confounded. He dared no reply. Though supported by the combined ecclesiastical and civil powers of Persia, he eventually found himself, in every contest he ventured against Bahá'u'lláh, completely defeated.

On a number of other occasions, Bahá'u'lláh's ascendancy over His opponents was likewise vindicated and recognised. These personal triumphs achieved by Him served to enhance His position, and spread abroad His fame. All classes of men marvelled at His miraculous success in emerging unscathed from the most perilous encounters. Nothing short of Divine protection, they thought, could have ensured His safety on such occasions. Not once did Bahá'u'lláh, beset though He was by the gravest perils, submit to the arrogance, the greed, and the treachery of those around Him. In His constant association, during those days, with the highest dignitaries of the realm, whether ecclesiastical or State officials, He was never content simply to accede to the views they expressed or the claims they advanced. He would, at their gatherings, fearlessly champion the cause of truth, would assert the rights of the downtrodden, defending the weak and protecting the innocent.

—NABÍL 4

Part 2/ DISCIPLESHIP

Chapter 3 / RECOGNITION OF THE BÁB'S PROPHETIC MISSION

In 1819, two years after Bahá'u'lláh was born, a child named Siyyid 'Alí-Muḥammad was born in the city of Shíráz in the southern province of Fárs. He was the son of a merchant who was descended through both parents from the Prophet Muḥammad, as the title Siyyid attests. As a child the dignity and serenity of His bearing and the fervor with which He performed His devotions distinguished Him from other boys, while His understanding and nobility of character so astonished His teacher that he took Him home one day and told His uncle that the boy was not in need of his instruction.

In 1844, when Bahá'u'lláh was twenty-six years old, Siyyid 'Alí-Muḥammad announced in Shíráz that He was the Báb, or Gate—the forerunner of the bearer of an even greater revelation, Whose advent was close at hand, by Whose will He moved, and in Whose path He longed to sacrifice His life. He also announced that He was the Qá'im—the Messenger of God promised in the Qur'án Who would usher in a new age of righteousness.

The person to whom the Báb first declared His mission on the evening of 22 May 1844 was Mullá Ḥusayn-i-Bushrú'í. He and the next seventeen disciples to seek out and find the Báb alone and unaided became known as Letters of the Living. The Báb sent them to various parts of Persia and Turkistán to raise the call of the new day. To Mullá Ḥusayn the Báb assigned the special mission of traveling to Ṭihrán, saying, "A secret lies hidden in that city. When made manifest, it shall turn the earth into paradise. My hope is that you may partake of its grace and recognise its splendour." The Báb assured Mullá Ḥusayn that the Mystery was of such transcendent holiness that neither Shíráz nor Ḥijáz, the home of Muḥammad, could hope to rival it.

When Mullá Ḥusayn reached Ṭihrán, he stayed at a seminary where he invited the director of the school to accept the Báb's claim. The director failed to respond to Mullá Ḥusayn's message, but a student, Mullá Muḥammad from Núr in the province of Mázindarán, became interested when he overheard their discussions. Mírzá Músá, Bahá'u'lláh's brother, related the following story, told to him by Mullá Muḥammad:

> *"Tell me," . . . enquired Mullá Ḥusayn, "is there to-day among the family of the late Mírzá Buzurg-i-Núrí, who was so renowned for his character, his charm, and artistic and intellectual attainments, anyone who has proved himself capable of maintaining the high traditions of that illustrious house?"*
>
> *"Yea," I replied, "among his sons now living, one has distinguished Himself by the very traits which characterised His father. By His virtuous life, His high attainments, His loving-kindness and liberality, He has proved Himself a noble descendant of a noble father."*
>
> *"What is His occupation?" he asked me.*
>
> *"He cheers the disconsolate and feeds the hungry," I replied.*
>
> *"What of His rank and position?"*
>
> *"He has none," I said, "apart from befriending the poor and the stranger."*
>
> *"What is His name?"*
>
> *"Ḥusayn-'Alí."*
>
> *"In which of the scripts of His father does He excel?"*
>
> *"His favourite script is shikastih-nasta'líq."*
>
> *"How does He spend His time?"*
>
> *"He roams the woods and delights in the beauties of the countryside."*
>
> *"What is His age?"*

"Eight and twenty."[1]

The eagerness with which Mullá Ḥusayn questioned me, and the sense of delight with which he welcomed every particular I gave him, greatly surprised me. Turning to me, with his face beaming with satisfaction and joy, he once more enquired: "I presume you often meet Him?"

"I frequently visit His home," I replied.

"Will you," he said, "deliver into His hands a trust from me?"

"Most assuredly," was my reply. He then gave me a scroll wrapped in a piece of cloth, and requested me to hand it to Him the next day at the hour of dawn.

"Should He deign to answer me," he added, "will you be kind enough to acquaint me with His reply?" I received the scroll from him and, at break of day, arose to carry out his desire.

As I approached the house of Bahá'u'lláh, I recognised His brother Mírzá Músá, who was standing at the gate, and to whom I communicated the object of my visit. He went into the house and soon reappeared bearing a message of welcome. I was ushered into His presence, and presented the scroll to Mírzá Músá, who laid it before Bahá'u'lláh. He bade us both be seated. Unfolding the scroll, He glanced at its contents and began to read aloud to us certain of its passages. I sat enraptured as I listened to the sound of His voice and the sweetness of its melody. He had read a page of the scroll when, turning to His brother, He said: "Músá, what have you to say? Verily I say, whoso believes in the Qur'án and recognises its Divine origin, and yet hesitates, though it be for a moment, to admit that these soul-stirring words are endowed with the same re-

1. According to the solar calendar, Bahá'u'lláh was twenty-six. The interview took place about three months after the Báb's declaration and about three months before Bahá'u'lláh's twenty-seventh birthday.

generating power, has most assuredly erred in his judgment and has strayed far from the path of justice." He spoke no more. Dismissing me from His presence, He charged me to take to Mullá Ḥusayn, as a gift from Him, a loaf of Russian sugar and a package of tea, and to convey to him the expression of His appreciation and love.[2]

I arose and, filled with joy, hastened back to Mullá Ḥusayn, and delivered to him the gift and message of Bahá'u'lláh. With what joy and exultation he received them from me! Words fail me to describe the intensity of his emotion. He started to his feet, received with bowed head the gift from my hand, and fervently kissed it. He then took me in his arms, kissed my eyes, and said: "My dearly beloved friend! I pray that even as you have rejoiced my heart, God may grant you eternal felicity and fill your heart with imperishable gladness."

I was amazed at the behaviour of Mullá Ḥusayn. What could be, I thought to myself, the nature of the bond that unites these two souls? What could have kindled so fervid a fellowship in their hearts? Why should Mullá Ḥusayn, in whose sight the pomp and circumstance of royalty were the merest trifle, have evinced such gladness at the sight of so inconsiderable a gift from the hands of Bahá'u'lláh? I was puzzled by this thought and could not unravel its mystery.

A few days later, Mullá Ḥusayn left for Khurásán. As he bade me farewell, he said: "Breathe not to anyone what you have heard and witnessed. Let this be a secret hidden within your breast. Divulge not His name, for they who envy His position will arise to harm Him. In your moments of meditation, pray that the Almighty may protect Him, that, through Him, He may exalt the downtrodden, enrich the poor, and redeem the fallen. The secret of things is concealed from our

2. Tea and this variety of sugar were extremely rare in Persia at the time and were often given as gifts among the higher classes of society.

eyes. Ours is the duty to raise the call of the New Day and to proclaim this Divine Message unto all people. Many a soul will, in this city, shed his blood in this path. That blood will water the Tree of God, will cause it to flourish, and to overshadow all mankind."[3]

He [Bahá'u'lláh] was in the heyday of His life when the call from Shíráz reached Him. At the age of twenty-seven, He arose to consecrate His life to its service, fearlessly identified Himself with its teachings, and distinguished Himself by the exemplary part He played in its diffusion. No effort was too great for the energy with which He was endowed, and no sacrifice too woful for the devotion with which His faith had inspired Him. He flung aside every consideration of fame, of wealth, and position, for the prosecution of the task He had set His heart to achieve. Neither the taunts of His friends nor the threats of His enemies could induce Him to cease championing a Cause which they alike regarded as that of an obscure and proscribed sect.[4]

—*NABÍL*

WE, VERILY, BELIEVE IN HIM WHO, in the person of the Báb, hath been sent down by the Will of the one true God, the King of Kings, the All-Praised. We, moreover, swear fealty to the One Who, in the time of Mustagháth,[5] is destined to be made manifest, as well as to those Who shall come after Him till the end that hath no end. We recognize in the manifestation of each one of them, whether

3. Mírzá Músá, quoted in *The Dawn-Breakers,* pp. 104–08.

4. *The Dawn-Breakers,* p. 376.

5. Literally, *He Who is Invoked for Help.* A term the Báb used to refer to the advent of the Promised One (Bahá'u'lláh).

outwardly or inwardly, the manifestation of none but God Himself, if ye be of those that comprehend. Every one of them is a mirror of God, reflecting naught else but His Self, His Beauty, His Might and Glory, if ye will understand. All else besides them are to be regarded as mirrors capable of reflecting the glory of these Manifestations Who are themselves the Primary Mirrors of the Divine Being, if ye be not devoid of understanding. No one hath ever escaped them, neither are they to be hindered from achieving their purpose. These Mirrors will everlastingly succeed each other, and will continue to reflect the light of the Ancient of Days. They that reflect their glory will, in like manner, continue to exist for evermore, for the Grace of God can never cease from flowing. This is a truth that none can disprove.

—BAHÁ'U'LLÁH 1

MAGNIFY THOU, O LORD MY GOD, Him Who is the Primal Point, the Divine Mystery, the Unseen Essence, the Day-Spring of Divinity, and the Manifestation of Thy Lordship, through Whom all the knowledge of the past and all the knowledge of the future were made plain, through Whom the pearls of Thy hidden wisdom were uncovered, and the mystery of Thy treasured name disclosed, Whom Thou hast appointed as the Announcer of the One through Whose name the letter B and the letter E have been joined and united, through Whom Thy majesty, Thy sovereignty and Thy might were made known, through Whom Thy words have been sent down, and Thy laws set forth with clearness, and

Thy signs spread abroad, and Thy Word established, through Whom the hearts of Thy chosen ones were laid bare, and all that were in the heavens and all that were on the earth were gathered together, Whom Thou hast called 'Alí-Muḥammad[6] in the kingdom of Thy names, and the Spirit of Spirits in the Tablets of Thine irrevocable decree, Whom Thou hast invested with Thine own title, unto Whose name all other names have, at Thy bidding and through the power of Thy might, been made to return, and in Whom Thou hast caused all Thine attributes and titles to attain their final consummation. To Him also belong such names as lay hid within Thy stainless tabernacles, in Thine invisible world and Thy sanctified cities.

Magnify Thou, moreover, such as have believed in Him and in His signs and have turned towards Him, from among those that have acknowledged Thy unity in His Latter Manifestation—a Manifestation whereof He hath made mention in His Tablets, and in His Books, and in His Scriptures, and in all the wondrous verses and gem-like utterances that have descended upon Him. It is this same Manifestation Whose covenant Thou hast bidden Him establish ere He had established His own covenant. He it is Whose praise the Bayán hath celebrated. In it His excellence hath been extolled, and His truth established, and His sovereignty proclaimed, and His Cause perfected. Blessed is the

6. The given name of the Báb.

man that hath turned unto Him, and fulfilled the things He hath commanded, O Thou Who art the Lord of the worlds and the Desire of all them that have known Thee!

Praised be Thou, O my God, inasmuch as Thou hast aided us to recognize and love Him. I, therefore, beseech Thee by Him and by Them Who are the Day-Springs of Thy Divinity, and the Manifestations of Thy Lordship, and the Treasuries of Thy Revelation, and the Depositories of Thine inspiration, to enable us to serve and obey Him, and to empower us to become the helpers of His Cause and the dispersers of His adversaries. Powerful art Thou to do all that pleaseth Thee. No God is there beside Thee, the Almighty, the All-Glorious, the One Whose help is sought by all men!

—BAHÁ'U'LLÁH 2

DO THOU BLESS, O LORD MY GOD, the Primal Point, through Whom the point of creation hath been made to revolve in both the visible and invisible worlds, Whom Thou hast designated as the One whereunto should return whatsoever must return unto Thee, and as the Revealer of whatsoever may be manifested by Thee. Do Thou also bless such of His Letters as have not turned away from Thee, who have been firmly established in Thy love, and clung steadfastly to Thy good-pleasure. Bless Thou, likewise, as long as Thine own Self endureth and Thine own Essence doth last, them that have suffered martyrdom in Thy path. Thou art, verily, the Ever-Forgiving, the Most Merciful.

Moreover, I beseech Thee, O my God, by Him Whom Thou hast announced unto us in all Thy Tablets and Thy Books and Thy Scrolls and Thy Scriptures, through Whom the kingdom of names hath been convulsed, and all that lay hid in the breasts of them that have followed their evil and corrupt desires hath been revealed,—I beseech Thee to strengthen us in our love for Him, to make us steadfast in His Cause, to help us befriend His loved ones and challenge His enemies. Shield us, then, O my God, from the mischief wrought by them that have denied Thy presence, and turned away from Thy face, and resolved to put an end to the life of Him Who is the Manifestation of Thine own Self.

—BAHÁ'U'LLÁH 3

Chapter 4 / IN THE SERVICE OF THE CAUSE OF THE BÁB

When the Báb received a letter from Mullá Ḥusayn reporting that His trust had been successfully delivered to Bahá'u'lláh, He undertook a pilgrimage to Mecca with Quddús, the eighteenth and most eminent Letter of the Living. While in Mecca, the Báb performed the usual rites of pilgrimage and then, in front of a great crowd of pilgrims, grasped the ring on the door to the Ka'bih and called aloud three times: "I am that Qá'im whose advent you have been awaiting." As the Báb's voice rang out, a sudden hush settled over the teeming crowd of pilgrims, the vast majority of whom failed to grasp the significance of His words.

Meanwhile, the Báb's disciples were busy spreading the news of His advent throughout Persia. The tumult raised by their activities led the governor of Fárs to send a squadron of soldiers to the seaport of Bushihr to arrest the Báb upon His return to Persia and bring Him to Shíráz, where He was severely rebuked in the governor's presence and violently struck in the face. Released on parole, the Báb spent a few months under house arrest in the home of an uncle. It was during this time that He granted three interviews to an emissary of the Sháh, Siyyid Yaḥyáy'-i-Dárábí, who had been sent to investigate the Báb's claims. As a result of his meetings with the Báb, Siyyid Yaḥyá (later given the name Vaḥíd) was wholeheartedly won over to His Cause.

The Báb's teachings threw Shíráz into a frenzy. The conversion of Vaḥíd, other prominent priests, and increasing numbers of people throughout the country provoked deep anxiety among the clergy, and in September 1846 the Báb was sent from Shíráz to

Iṣfahán, where He enjoyed several months of relative calm. But as increasing numbers of people in Iṣfahán, including the governor, gave the Báb their allegiance, Ḥájí Mírzá Áqásí, the prime minister, began to fear that an interview which the governor sought to arrange between the Báb and Muḥammad Sh͟áh would draw the Sh͟áh under the Báb's spell. Blocking the Sh͟áh's order that the Báb be brought to Ṭihrán, Ḥájí Mírzá Áqásí arranged for the Báb to be sent to the castle of Máh-Kú in the remote and mountainous region of Ád͟hirbáyján, where He arrived in July 1847. The strict terms of His confinement were soon relaxed as the warden and the people surrounding the castle became mesmerized by the Báb's loving influence, and Bábí pilgrims, including Mullá Ḥusayn, made their way to see Him. Learning of these developments, Ḥájí Mírzá Áqásí transferred the Báb in April 1848 to the fortress of C͟hihríq, where He remained until shortly before His execution on 9 July 1850 in Tabríz.

Ṭáhirih and the Conference of Badas͟ht

Shortly after the Báb's arrival at the prison-fortress of C͟hihríq, He sent a letter to all the Bábís of Persia, summoning them to K͟hurásán. Ṭáhirih, one of the Letters of the Living and the most outstanding woman of the Bábí Dispensation, was on her way to K͟hurásán from Baghdád when she was met by a delegation her father had sent to persuade her to delay her trip and visit her family in Qazvín. She reluctantly agreed and stayed in her father's home, refusing to be reunited with her husband, an arrogant and devious clergyman.

Ṭáhirih's father-in-law and uncle, Ḥájí Mullá Taqí, was a prominent member of the Muslim clergy who bitterly opposed the Faith of the Báb. Angered by Ṭáhirih's convictions and her refusal to reconcile with his son, he escalated his attacks from the pulpit on the Báb and the Báb's heralds, S͟hayk͟h Aḥmad and Siyyid

Káẓim. An admirer of Shaykh Aḥmad and Siyyid Káẓim became incensed at Ḥájí Mullá Taqí's venomous sermons and stabbed him to death in the mosque.

Although the Bábís of Qazvín were innocent of any involvement in the murder, three were arrested and summarily executed. Bahá'u'lláh, Who had given financial assistance to the wrongly accused Bábís, was arrested and imprisoned briefly in Ṭihrán after Ḥájí Mullá Taqí's family falsely accused Him of complicity in the murder. Ṭáhirih was put under house arrest but, as a result of Bahá'u'lláh's intervention, was freed. She joined her fellow believers in Khurásán in the hamlet of Badasht in June 1848. There, in gardens rented by Bahá'u'lláh, a conference was held to implement the Báb's revelation by making a sudden and dramatic break with Islám. A secondary purpose of the conference, which from the beginning was destined to fail, was to devise a plan to free the Báb from captivity.

Ṭáhirih was the instrument through which the break with Islamic laws and customs would be made. Bahá'u'lláh, Who corresponded continually with the Báb and was the guiding hand behind the activities of the Bábís, quietly but effectively presided over and controlled the conference proceedings. Each day He revealed a Tablet that was chanted before the assembled gathering, and on each believer who was present He bestowed a new name without making known the source from which the names came. He Himself became known by the title Bahá (Glory).

Ṭáhirih, who previously had been known by the title Qurratu'l-'Ayn (Solace of the Eyes), and who was regarded as the quintessence of chastity and the incarnation of Fáṭimih (Muḥammad's daughter), stunned the participants by appearing before them unveiled. The violation of so central a code of Islamic conduct threw the conference into disarray. One man was so horrified that he cut his throat, while others renounced their faith. Standing her ground, Ṭáhirih eloquently proclaimed the inauguration of a new Dispensation and invited her fellow believers to celebrate so momentous an occasion.

Despite the furor Ṭáhirih caused, the primary purpose of the conference was fully realized, and from that point onward the independent character of the Báb's revelation was asserted.

We were celebrating, in the company of a number of distinguished notables, the nuptials of one of the princes of royal blood in Ṭihrán, when Siyyid Aḥmad-i-Yazdí, father of Siyyid Ḥusayn, the Báb's amanuensis, appeared suddenly at the door. He beckoned to Us, and seemed to be the bearer of an important message which he wished immediately to deliver. We were, however, unable at that moment to leave the gathering, and motioned to him to wait. When the meeting had dispersed, he informed Us that Ṭáhirih had been placed in strict confinement in Qazvín, and that her life was in great danger. We immediately summoned Muḥammad-Hádiy-i-Farhádí, and gave him the necessary directions to release her from her captivity, and escort her to the capital. As the enemy had seized Our house, We were unable to accommodate her indefinitely in Our home. Accordingly, We arranged for her transference from Our house to that of the Minister of War,[1] who, in those days, had been disgraced by his sovereign and had been deported to Káshán. We requested his sister, who still was numbered among Our friends, to act as hostess to Ṭáhirih.

She remained in her company until the call of the Báb, bidding Us to proceed to Khurásán, reached

1. Mírzá Áqá Khán-i-Núrí, a distant relative of Bahá'u'lláh who later became Grand Vazír (prime minister) under Náṣiri'd-Dín Sháh.

Our ears. We decided that Ṭáhirih should proceed immediately to that province, and commissioned Mírzá[2] to conduct her to a place outside the gate of the city, and from thence to any locality he deemed advisable in that neighbourhood. She was taken to an orchard in the vicinity of which was a deserted building, where they found an old man who acted as its caretaker. Mírzá Músá returned and informed Us of the reception which had been accorded to them, and highly praised the beauty of the surrounding landscape. We subsequently arranged for her departure for Khurásán, and promised that We would follow within the space of a few days.

We soon joined her at Badasht, where We rented a garden for her use, and appointed the same Muḥammad-Hádí who had achieved her deliverance, as her doorkeeper. About seventy of Our companions were with Us and lodged in a place in the vicinity of that garden.

We fell ill one day, and were confined to bed. Ṭáhirih sent a request to call upon Us. We were surprised at her message, and were at a loss as to what We should reply. Suddenly We saw her at the door, her face unveiled before Us. How well has Mírzá Áqá Ján[3] commented upon that incident. "The face of Fáṭimih," he said, "must needs be revealed on the Day of Judgment and appear unveiled before the eyes of men. At that moment the

2. Mírzá Músá, also known as Áqáy-i-Kalím, a faithful younger brother of Bahá'u'lláh who accompanied Him in His exiles.

3. Bahá'u'lláh's amanuensis.

voice of the Unseen shall be heard saying: 'Turn your eyes away from that which ye have seen.'"

How great was the consternation that seized the companions on that day! Fear and bewilderment filled their hearts. A few, unable to tolerate that which was to them so revolting a departure from the established customs of Islám, fled in horror from before her face. Dismayed, they sought refuge in a deserted castle in that neighbourhood. Among those who were scandalised by her behaviour and severed from her entirely were the Siyyid-i-Nahrí and his brother Mírzá Hádí, to both of whom We sent word that it was unnecessary for them to desert their companions and seek refuge in a castle.

Our friends eventually dispersed, leaving Us at the mercy of Our enemies.

. . . .

At the time We purposed to send Muḥammad-Hádiy-i-Farhádí to Qazvín, in order to achieve the deliverance of Ṭáhirih and conduct her to Ṭihrán, Shaykh Abú-Turáb wrote Us, insisting that such an attempt was fraught with grave risks and might occasion an unprecedented tumult. We refused to be deflected from Our purpose. That Shaykh was a kind-hearted man, was simple and lowly in temper, and behaved with great dignity. He lacked courage and determination, however, and betrayed weakness on certain occasions.

—BAHÁ'U'LLÁH 1

The Incident at Níyálá

Following the conference of Badasht, Bahá'u'lláh, Ṭáhirih, and Quddús decided to go to Mázindarán. On their way they passed through the village of Níyálá, where they encountered more than five hundred hostile villagers whose opposition had been aroused by the excesses committed by a few of the Bábís who had attended the conference of Badasht. Misinterpreting Ṭáhirih's act of discarding her veil as a license for self-indulgence, these Bábís had abused the liberty that the Báb's abrogation of Islamic law had conferred upon them. Although, as Nabíl says, their conduct "provoked the wrath of the Almighty and caused their immediate dispersion," it had unfortunate consequences for Bahá'u'lláh and His companions.

WE WERE ALL GATHERED IN THE VILLAGE of Níyálá and were resting at the foot of a mountain, when, at the hour of dawn, we were suddenly awakened by the stones which the people of the neighbourhood were hurling upon us from the top of the mountain. The fierceness of their attack induced our companions to flee in terror and consternation. I clothed Quddús in my own garments and despatched him to a place of safety, where I intended to join him. When I arrived, I found that he had gone. None of our companions had remained in Níyálá except Ṭáhirih and a young man from Shíráz, Mírzá 'Abdu'lláh. The violence with which we were assailed had brought desolation into our camp. I found no one into whose custody I could deliver Ṭáhirih except that young man, who displayed on that occasion a courage and determination that were truly surprising. Sword in hand, undaunted by the savage assault of the inhabitants of the village, who had rushed to plunder our property, he sprang forward to stay the hand of the assailants. Though himself wounded in several parts of his body, he risked his life to protect our property. I bade him desist from his act. When the tumult had subsided, I approached a number of the inhabitants of the village and was able to convince them of the cruelty and shamefulness of their behaviour. I subsequently succeeded in restoring a part of our plundered property.

—*BAHÁ'U'LLÁH 2*

Arrest, Detention, and Bastinado in Ámul

After the incident at Níyálá, Bahá'u'lláh continued His journey to Núr, where He stayed for the remainder of the summer and early fall of 1848. Ṭáhirih was detained under house arrest in Ṭihrán, where she remained until August 1852, when she was martyred, while Quddús had been arrested and imprisoned in Sárí. Amidst these happenings, Muḥammad Sháh had issued an edict for Bahá'u'lláh's arrest and had expressed his intention of executing Him. However, the Sháh's death shortly thereafter, on 4 September 1848, nullified the edict.

Meanwhile, in Khurásán a messenger of the Báb delivered to Mullá Ḥusayn the Báb's green turban (a symbol of His descent from the Prophet Muḥammad) and a Tablet bidding him to hasten to Mázindarán to aid Quddús. As he marched to Mázindarán, more than three hundred Bábís joined him. Encountering opposition in Bárfurúsh, the home of Quddús, the Bábís hastily built a fortress about fourteen miles away around the mausoleum of a Muslim saint named Shaykh Ṭabarsí to protect themselves from the onslaught of the clergy, who had inflamed the anti-Bábí sentiments of the local populace. Hearing of these developments while in Núr, Bahá'u'lláh decided to visit the Bábís at Ṭabarsí, where He provided them with a sumptuous dinner and approved the arrangements they had made. Observing that the one thing that was missing was the presence of Quddús, Bahá'u'lláh directed one of the Bábís to go with six men to Sárí and demand the release of Quddús. The leading cleric of Sárí complied with the demand, and Quddús joined the Bábís at Ṭabarsí. Bahá'u'lláh left for His home in Ṭihrán, promising to return with provisions. On the return trip in December 1848 Bahá'u'lláh and His companions—who included His younger half-brother Mírzá Yaḥyá—were arrested outside the village of Ámul by guards who had been ordered to prevent anyone from joining the Bábís at the fort.

The guards escorted Bahá'u'lláh and His companions to Ámul, where the acting governor, having been notified of the Bábís' approach, had asked the clergy to assemble at the mosque. When he recognized Bahá'u'lláh, he was filled with regret at having summoned the clergy and tried to appease them by feigning to reprimand Bahá'u'lláh. The clergy then put questions to Bahá'u'lláh. His masterful answers so inflamed their bigoted animosity that they demanded the captives' immediate execution. The acting governor sought to defuse the situation by ordering that the captives be punished with the bastinado (a form of torture that involves being beaten on the soles of the feet with a rod) and by promising to keep the Bábís in custody until the governor returned. However, Bahá'u'lláh intervened, requesting that He be punished in the place of His companions. The acting governor reluctantly agreed. Five months earlier, the Báb had suffered the same treatment after being brought from the prison-fortress of Chihríq to Tabríz for interrogation by the clergy before the crown prince, heir to the throne, one of several instances in which the tribulations suffered by Bahá'u'lláh were preceded by similar tribulations suffered by the Báb.

God knows that at no time did We attempt to conceal Ourself or hide the Cause which We have been bidden to proclaim. Though not wearing the garb of the people of learning, We have again and again faced and reasoned with men of great scholarship in both Núr and Mázindarán, and have succeeded in persuading them of the truth of this Revelation. We never flinched in Our determination; We never hesitated to accept the challenge from whatever direction it came. To whomsoever We spoke in those days, We found him receptive to our Call and ready to identify himself with its precepts. But for the shameful behaviour of the people of the Bayán,[4] who sullied by their deeds the work We had accomplished, Núr and Mázindarán would have been entirely won to this Cause and would have been accounted by this time among its leading strongholds.

At a time when the forces of Prince Mihdí-Qulí Mírzá had besieged the fort of Ṭabarsí, We resolved to depart from Núr and lend Our assistance to its heroic defenders. We had intended to send 'Abdu'l-Vahháb, one of Our companions, in advance of Us, and to request him to announce Our approach to the besieged. Though encompassed by the forces of the enemy, We had decided to throw in Our lot with those steadfast companions, and to risk the dangers with which they were confronted. This, however, was not to be. The hand of Omnipotence spared Us from their fate and preserved Us for the work We were

4. The followers of the Báb.

destined to accomplish. In pursuance of God's inscrutable wisdom, the intention We had formed was, before Our arrival at the fort, communicated by certain inhabitants of Núr to Mírzá Taqí, the [acting] governor of Ámul, who sent his men to intercept Us. While We were resting and taking Our tea, We found Ourselves suddenly surrounded by a number of horsemen, who seized Our belongings and captured Our steeds. We were given, in exchange for Our own horse, a poorly saddled animal which We found it extremely uncomfortable to ride. The rest of Our companions were conducted, handcuffed, to Ámul.

—BAHÁ'U'LLÁH 3

THAT WHICH HATH TOUCHED this Wronged One is beyond compare or equal. We have borne it all with the utmost willingness and resignation, so that the souls of men may be edified, and the Word of God be exalted. While confined in the prison of the Land of Mím [Mázindarán] We were one day delivered into the hands of the divines. Thou canst well imagine what befell Us.

—BAHÁ'U'LLÁH 4

WHEN . . . WE WENT TO ÁMUL, such was the turmoil which the people had raised that above four thousand persons had congregated in the masjid[5] and had crowded onto the roofs of their houses. The leading mullá of the town denounced Us bitterly.

5. Mosque.

"You have perverted the Faith of Islám," he cried in his Mázindaráni dialect, "and sullied its fame! Last night I saw you in a dream enter the masjid, which was thronged by an eager multitude that had gathered to witness your arrival. As the crowd pressed round you, I beheld, and, lo, the Qá'im[6] was standing in a corner with His gaze fixed upon your countenance, His features betraying great surprise. This dream I regard as evidence of your having deviated from the path of Truth." We assured him that the expression of surprise on that countenance was a sign of the Qá'im's strong disapproval of the treatment he and his fellow-townsmen had accorded Us. He questioned Us regarding the Mission of the Báb. We informed him that, although We had never met Him face to face, yet We cherished, none the less, a great affection for Him. We expressed Our profound conviction that He had, under no circumstances, acted contrary to the Faith of Islám.

The mullá and his followers, however, refused to believe Us, and rejected Our testimony as a perversion of the truth. They eventually placed Us in confinement, and forbade Our friends to meet Us. The acting governor of Ámul succeeded in effecting Our release from captivity. Through an opening in the wall that he ordered his men to make, he enabled Us to leave that room, and conducted Us to

---

6. He who shall arise; the Twelfth Imám, or Mihdí, awaited by Shí'ah Muslims and expected to inaugurate a new era of righteousness in the world. The Báb declared Himself to be the Qá'im and the Gate to another divine Messenger, "Him Whom God shall make manifest."

his house. No sooner were the inhabitants informed of this act than they arose against Us, besieged the governor's residence, pelted Us with stones, and hurled in Our face the foulest invectives.

—*BAHÁ'U'LLÁH 5*

MÍRZÁ TAQÍ SUCCEEDED, in spite of the tumult Our arrival had raised, and in the face of the opposition of the 'ulamás, in releasing Us from their grasp and in conducting Us to his own house. He extended to Us the warmest hospitality. Occasionally he yielded to the pressure which the 'ulamás were continuously bringing to bear upon him, and felt himself powerless to defeat their attempts to harm Us.[7] We were still in his house when the Sardár,[8] who had joined the army in Mázindarán, returned to Ámul. No sooner was he informed of the indignities We had suffered than he rebuked Mírzá Taqí for the weakness he had shown in protecting Us from Our enemies. "Of what importance," he indignantly demanded, "are the denunciations of this ignorant people? Why is it that you have allowed yourself to be swayed by their clamour? You should have been satisfied with preventing the party from reaching their destination and, instead of detaining them in this house, you should have arranged for their safe and immediate return to Ṭihrán."

—*BAHÁ'U'LLÁH 6*

7. A reference to being bastinadoed.
8. Military commander.

NO PRISONER HAS EVER BEEN accorded the treatment which I received at the hands of the acting governor of Ámul. He treated Me with the utmost consideration and esteem. I was generously entertained by him, and the fullest attention was given to everything that affected My security and comfort. I was, however, unable to leave the gate of the house. My host was afraid lest the governor, who was related to 'Abbás-Qulí Khán-i-Láríjání,[9] might return from the fort of Ṭabarsí and inflict injury upon Me. I tried to dispel his apprehensions. "The same Omnipotence," I assured him, "who has delivered us from the hands of the mischief-makers of Ámul, and has enabled us to be received with such hospitality by you in this house, is able to change the heart of the governor and to cause him to treat us with no less consideration and love."

One night we were suddenly awakened by the clamour of the people who had gathered outside the gate of the house. The door was opened, and it was announced that the governor had returned to Ámul. Our companions, who were anticipating a fresh attack upon them, were completely surprised to hear the voice of the governor rebuking those who had denounced us so bitterly on the day of our arrival. "For what reason," we heard him loudly remonstrating, "have these miserable wretches chosen to treat so disrespectfully a guest whose

9. A prominent military commander who led troops in battle against the Bábís gathered at Shaykh Ṭabarsí.

> hands are tied and who has not been given the chance to defend himself? What is their justification for having demanded that he be immediately put to death? What evidence have they with which to support their contention? If they be sincere in their claims to be devotedly attached to Islám and to be the guardians of its interests, let them betake themselves to the fort of Shaykh Ṭabarsí and there demonstrate their capacity to defend the Faith of which they profess to be the champions."
>
> —*BAHÁ'U'LLÁH* 7

The Martyrdom of the Báb

Having been prevented from joining the Bábís at the fort of Shaykh Ṭabarsí, Bahá'u'lláh returned to Ṭihrán, where His home became a center of Bábí activity. Among those to receive His hospitality were Ṭáhirih, Vaḥíd, and Nabíl.

At Shaykh Ṭabarsí the 313 Bábís who had gathered there withstood for eight months with extraordinary heroism the attacks of the royal army, whose numbers had swelled to twelve thousand. Devoid of food, the Bábís resorted to eating grass, the leather of their belts and shoes, and the skin and ground bones of their horses. Under mounting pressure from the newly enthroned Náṣiri'd-Dín Sháh to defeat the Bábís, the commander of the army in May 1849 proposed a truce, swearing on the Qur'án that the Bábís would be allowed to return to their homes in safety. Although aware of his treacherous intent, the Bábís laid down their arms, came out of the fort, and were massacred.

The humiliation the Sháh's army had suffered in its inability to defeat the Bábís swiftly and without deceit at Shaykh Ṭabarsí inflamed the animosity that the Sháh's prime minister, Mírzá Táqí

Khán, held for the Báb and His followers. Throughout the country the venomous attacks of the government and clergy plunged the Bábís into a maelstrom of persecution in which thousands perished. In February 1850 seven Bábís were publicly executed in Ṭihrán after refusing to recant their faith. Shortly thereafter about seventy Bábís in Nayríz, under the leadership of Vaḥíd, and eighteen hundred Bábís in Zanján under Ḥujjat, an eminent priest who had become one of the Báb's leading followers, sought protection by banding together in forts. After bloody and protracted battles, they, too, were slaughtered. Further shaken and alarmed by these events, the prime minister resolved to destroy the Bábí Cause completely and ordered that the Báb be brought from the prison-fortress of Chihríq to Tabríz for execution.

Forty days before the officer bearing the order summoning the Báb to Tabríz arrived in Chihríq, the Báb, aware of His impending death, placed His documents, seals, and rings in a coffer and dispatched them in the care of a trusted disciple to Bahá'u'lláh in Ṭihrán. Among the documents was a Tablet of about five hundred verses, all of which were derivatives of the word Bahá,[10] *recorded on a scroll of blue paper in the form of a pentacle in the Báb's exquisite handwriting.*

On 9 July 1850 the Báb was suspended by a rope fixed to a nail on the wall of the barracks square of Tabríz and shot by a firing squad of 750 soldiers. His execution brought to an end, Shoghi Effendi says, "the tumultuous and tragic ministry of One Whose age inaugurated the consummation of all ages, and Whose Revelation fulfilled the promise of all Revelations."

AND NOW CONSIDER how this Sadrih of the Riḍván of God hath, in the prime of youth, risen to proclaim

10. *Bahá* means glory, splendor, or light and is the root of the title Bahá'u'lláh, which means the Glory of God.

the Cause of God.[11] Behold what steadfastness that Beauty of God hath revealed. The whole world rose to hinder Him, yet it utterly failed. The more severe the persecution they inflicted on that Sadrih of Blessedness, the more His fervour increased, and the brighter burned the flame of His love. All this is evident, and none disputeth its truth. Finally, He surrendered His soul, and winged His flight unto the realms above.

—BAHÁ'U'LLÁH 8

AGES ROLLED AWAY, until they attained their consummation in this, the Lord of days, the Day whereon the Day Star of the Bayán manifested itself above the horizon of mercy, the Day in which the Beauty of the All-Glorious shone forth in the exalted person of 'Alí-Muḥammad, the Báb. No sooner did He reveal Himself, than all the people rose up against Him. By some He was denounced as one that hath uttered slanders against God, the Almighty, the Ancient of Days. Others regarded Him as a man smitten with madness, an allegation which I, Myself, have heard from the lips of one of the divines. Still others disputed His claim to be the Mouthpiece of God, and stigmatized Him as one who had stolen and used as his the words of the Almighty, who had perverted their meaning, and mingled them with his own. The Eye of Grandeur weepeth sore for the things which their mouths have uttered, while they

---

11. "Sadrih" means "Tree," and "Riḍván," "Paradise"—a reference to the Báb.

continue to rejoice upon their seats.

"God," said He, "is My witness, O people! I am come to you with a Revelation from the Lord, your God, the Lord of your fathers of old. Look not, O people, at the things ye possess. Look rather at the things God hath sent down unto you. This, surely, will be better for you than the whole of creation, could ye but perceive it. Repeat the gaze, O people, and consider the testimony of God and His proof which are in your possession, and compare them unto the Revelation sent down unto you in this Day, that the truth, the infallible truth, may be indubitably manifested unto you. Follow not, O people, the steps of the Evil One; follow ye the Faith of the All-Merciful, and be ye of them that truly believe. What would it profit man, if he were to fail to recognize the Revelation of God? Nothing whatever. To this Mine own Self, the Omnipotent, the Omniscient, the All-Wise, will testify."

The more He exhorted them, the fiercer grew their enmity, till, at the last, they put Him to death with shameful cruelty. The curse of God be upon the oppressors!

—BAHÁ'U'LLÁH 9

REFLECT, O SHAYKH, upon the Shí'ih sect.[12] How many the edifices which they reared with the hands of idle fancies and vain imaginings, and how

---

12. Shaykh Muḥammad Taqíy-i-Najafí, a Shí'ah divine of Iṣfahán to whom Bahá'u'lláh addressed *Epistle to the Son of the Wolf.* Both father and son were bitter opponents of the Bábí and Bahá'í Faiths.

numerous the cities which they built! At length those vain imaginings were converted into bullets and aimed at Him Who is the Prince of the world. Not one single soul among the leaders of that sect acknowledged Him in the Day of His Revelation! Whenever His blessed name was mentioned, all would say: "May God hasten the joy His coming will bring!" On the day of the Revelation of that Sun of Truth, however, all, as hath been observed, have exclaimed, saying: "May God hasten His chastisement!" He Who was the Essence of being and Lord of the seen and unseen they suspended, and committed what made the Tablet to weep, and the Pen to groan, and the cries of the sincere to break forth, and the tears of the favored ones to flow.

—BAHÁ'U'LLÁH 10

Tributes to the Bábí Martyrs

The systematic campaign waged against the Báb and His followers by the civil and religious authorities of Persia had succeeded in depriving the newborn Faith of its chief protagonists and had culminated in the execution of the Báb Himself. These tragic events were followed in the ensuing years by the extermination of more than ten thousand Bábís, including virtually all of the Báb's leading supporters, with the exception of One Who, through the mysterious workings of Providence, had been spared the fate of His fellow believers and Who would at a later date arise to redeem the Cause for which they had sacrificed their lives. In numerous Tablets Bahá'u'lláh extols the heroism of the Bábí martyrs, whose blood watered the seeds of His Administrative Order, which in the fullness of time will overshadow all humankind.

Among the evidences of the truth of His manifestation were the ascendancy, the transcendent power, and supremacy which He, the Revealer of being and Manifestation of the Adored, hath, unaided and alone, revealed throughout the world. No sooner had that eternal Beauty revealed Himself in Shíráz, in the year sixty,[13] and rent asunder the veil of concealment, than the signs of the ascendancy, the might, the sovereignty, and power, emanating from that Essence of Essences and Sea of Seas, were manifest in every land. So much so, that from every city there appeared the signs, the evidences, the tokens, the testimonies of that divine Luminary. How many were those pure and kindly hearts which faithfully reflected the light of that eternal Sun, and how manifold the emanations of knowledge from that Ocean of divine wisdom which encompassed all beings! In every city, all the divines and dignitaries rose to hinder and repress them, and girded up the loins of malice, of envy, and tyranny for their suppression. How great the number of those holy souls, those essences of justice, who, accused of tyranny, were put to death! And how many embodiments of purity, who showed forth naught but true knowledge and stainless deeds, suffered an agonizing death! Notwithstanding all this, each of these holy beings, up to his last moment, breathed the Name of God, and soared in the realm of submission and resignation. Such was the potency

13. 1844.

and transmuting influence which He exercised over them, that they ceased to cherish any desire but His will, and wedded their soul to His remembrance.

Reflect: Who in this world is able to manifest such transcendent power, such pervading influence? All these stainless hearts and sanctified souls have, with absolute resignation, responded to the summons of His decree. Instead of complaining, they rendered thanks unto God, and amidst the darkness of their anguish they revealed naught but radiant acquiescence to His will. It is evident how relentless was the hate, and how bitter the malice and enmity entertained by all the peoples of the earth towards these companions. The persecution and pain they inflicted on these holy and spiritual beings were regarded by them as means unto salvation, prosperity, and everlasting success. Hath the world, since the days of Adam, witnessed such tumult, such violent commotion? Notwithstanding all the torture they suffered, and manifold the afflictions they endured, they became the object of universal opprobrium and execration. Methinks, patience was revealed only by virtue of their fortitude, and faithfulness itself was begotten only by their deeds.

Do thou ponder these momentous happenings in thy heart, so that thou mayest apprehend the greatness of this Revelation, and perceive its stupendous glory.

—BAHÁ'U'LLÁH 11

IN THIS MOST RESPLENDENT DISPENSATION . . . this most mighty Sovereignty, a number of illumined divines, of men of consummate learning, of doctors of mature wisdom, have attained unto His Court, drunk the cup of His divine Presence, and been invested with the honour of His most excellent favour. They have renounced, for the sake of the Beloved, the world and all that is therein. We will mention the names of some of them, that perchance it may strengthen the faint-hearted, and encourage the timorous.

Among them was Mullá Ḥusayn, who became the recipient of the effulgent glory of the Sun of divine Revelation. But for him, God would not have been established upon the seat of His mercy, nor ascended the throne of eternal glory. Among them also was Siyyid Yaḥyá,[14] that unique and peerless figure of his age,

Mullá Muḥammad 'Alíy-i-Zanjání[15]
Mullá 'Alíy-i-Bastámí
Mullá Sa'íd-i-Bárfurúshí
Mullá Ni'matu'llah-i-Mázindarání
Mullá Yúsuf-i-Ardibílí
Mullá Mihdíy-i-Khu'í
Siyyid Ḥusayn-i-Turshízí
Mullá Mihdíy-i-Kandí
Mullá Báqir
Mullá 'Abdu'l-Kháliq-i-Yazdí
Mullá 'Alíy-i-Baraqání

14. Vaḥíd.
15. Ḥujjat.

and others, well nigh four hundred in number, whose names are all inscribed upon the "Guarded Tablet" of God.

All these were guided by the light of that Sun of divine Revelation, confessed and acknowledged His truth. Such was their faith, that most of them renounced their substance and kindred, and cleaved to the good-pleasure of the All-Glorious. They laid down their lives for their Well-Beloved, and surrendered their all in His path. Their breasts were made targets for the darts of the enemy, and their heads adorned the spears of the infidel. No land remained which did not drink the blood of these embodiments of detachment, and no sword that did not bruise their necks. Their deeds, alone, testify to the truth of their words. Doth not the testimony of these holy souls, who have so gloriously risen to offer up their lives for their Beloved that the whole world marvelled at the manner of their sacrifice, suffice the people of this day?

—BAHÁ'U'LLÁH 12

THE MIND IS BEWILDERED AT THEIR DEEDS, and the soul marvelleth at their fortitude and bodily endurance. . . .

Were not the happenings of the life of the "Prince of Martyrs"[16] regarded as the greatest of all events, as the supreme evidence of his truth? Did not

---

16. Imám Ḥusayn, the third Imám of Shí'ah Islám, who was martyred on the plain of Karbilá in 680 A.D. He was the grandson of Muḥammad and the son of His daughter Fáṭimih and her husband 'Alí, who was the first Imám and, the Shí'ahs believe, Muḥammad's rightful successor.

the people of old declare those happenings to be unprecedented? Did they not maintain that no manifestation of truth hath ever evinced such constancy, such conspicuous glory? And yet, that episode of his life, commencing as it did in the morning, was brought to a close by the middle of the same day, whereas, these holy lights have, for eighteen years, heroically endured the showers of afflictions which, from every side, have rained upon them. With what love, what devotion, what exultation and holy rapture, they sacrificed their lives in the path of the All-Glorious! To the truth of this all witness. And yet, how can they belittle this Revelation? Hath any age witnessed such momentous happenings? If these companions be not the true strivers after God, who else could be called by this name? Have these companions been seekers after power or glory? Have they ever yearned for riches? Have they cherished any desire except the good-pleasure of God? If these companions, with all their marvellous testimonies and wondrous works, be false, who then is worthy to claim for himself the truth? I swear by God! Their very deeds are a sufficient testimony, and an irrefutable proof unto all the peoples of the earth, were men to ponder in their hearts the mysteries of divine Revelation.

—*BAHÁ'U'LLÁH 13*

The death of the Báb brought to an end the first, the bloodiest, and the most turbulent stage of the Heroic Age of the Bahá'í Dispensation. It also ushered in a new phase in the life of Bahá'u'lláh.

As a disciple of the Báb, Bahá'u'lláh had been imprisoned in Ṭihrán for assisting the Bábís held captive in Qazvín and had freed Ṭáhirih from detention and vigilantly protected her. At Badas͟ht He had steered the course of the conference and had wisely handled the volatile situation Ṭáhirih's impetuosity created. At the fort of S͟hayk͟h Ṭabarsí He had counseled and supported the Bábís and engineered Quddús's release from captivity as well as his arrival at the fort. In Ámul, where the clergy had clamored for the death of His companions, Bahá'u'lláh had magnanimously offered Himself as a substitute and endured the bastinado. These acts, Nabíl says, "are but a few instances that eloquently testify to the unique position which He occupied as the prime Mover of the forces which were destined to reshape the face of His native land. It was He who had released these forces, who steered their course, harmonised their action, and brought them finally to their highest consummation in the Cause He Himself was destined at a later time to reveal."

Part 3 / PROMISED DAWN

Chapter 5 / ṬIHRÁN

Arrest and Imprisonment

Shortly after the execution of the Báb, Mírzá Taqí Khán, the prime minister, sought a meeting with Bahá'u'lláh. The prime minister opened the interview by asserting that, were it not for Bahá'u'lláh's support and assistance, the Bábís at Fort Shaykh Ṭabarsí would not have been able to resist the imperial government's forces for so long. As convinced as he was of Bahá'u'lláh's complicity, he admitted he had no evidence. Mírzá Taqí Khán expressed his regret that the government should be deprived of the services of such a resourceful person as Bahá'u'lláh and declared his intention of securing from the Sháh Bahá'u'lláh's appointment as Head of the Court (Amír-i-Díván) upon the Sháh's return from a journey to Iṣfahán. The prime minister also diplomatically suggested that it would be timely for Bahá'u'lláh to leave the capital for a while. Bahá'u'lláh courteously refused to accept the position but advised Mírzá Taqí Khán of His desire to visit the holy cities of Karbilá and Najaf in 'Iráq. A few days later Bahá'u'lláh left for Karbilá, arriving on 28 August 1851. While there, Shoghi Effendi says, He was engaged in "spreading, with that same enthusiasm and ability that had distinguished His earlier exertions in Mázindarán, the teachings of His departed Leader, in safeguarding the interests of His Faith, in reviving the zeal of its grief-stricken followers, and in organizing the forces of its scattered and bewildered adherents."

While Bahá'u'lláh was in Karbilá, the young Náṣiri'd-Dín Shah, jealous and fearful of Mírzá Taqí Khán's rising power, dismissed him and ordered his execution. The new prime minister, Mírzá Áqá Khán-i-Núrí, whose cousin had married an elder brother of Bahá'u'lláh, hoped to effect a reconciliation between the government and Bahá'u'lláh, Whom he recognized as the most capable of the Báb's followers. Thus he wrote to Bahá'u'lláh, asking Him to return to Ṭihrán. However, Bahá'u'lláh had already decided to return of His own accord.

Shortly after Bahá'u'lláh's arrival in Ṭihrán, three Bábí youths, obsessed by the tragedy of the Báb's martyrdom and driven by their despair to avenge His death, attempted to assassinate the Sháh on 15 August 1852. The event engulfed the Bábí community in what Shoghi Effendi terms "a fresh calamity, unprecedented in its gravity, disgraceful in its character, and devastating in its immediate consequences."

At the time, Bahá'u'lláh was staying in Afchih, outside of Ṭihrán, as the prime minister's guest. Mírzá Áqá Khán sent word of the storm about to break and referred to the venomous attacks on Bahá'u'lláh made by the Sháh's mother, who accused Bahá'u'lláh of being the chief instigator of the plot to murder her son. Friends offered to hide Him until the danger passed, but Bahá'u'lláh refused and rode the next day with calm and confidence toward the imperial army's headquarters. News of His movements was conveyed to the Sháh, who, greatly amazed at Bahá'u'lláh's action, ordered His immediate arrest. Bahá'u'lláh was taken to the notorious Síyáh-Chál, the "Black Pit" of Ṭihrán, a subterranean dungeon in which He was imprisoned for four months. Along the way He was stoned, ridiculed, and stripped of His outer garments.

IN ṬIHRÁN WE WERE TWICE IMPRISONED as a result of Our having risen to defend the cause of the innocent against a ruthless oppressor. The first confinement to which We were subjected followed the slaying of

Mullá Taqíy-i-Qazvíní,[1] and was occasioned by the assistance We were moved to extend to those upon whom a severe punishment had been undeservedly inflicted. Our second imprisonment, infinitely more severe, was precipitated by the attempt which irresponsible followers of the Faith made on the life of the Sháh.

—*BAHÁ'U'LLÁH 1*

AT THE TIME WHEN HIS MAJESTY the Sháh, may God, his Lord, the Most Merciful, aid him through His strengthening grace, was planning a journey to Iṣfahán, this Wronged One, having obtained his permission, visited the holy and luminous resting-places of the Imáms, may the blessings of God be upon them! Upon Our return, We proceeded to Lavásán on account of the excessive heat prevailing in the capital. Following Our departure, there occurred the attempt upon the life of His Majesty, may God, exalted and glorified be He, assist him. Those days were troublous days, and the fires of hatred burned high. Many were arrested, among them this Wronged One. By the righteousness of God! We were in no wise connected with that evil deed, and Our innocence was indisputably established by the tribunals. Nevertheless, they apprehended Us, and from Níyávarán, which was then the residence of His Majesty, conducted Us, on

1. Ṭáhirih's uncle and father-in-law. He was also known as Ḥájí Mullá Taqí.

foot and in chains, with bared head and bare feet, to the dungeon of Ṭihrán. A brutal man, accompanying Us on horseback, snatched off Our hat, whilst We were being hurried along by a troop of executioners and officials. We were consigned for four months to a place foul beyond comparison. As to the dungeon in which this Wronged One and others similarly wronged were confined, a dark and narrow pit were preferable. Upon Our arrival We were first conducted along a pitch-black corridor, from whence We descended three steep flights of stairs to the place of confinement assigned to Us. The dungeon was wrapped in thick darkness, and Our fellow-prisoners numbered nearly a hundred and fifty souls: thieves, assassins and highwaymen. Though crowded, it had no other outlet than the passage by which We entered. No pen can depict that place, nor any tongue describe its loathsome smell. Most of these men had neither clothes nor bedding to lie on. God alone knoweth what befell Us in that most foul-smelling and gloomy place!

Day and night, while confined in that dungeon, We meditated upon the deeds, the condition, and the conduct of the Bábís, wondering what could have led a people so high-minded, so noble, and of such intelligence, to perpetrate such an audacious and outrageous act against the person of His Majesty. This Wronged One, thereupon, decided to arise, after His release from prison, and undertake, with the utmost vigor, the task of regenerating this people.

—BAHÁ'U'LLÁH 2

O SHAYKH![2] . . . SHOULDST THOU at some time happen to visit the dungeon of His Majesty the Sháh, ask the director and chief jailer to show thee those two chains, one of which is known as Qará-Guhar, and the other as Salásil.[3] I swear by the Day-Star of Justice that for four months this Wronged One was tormented and chained by one or the other of them. "My grief exceedeth all the woes to which Jacob gave vent, and all the afflictions of Job are but a part of My sorrows!"

—BAHÁ'U'LLÁH 3

ALL THIS GENERATION COULD OFFER US were wounds from its darts, and the only cup it proffered to Our lips was the cup of its venom. On our neck We still bear the scar of chains, and upon Our body are imprinted the evidences of an unyielding cruelty.

—BAHÁ'U'LLÁH 4

Events in the Síyáh-Chál

ALL THOSE WHO WERE STRUCK DOWN by the storm that raged during that memorable year in Ṭihrán were Our fellow-prisoners in the Síyáh-Chál, where We

---

2. Shaykh Muḥammad Taqíy-i-Najafí, a Shí'ah divine of Iṣfahán and bitter opponent of the Bábí and Bahá'í Faiths.

3. One of the two chains was placed around Bahá'u'lláh's neck at all times. They cut into His flesh and were so heavy that they had to be supported by a special wooden fork. The heaviest, Qará-Guhar, weighed 112 pounds (51 kilograms).

were confined. We were all huddled together in one cell, our feet in stocks, and around our necks fastened the most galling of chains. The air we breathed was laden with the foulest impurities, while the floor on which we sat was covered with filth and infested with vermin. No ray of light was allowed to penetrate that pestilential dungeon or to warm its icy-coldness. We were placed in two rows, each facing the other. We had taught them to repeat certain verses which, every night, they chanted with extreme fervour. "God is sufficient unto me; He verily is the All-sufficing!" one row would intone, while the other would reply: "In Him let the trusting trust." The chorus of these gladsome voices would continue to peal out until the early hours of the morning. Their reverberation would fill the dungeon, and, piercing its massive walls, would reach the ears of Náṣiri'd-Dín Sh̲áh, whose palace was not far distant from the place where we were imprisoned. "What means this sound?" he was reported to have exclaimed. "It is the anthem the Bábís are intoning in their prison," they replied. The Sh̲áh made no further remarks, nor did he attempt to restrain the enthusiasm his prisoners, despite the horrors of their confinement, continued to display.

One day, there was brought to Our prison a tray of roasted meat, which they informed Us the Sh̲áh had ordered to be distributed among the prisoners. "The Sh̲áh," We were told, "faithful to a vow he made, has chosen this day to offer to you all this lamb in fulfilment of his pledge." A deep silence fell upon Our companions, who expected Us to make answer on their behalf. "We return this gift to you," We replied; "we can well dispense with this offer." The answer We made would have greatly irritated the guards had they not been eager to devour the food we had refused to touch. Despite the hunger with which Our companions were afflicted, only one among them, a certain Mírzá Ḥusayn-i-Mutavallíy-i-Qumí, showed any desire to eat of the food the sovereign had chosen to spread before us. With a fortitude that was truly heroic, Our fellow-prisoners submitted, without a murmur, to endure the piteous plight to which they were reduced. Praise of God, instead of complaint of the treatment meted out to them by the Sháh, fell unceasingly from their lips—praise with which they sought to beguile the hardships of a cruel captivity.

Every day Our gaolers, entering Our cell, would call the name of one of Our companions, bidding him arise and follow them to the foot of the gallows. With what eagerness would the owner of that name respond to that solemn call! Relieved of his chains, he would spring to his feet and, in a state of uncontrollable delight, would approach and embrace Us. We would seek to comfort him with the assurance of an everlasting life in the world beyond, and, filling his heart with hope and joy, would send him forth to win the crown of glory. He would embrace, in turn, the rest of his fellow-prisoners and then proceed to die as dauntlessly as he had lived. Soon after the martyrdom of each of these companions, We would be informed by the executioner, who had grown to be friendly to Us, of the circumstances of the death of his victim, and of the joy with which he had endured his sufferings to the very end.

We were awakened one night, ere break of day, by Mírzá 'Abdu'l-Vahháb-i-Shírází, who was bound with Us to the same chains. He had left Káẓimayn and followed Us to Ṭihrán, where he was arrested and thrown into prison. He asked Us whether We were awake, and proceeded to relate to Us his dream. "I have this night," he said, "been soaring into a space of infinite vastness and beauty. I seemed to be uplifted on wings that carried me wherever I desired to go. A feeling of rapturous delight filled my soul. I flew in the midst of that immensity with a swiftness and ease that I cannot describe." "To-day," We replied, "it will be your turn to sacrifice yourself for this Cause. May you remain firm and steadfast to the end. You will then find yourself soaring in that same limitless space of which you dreamed, traversing with the same ease and swiftness the realm of immortal sovereignty, and gazing with that same rapture upon the Infinite Horizon."

That morning saw the gaoler again enter Our cell and call out the name of 'Abdu'l-Vahháb. Throwing off his chains, he sprang to his feet, embraced each of his fellow-prisoners, and, taking Us into his arms, pressed Us lovingly to his heart. That moment We discovered that he had no shoes to wear. We gave him Our own, and, speaking a last word of encouragement and cheer, sent him forth to the scene of his martyrdom. Later on, his executioner came to Us, praising in glowing language the spirit which that youth had shown. How thankful We

were to God for this testimony which the
executioner himself had given!

—*BAHÁ'U'LLÁH 5*

The Intimation

A Revelation, hailed as the promise and crowning glory of past ages and centuries, as the consummation of all the Dispensations within the Adamic Cycle, inaugurating an era of at least a thousand years' duration, and a cycle destined to last no less than five thousand centuries, signalizing the end of the Prophetic Era and the beginning of the Era of Fulfillment, unsurpassed alike in the duration of its Author's ministry and the fecundity and splendor of His mission—such a Revelation was . . . born amidst the darkness of a subterranean dungeon in Ṭihrán—an abominable pit that had once served as a reservoir of water for one of the public baths of the city. Wrapped in its stygian gloom, breathing its fetid air, numbed by its humid and icy atmosphere, His feet in stocks, His neck weighed down by a mighty chain, surrounded by criminals and miscreants of the worst order, oppressed by the consciousness of the terrible blot that had stained the fair name of His beloved Faith, painfully aware of the dire distress that had overtaken its champions, and of the grave dangers that faced the remnant of its followers—at so critical an hour and under such appalling circumstances the "Most Great Spirit," *as designated by Himself, and symbolized in the Zoroastrian, the Mosaic, the Christian, and Muḥammadan Dispensations by the Sacred Fire, the Burning Bush, the Dove and the Angel Gabriel respectively, descended upon, and revealed itself, personated by a* "Maiden," *to the agonized soul of Bahá'u'lláh.*[4]

—*SHOGHI EFFENDI*

4. *God Passes By,* pp. 100–01.

DURING THE DAYS I LAY IN THE PRISON of Ṭihrán, though the galling weight of the chains and the stench-filled air allowed Me but little sleep, still in those infrequent moments of slumber I felt as if something flowed from the crown of My head over My breast, even as a mighty torrent that precipitateth itself upon the earth from the summit of a lofty mountain. Every limb of My body would, as a result, be set afire. At such moments My tongue recited what no man could bear to hear.

—BAHÁ'U'LLÁH 6

WHILE ENGULFED IN TRIBULATIONS I heard a most wondrous, a most sweet voice, calling above My head. Turning My face, I beheld a Maiden—the embodiment of the remembrance of the name of My Lord—suspended in the air before Me. So rejoiced was she in her very soul that her countenance shone with the ornament of the good-pleasure of God, and her cheeks glowed with the brightness of the All-Merciful. Betwixt earth and heaven she was raising a call which captivated the hearts and minds of men. She was imparting to both My inward and outer being tidings which rejoiced My soul, and the souls of God's honored servants. Pointing with her finger unto My head, she addressed all who are in heaven and all who are on earth, saying: "By God! This is the Best-Beloved of the worlds, and yet ye comprehend not. This is the Beauty of God amongst you, and the power of His sovereignty within you, could ye but understand. This is the Mystery of God and His Treasure, the

Cause of God and His glory unto all who are in the kingdoms of Revelation and of creation, if ye be of them that perceive."

—BAHÁ'U'LLÁH 7

ONE NIGHT, IN A DREAM, these exalted words were heard on every side: "Verily, We shall render Thee victorious by Thyself and by Thy Pen. Grieve Thou not for that which hath befallen Thee, neither be Thou afraid, for Thou art in safety. Erelong will God raise up the treasures of the earth—men who will aid Thee through Thyself and through Thy Name, wherewith God hath revived the hearts of such as have recognized Him."

—BAHÁ'U'LLÁH 8

I WAS BUT A MAN LIKE OTHERS, asleep upon My couch, when lo, the breezes of the All-Glorious were wafted over Me, and taught Me the knowledge of all that hath been. This thing is not from Me, but from One Who is Almighty and All-Knowing. And He bade Me lift up My voice between earth and heaven, and for this there befell Me what hath caused the tears of every man of understanding to flow. The learning current amongst men I studied not; their schools I entered not. Ask of the city wherein I dwelt, that thou mayest be well assured that I am not of them who speak falsely. This is but a leaf which the winds of the will of thy Lord, the Almighty, the All-Praised, have stirred. Can it be still when the tempestuous winds are blowing? Nay, by Him Who is the Lord of all Names and Attributes! They move it as they list. The evanescent is as nothing before

Him Who is the Ever-Abiding. His all-compelling summons hath reached Me, and caused Me to speak His praise amidst all people. I was indeed as one dead when His behest was uttered. The hand of the will of thy Lord, the Compassionate, the Merciful, transformed Me.

—BAHÁ'U'LLÁH 9

THE DAY STAR OF ETERNAL GUIDANCE beareth me witness: Had it been in my power, I would have, under no circumstances, consented to distinguish myself amongst men, for the Name I bear utterly disdaineth to associate itself with this generation whose tongues are sullied and whose hearts are false. And whenever I chose to hold my peace and be still, lo, the voice of the Holy Ghost, standing on my right hand, aroused me, and the Supreme Spirit appeared before my face, and Gabriel overshadowed me, and the Spirit of Glory stirred within my bosom, bidding me arise and break my silence. If your hearing be purged and your ears be attentive, ye will assuredly perceive that every limb of my body, nay all the atoms of my being, proclaim and bear witness to this call: "God, besides Whom is none other God, and He, Whose beauty is now manifest, is the reflection of His glory unto all that are in heaven and on earth."

—BAHÁ'U'LLÁH 10

THAT SO BRIEF A SPAN should have separated this most mighty and wondrous Revelation from Mine own previous Manifestation, is a secret that no man can unravel and a mystery such as no mind can fathom. Its duration had been foreordained, and no man shall ever discover its reason unless and until he be informed of the contents of My Hidden Book.

—BAHÁ'U'LLÁH 11

Prayer from the Síyáh-Chál

MY GOD, MY MASTER, MY HIGHEST HOPE, and the Goal of my desire! Thou seest and hearest the sighing of this wronged One, from this darksome well which the vain imaginations of Thine adversaries have built, and from this blind pit which the idle fancies of the wicked among Thy creatures have digged. By Thy Beauty, O Thou Whose glory is uncovered to the face of men! I am not impatient in the troubles that touch me in my love for Thee, neither in the adversities which I suffer in Thy path. Nay, I have, by Thy power, chosen them for mine own self, and I glory in them amongst such of Thy creatures as enjoy near access to Thee, and those of Thy servants that are wholly devoted to Thy Self.

I beseech Thee, however, O Thou Who art the Enlightener of the world and the Lord of the nations, at this very moment when, with the hands of hope, I have clung to the hem of the raiment of Thy mercy and Thy bounty, to forgive Thy servants who have soared in the atmosphere of Thy nearness, and set their faces towards the splendors of the light of Thy countenance, and turned unto the horizon of Thy good pleasure, and approached the ocean of Thy mercy, and all their lives long have spoken forth Thy praise, and have been inflamed with the fire of their love for Thee. Do Thou ordain for them, O Lord my God, both before and after their death, what becometh the loftiness of Thy bounty and the excellence of Thy loving-kindness.

—BAHÁ'U'LLÁH 12

Prayers and Meditations of Praise and Gratitude

PRAISED BE THOU, O MY GOD! How can I thank Thee for having singled me out and chosen me above all Thy servants to reveal Thee, at a time when all had turned away from Thy beauty! I testify, O my God, that if I were given a thousand lives by Thee, and offered them up all in Thy path, I would still have failed to repay the least of the gifts which, by Thy grace, Thou hast bestowed upon me.

I lay asleep on the bed of self when lo, Thou didst waken me with the divine accents of Thy voice, and didst unveil to me Thy beauty, and didst enable me to listen to Thine utterances, and to recognize Thy Self, and to speak forth Thy praise, and to extol Thy virtues, and to be steadfast in Thy love. Finally I fell a captive into the hands of the wayward among Thy servants.

. . . .

I entreat Thee, O Thou Who art the Ruler of the kingdoms of creation and the Author of all names, to write down my name with the names of them who, from eternity, have circled round the Tabernacle of Thy majesty, and clung to the hem of Thy loving-kindness, and held fast the cord of Thy tender mercy.

Thou art, in truth, the Help in Peril, the Self-Subsisting.

—BAHÁ'U'LLÁH 13

GLORIFIED ART THOU, O LORD MY GOD! Look Thou upon this wronged one, who hath been sorely afflicted by the oppressors among Thy creatures and the infidels among Thine enemies, though he himself hath refused to breathe a single breath but by Thy leave and at Thy bidding. I lay asleep on my couch, O my God, when lo, the gentle winds of Thy grace and Thy loving-kindness passed over me, and wakened me through the power of Thy sovereignty and Thy gifts, and bade me arise before Thy servants, and speak forth Thy praise, and glorify Thy word. Thereupon most of Thy people reviled me. I swear by Thy glory, O my God! I never thought that they would show forth such deeds, aware as I am that Thou hast Thyself announced this Revelation unto them in the Scrolls of Thy commandment and the Tablets of Thy decree, and hast covenanted with them concerning this youth in every word sent down by Thee unto Thy creatures and Thy people.

I am bewildered, therefore, O my God, and know not how to act toward them. Every time I hold my peace, and cease to extol Thy wondrous virtues, Thy Spirit impelleth me to cry out before all who are in Thy heaven and on Thy earth; and every time I am still, the breaths wafted from the right hand of Thy will and purpose pass over me, and stir me up, and I find myself to be as a leaf which lieth at the mercy of the winds of Thy decree, and is carried away whithersoever Thou dost permit or command it. Every man of insight who considereth what hath been revealed by me, will be persuaded that Thy Cause is not in my hands, but in Thy hands, and will recognize that the reins of power are held not in my grasp but in Thy grasp, and are subject to Thy sovereign might. And yet, Thou seest, O my God, how the inhabitants of Thy realm have arrayed themselves against me, and inflict upon me every moment of my life what causeth the realities of Thy chosen ones and trusted ones to tremble.

I entreat Thee, therefore, O my God, by Thy Name through which Thou hast guided Thy lovers to the living waters of Thy grace and Thy favors, and attracted them that long for Thee to the Paradise of Thy nearness and Thy presence, to open the eyes of Thy people that they may recognize in this Revelation the manifestation of Thy transcendent unity, and the dawning of the lights of Thy countenance and Thy beauty. Cleanse them, then, O my God, from all idle fancies and vain imaginations, that they may inhale the fragrances of sanctity from the robe of Thy Revelation and Thy commandment, that haply they may cease to inflict upon me what will deprive their souls of the fragrances of the manifold tokens of Thy mercy, that are wafted in the days of Him Who is the Manifestation of Thyself, and the Day-Spring of

Thy Cause, and that they may not perpetrate what will call down Thy wrath and anger.

—BAHÁ'U'LLÁH 14

EVER SINCE THE DAY THOU DIDST create me at Thy bidding, O my God, and didst arouse me through the gentle winds of Thy tender mercies, I have refused to turn to any one except Thee, and have, through the power of Thy sovereignty and Thy might, arisen to face Thine enemies, and have summoned all mankind unto the shores of the ocean of Thy oneness and the heaven of Thine all-glorious unity. I have sought, all my days, not to guard myself from the mischief of the rebellious among Thy creatures, but rather to exalt Thy name amidst Thy people. I have, thereby, suffered what none of Thy creatures hath suffered.

How many the days, O my God, which I have spent in utter loneliness with the transgressors amongst Thy servants, and how many the nights, O my Best-Beloved, during which I lay a captive in the hands of the wayward amidst Thy creatures! In the midst of my troubles and tribulations I have continued to celebrate Thy praise before all who are in Thy heaven and on Thy earth, and have not ceased to extol Thy wondrous glory in the kingdoms of Thy Revelation and of Thy creation, though all that I have been capable of showing forth hath fallen short of the greatness and the majesty of Thy oneness, and is unworthy of Thine exaltation and of Thine omnipotence.

—BAHÁ'U'LLÁH 15

LAUDED BE THY NAME, O MY GOD! I am so carried away by the breezes blowing from Thy presence that I have forgotten my self and all that I possess. This is but a sign of the wonders of Thy grace and bountiful favors vouchsafed unto me. I give praise to Thee, O my God, that Thou hast chosen me out of all Thy creatures, and made me to be the Day-Spring of Thy strength and the Manifestation of Thy might, and empowered me to reveal such of Thy signs and such tokens of Thy majesty and power as none, whether in Thy heaven or on Thy earth, can produce.

I beseech Thee, O my Lord, by Thy most effulgent Name, to acquaint my people with the things Thou didst destine for them. Do Thou, then, preserve them within the stronghold of Thy guardianship and the tabernacle of Thine unerring protection, lest through them may appear what will divide Thy servants. Assemble them, O my Lord, on the shores of this Ocean, every drop of which proclaimeth Thee to be God, besides Whom there is none other God, the All-Glorious, the All-Wise.

Uncover before them, O my Lord, the majesty of Thy Cause, lest they be led to doubt Thy sovereignty and the power of Thy might. I swear by Thy glory, O Thou Who art the Beloved of the worlds! Had they been aware of Thy power they would of a certainty have refused to utter what Thou didst not ordain for them in the heaven of Thy will.

Inspire them, O my Lord, with a sense of their own powerlessness before Him Who is the Manifestation of Thy Self, and teach them to recognize the poverty of their own nature in the face of the manifold tokens of Thy self-sufficiency and riches, that they may gather together round Thy Cause, and cling to the hem of Thy mercy, and cleave to the cord of the good-pleasure of Thy will.

Thou art the Lord of the worlds, and of all those who show mercy, art the Most Merciful.

—BAHÁ'U'LLÁH 16

Release and Exile

Bahá'u'lláh was released from prison in December 1852 and was immediately notified of the Sháh's decree banishing Him from Persia. While He was in prison, His wealth had been confiscated, and His home and possessions had been pillaged. Given no more than one month to recover from the debilitating effects of His imprisonment in the Síyáh-Chál and to leave for a land of His choosing, Bahá'u'lláh declined the protection the government of Russia extended through its minister, Prince Dolgorukov, and chose instead to proceed to Baghdád, 'Iráq.

Bahá'u'lláh and His family left Ṭihrán on 12 January 1853, escorted by an officer of the Imperial bodyguard and an official representing the Russian Legation. The exiles traveled on horseback over the snow-covered mountains of western Persia, poorly equipped for the bitter cold of winter and the hardships of such a demanding journey.

IN THE DAYS WHEN THIS WRONGED ONE was sore-afflicted in prison, the minister of the highly esteemed government—may God, glorified and exalted be He, assist him!—exerted his utmost endeavor to compass My deliverance. Several times permission for My release was granted. Some of the 'ulamás of the city, however, would prevent it.

Finally, My freedom was gained through the solicitude and the endeavor of His Excellency the Minister. . . . His Imperial Majesty, the Most Great Emperor[5]—may God, exalted and glorified be He, assist him!—extended to Me for the sake of God his protection—a protection which has excited the envy and enmity of the foolish ones of the earth.

—BAHÁ'U'LLÁH 17

MY GOD, MY MASTER, MY DESIRE! . . . Thou hast created this atom of dust through the consummate power of Thy might, and nurtured Him with Thine hands which none can chain up. . . . Thou hast destined for Him trials and tribulations which no tongue can describe, nor any of Thy Tablets adequately recount. The throat Thou didst accustom to the touch of silk Thou hast, in the end, clasped with strong chains, and the body Thou didst ease with brocades and velvets Thou hast at last subjected to the abasement of a dungeon. Thy decree hath shackled Me with unnumbered fetters, and cast about My neck chains that none can sunder. A number of years have passed during which afflictions have, like showers of mercy, rained upon Me. . . . How many the nights during which the weight of chains and fetters allowed Me no rest, and how numerous the days during which peace and tranquillity were denied Me, by reason of that

5. Czar Alexander II of Russia.

wherewith the hands and tongues of men have afflicted Me! Both bread and water which Thou hast, through Thy all-embracing mercy, allowed unto the beasts of the field, they have, for a time, forbidden unto this servant, and the things they refused to inflict upon such as have seceded from Thy Cause, the same have they suffered to be inflicted upon Me, until, finally, Thy decree was irrevocably fixed, and Thy behest summoned this servant to depart out of Persia, accompanied by a number of frail-bodied men and children of tender age, at this time when the cold is so intense that one cannot even speak, and ice and snow so abundant that it is impossible to move.

—BAHÁ'U'LLÁH 18

Part 4 / UNFOLDING REVELATION

Chapter 6 / BAGHDÁD

Arrival in Baghdád

Accompanying Bahá'u'lláh on the journey to Baghdád were His wife, Navváb, later known as "the Most Exalted Leaf"; His nine-year-old son 'Abbás, later titled "the Most Great Branch" and known as 'Abdu'l-Bahá; His seven-year-old daughter Bahíyyih, later known as "the Greatest Holy Leaf"; and Bahá'u'lláh's two faithful brothers, Mírzá Músá and Mírzá Muḥammad-Qulí, the latter being about sixteen years old. A two-year-old son, Mihdí, later given the title "the Purest Branch," was left in the care of Navváb's grandmother. The party was escorted by an officer of the Imperial bodyguard and an official representing the Russian Legation.

The exiles arrived in Baghdád on 8 April 1853. A few days later they moved about three miles outside the city to the township of Káẓimayn, where the shrines for the seventh and eighth Imáms of Shí'ah Islám are located. The Persian consul called to pay his respects and suggested that, in view of the fanaticism of the residents and pilgrims visiting the shrines, Bahá'u'lláh might find the old quarter within the city of Baghdád more agreeable. About a month later a house was found, and Bahá'u'lláh and His family returned to the city.

The edict exiling Bahá'u'lláh to Baghdád, Shoghi Effendi explains, opened "a new and glorious chapter in the history of the first Bahá'í century." This new chapter set in motion a gradually and progressively unfolding process that "ushered in one of the most eventful and momentous epochs in the world's religious history. It coincides with the inauguration of a ministry extending over a period of almost forty years—a ministry which, by virtue of its creative power, its cleansing force, its healing influences, and the irresistible operation of the world-directing, world-shaping forces it released, stands unparalleled in the religious annals of the entire human race. It marks the opening phase in a series of banishments, ranging over a period of four decades, and terminating only with the death of Him Who was the Object of that cruel edict."

AND WHEN THIS WRONGED ONE went forth out of His prison, We journeyed, in pursuance of the order of His Majesty the Sháh—may God, exalted be He, protect him—to 'Iráq, escorted by officers in the service of the esteemed and honored governments of Persia and Russia. After Our arrival, We revealed, as a copious rain, by the aid of God and His Divine Grace and mercy, Our verses, and sent them to various parts of the world. We exhorted all men, and particularly this people, through Our wise counsels and loving admonitions, and forbade them to engage in sedition, quarrels, disputes and conflict. As a result of this, and by the grace of God, waywardness and folly were changed into piety and understanding, and weapons converted into instruments of peace.

—BAHÁ'U'LLÁH 1

WE DEPARTED OUT OF ṬIHRÁN, at the bidding of the King, and, by his leave, transferred Our residence to 'Iráq. If I had transgressed against him, why, then, did he release Me? And if I were innocent of guilt, wherefore did ye[1] afflict Us with such tribulation as none among them that profess your faith hath suffered? Hath any of Mine acts, after Mine arrival in 'Iráq, been such as to subvert the authority of the government? Who is it that can be said to have detected any thing reprehensible in Our behavior? Enquire for thyself of its people, that thou mayest be of them who have discerned the truth.

—BAHÁ'U'LLÁH 2

UPON OUR ARRIVAL IN 'IRÁQ WE FOUND the Cause of God sunk in deep apathy and the breeze of divine revelation stilled. Most of the believers were faint and dispirited, nay utterly lost and dead. Hence there was a second blast on the Trumpet, whereupon the Tongue of Grandeur uttered these blessed words: "We have sounded the Trumpet for the second time." Thus the whole world was quickened through the vitalizing breaths of divine revelation and inspiration.

—BAHÁ'U'LLÁH 3

1. The minister of the Sháh in Constantinople, Ḥájí Mírzá Ḥusayn Khán-i-Qazvíní.

The Machinations of Mírzá Yaḥyá and Siyyid Muḥammad

Soon after Bahá'u'lláh's arrival in Baghdád an internal crisis, the first signs of which had begun to appear after the Báb's martyrdom, arose within the community of exiles. At the center of the crisis was Bahá'u'lláh's half-brother Mírzá Yaḥyá.

Because the Báb's many references to the Promised One were so transparently clear and because the Báb's own Dispensation was to be so short, He had deemed it unnecessary to appoint a successor. He had, however, named Mírzá Yaḥyá as the figurehead of the Bábí community in order to deflect attention from Bahá'u'lláh and to leave Him free to promote the Cause in relative security.

The growing veneration the Bábís showed toward Bahá'u'lláh, Whom some already recognized as the Promised One, aroused the jealousy that Mírzá Yaḥyá had long harbored against his older Brother. Feeling the need to assert himself in view of his weakening position, he formed an alliance with Siyyid Muḥammad of Iṣfahán, whom Shoghi Effendi designates as the "Antichrist of the Bahá'í Revelation" and describes as a scheming and "black-hearted scoundrel" who manipulated Mírzá Yaḥyá's vanity to fulfill his own ambitions. The two men, acting in concert, initiated a campaign of subtle criticism in which they distorted Bahá'u'lláh's interpretations and commentaries and circulated rumors about His actions, portraying Him as a usurper, sowing seeds of doubt about Him, and creating controversy and division among the Bábís.

THIS WRONGED ONE hath been perpetually afflicted, and found no place of safety in which He could peruse either the writings of the Most Exalted One [the Báb] or those of any one else. About two months after Our arrival in 'Iráq, following the command of His Majesty the Sháh of Persia—may God assist him—Mírzá Yaḥyá joined Us. We said unto him: "In accordance with the Royal command We have been sent unto this place. It is advisable for thee to remain in Persia. We will send Our brother, Mírzá Músá, to some other place. As your names have not been mentioned in the Royal decree, you can arise and render some service." Subsequently, this Wronged One departed from Baghdád,[2] and for two years withdrew from the world. Upon Our return, We found that he had not left, and had postponed his departure. This Wronged One was greatly saddened. God testifieth and beareth Us witness that We have, at all times, been busied with the propagation of this Cause. Neither chains nor bonds, stocks nor imprisonment, have succeeded in withholding Us from revealing Our Self. In that land We forbad all mischief, and all unseemly and unholy deeds. Day and night We sent forth Our Tablets in every direction. We had no other purpose except to edify the souls of men, and to exalt the blessed Word.

—BAHÁ'U'LLÁH 4

WHEREVER THIS WRONGED ONE WENT Mírzá Yaḥyá followed Him. Thou[3] art thyself a witness and well knowest that whatever hath been said is the truth.

---

2. To the mountains of Kurdistán.

3. Mírzá Hádí Dawlat-Ábádí, a Muslim clergyman who became a Bábí and later a supporter of Mírzá Yaḥyá, who appointed him his representative in Persia and his successor. In 1888, when the Bábís of Persia were undergoing persecution, he recanted his faith.

The Siyyid of Iṣfahán, however, surreptitiously duped him. They committed that which caused the greatest consternation. Would that thou wouldst inquire from the officials of the government concerning the conduct of Mírzá Yaḥyá in that land. Aside from all this, I adjure thee by God, the One, the Incomparable, the Lord of Strength, the Most Powerful, to carefully look into the communications addressed in his name to the Primal Point, that thou mayest behold the evidences of Him Who is the Truth as clear as the sun. Likewise, there proceeded from the words of the Point of the Bayán—may the souls of all else but Him be sacrificed for His sake—that which no veil can obscure, and which neither the veils of glory nor the veils interposed by such as have gone astray can hide. The veils have, verily, been rent asunder by the finger of the will of thy Lord, the Strong, the All-Subduing, the All-Powerful. Yea, desperate is the state of such as have calumniated Me and envied Me.

—*BAHÁ'U'LLÁH* 5

The Heedlessness of the People of the Bayán

WE FAIN WOULD HOPE THAT THE PEOPLE of the Bayán will be enlightened, will soar in the realm of the spirit and abide therein, will discern the Truth, and recognize with the eye of insight dissembling falsehood. In these days, however, such odours of jealousy are diffused, that—I swear by the Educator of all beings, visible and invisible—from the beginning of the foundation of the world—though it hath no beginning—until the present day, such malice, envy, and hate have in no wise appeared, nor will they ever be witnessed in the future. For a number of people who have never inhaled the fragrance of justice, have raised the standard of sedition, and have leagued themselves against Us. On every side We witness the menace of their spears, and in all directions We recognize the shafts of their arrows. This, although We have never gloried in any thing, nor did We seek preference over any soul. To everyone We have been a most kindly companion, a most forbearing and affectionate friend. In the company of the poor We have sought their fellowship, and amidst the exalted and learned We have been submissive and resigned. I swear by God, the one true God! grievous as have been the woes and sufferings which the hand of the enemy and the people of the Book inflicted upon Us, yet all these fade into utter nothingness when compared with that which hath befallen Us at the hand of those who profess to be Our friends.

—BAHÁ'U'LLÁH 6

Counsel to the People of the Bayán

THE DAYS OF TESTS ARE NOW COME. Oceans of dissension and tribulation are surging, and the Banners of Doubt are, in every nook and corner, occupied in stirring up mischief and in leading men to perdition. . . . Suffer not the voice of some of the soldiers of negation to cast doubt into your midst, neither allow yourselves to become heedless of Him Who is the Truth, inasmuch as in every Dispensation such contentions have been raised. God, however, will establish His Faith, and manifest His light albeit the stirrers of sedition abhor it. . . . Watch ye every day for the Cause of God. . . . All are held captive in His grasp. No place is there for any one to flee to. Think not the Cause of God to be a thing lightly taken, in which any one can gratify his whims. In various quarters a number of souls have, at the present time, advanced this same claim. The time is approaching when . . . every one of them will have perished and been lost, nay will have come to naught and become a thing unremembered, even as the dust itself.

—BAHÁ'U'LLÁH 7

Prayer for the People of the Bayán

THOU WELL KNOWEST, O MY GOD, that I was regarded as one of the people of the Bayán, and consorted with them with love and fellowship, and summoned them to Thee in the daytime and in the night season, through the wonders of Thy Revelation and Thine inspiration, and sustained at their hands what the inmates of the cities of Thine invention are powerless to recount. I swear by Thy might, O my Beloved! Every morning I waken to find that I am made a target for the darts of their envy, and every night, when I lie down to rest, I discover that I have fallen a victim to the spears of their hate. Though

Thou hast made known unto me the secrets of their hearts, and hast set me above them, I have refused to uncover their deeds, and have dealt patiently with them, mindful of the time which Thou hast fixed. And when Thy promise came to pass, and the set time was fulfilled, Thou didst lift, to an imperceptible degree, the veil of concealment, and lo, all the inmates of the kingdoms of Thy Revelation and of Thy creation shook and trembled, except those who were created by Thee, through the fire of Thy love, and the breath of Thine eagerness, and the water of Thy loving-kindness, and the clay of Thy grace. These are they who are glorified by the Concourse on high and the denizens of the Cities of eternity.

I give praise to Thee, therefore, O my God, that Thou hast preserved them that have acknowledged Thy unity, and hast destroyed them that have joined partners with Thee, and hast divided the one from the other through yet another word that hath proceeded out of the mouth of Thy will, and flowed down from the pen of Thy purpose. Thereby have Thy servants, who were created through the word of Thy commandment, and were begotten by Thy will, caviled at me, and so fiercely opposed me that they repudiated Thee, and have rejected Thy signs, and have risen up against Thee.

Thy glory beareth me witness, O my Beloved! My pen is powerless to describe what their hands have wrought against Him Who is the Manifestation of Thy Cause, and the Day-Spring of Thy Revelation, and the Dawning-Place of Thine inspiration. For all this I give praise to Thee. I swear by Thy glory, O my God! My heart yearneth after the things ordained by Thee in the heaven of Thy decree and the kingdom of Thine appointment. For whatsoever befalleth me in Thy path is the beloved of my soul and the goal of my desire. This, verily, is to be ascribed to naught except Thy power and Thy might.

I am the one, O my God, who, through the love I bear to Thee, hath been able to dispense with all who are in heaven and on earth. Armed with this love, I am afraid of no one, though all the peoples of the world unite to hurt me. Oh, that my blood could, this very moment, be shed on the face of the earth before Thee, and Thou wouldst behold me in the condition in which Thou didst behold such of Thy servants as have drawn nigh unto Thee, and those of Thy righteous creatures as have been chosen by Thee!

I give Thee thanks, O my God, that Thou hast decided through the power of Thy decree, and wilt continue to decide through Thine irrevocable appointment and purpose. I entreat Thee, O my Beloved, by Thy Name through which Thou didst lift up the ensigns of Thy Cause, and shed the splendors of the light of Thy countenance, to send down upon me and upon such of Thy servants as are wholly devoted to Thee all the good Thou hast ordained in Thy Tablets. Establish us, then, upon the seats of truth in Thy presence, O Thou in Whose hands is the kingdom of all things!

Thou art, verily, the Almighty, the All-Glorious, the Most Merciful.

—BAHÁ'U'LLÁH 8

Prayers and Meditations on Bahá'u'lláh's Sufferings in Baghdád

OCEANS OF SADNESS HAVE SURGED over Me, a drop of which no soul could bear to drink. Such is My grief that My soul hath well nigh departed from My body. . . . Give ear, O Kamál![4] to the voice of this lowly, this forsaken ant, that hath hid itself in its hole, and whose desire is to depart from your midst, and vanish from your sight, by reason of that which the hands of men have wrought. God, verily, hath been witness between Me and His servants. . . . Woe is Me, woe is Me! . . . all that I have seen from the day on which I first drank the pure milk from the breast of My mother until this moment hath been effaced from My memory, in consequence of that which the hands of the people have committed.

—*BAHÁ'U'LLÁH 9*

NOAH'S FLOOD IS BUT THE MEASURE of the tears I have shed, and Abraham's fire an ebullition of My soul. Jacob's grief is but a reflection of My sorrows, and Job's afflictions a fraction of my calamity.

—*BAHÁ'U'LLÁH 10*

O GOD, MY GOD! Be Thou not far from me, for tribulation upon tribulation hath gathered about me. O God, my God! Leave me not to myself, for

4. Ḥájí Mírzá Kamálu'd-Dín. See glossary.

the extreme of adversity hath come upon me. Out of the pure milk, drawn from the breasts of Thy loving-kindness, give me to drink, for my thirst hath utterly consumed me. Beneath the shadow of the wings of Thy mercy shelter me, for all mine adversaries with one consent have fallen upon me. Keep me near to the throne of Thy majesty, face to face with the revelation of the signs of Thy glory, for wretchedness hath grievously touched me. With the fruits of the Tree of Thine Eternity nourish me, for uttermost weakness hath overtaken me. From the cups of joy, proffered by the hands of Thy tender mercies, feed me, for manifold sorrows have laid mighty hold upon me. With the broidered robe of Thine omnipotent sovereignty attire me, for poverty hath altogether despoiled me. Lulled by the cooing of the Dove of Thine Eternity, suffer me to sleep, for woes at their blackest have befallen me. Before the throne of Thy oneness, amid the blaze of the beauty of Thy countenance, cause me to abide, for fear and trembling have violently crushed me. Beneath the ocean of Thy forgiveness, faced with the restlessness of the leviathan of glory, immerse me, for my sins have utterly doomed me.

—BAHÁ'U'LLÁH 11

The Mountains of Kurdistán

One morning Bahá'u'lláh's family arose to find that He was gone. Burdened with grief over the malicious allegations made by Mírzá Yaḥyá and Siyyid Muḥammad, and distraught over the division their campaign of slander was creating within the Bábí community, Bahá'u'lláh, without informing anyone, left Baghdád on 10

April 1854 for the remote wilderness of Kurdistán, accompanied only by a Muslim attendant who was soon attacked by thieves and killed.

Bahá'u'lláh's departure to Kurdistán recalls the retreats other Manifestations of God took in preparation for the prosecution of their Prophetic Missions. Just as Moses stayed in the desert of Paran, Jesus spent forty days and nights in the wilderness, and Muḥammad dwelt in the caves of Mount Hira, so Bahá'u'lláh withdrew to the mountains of Kurdistán, where He lived in solitude for two years.

Dressed as a dervish (darvísh), *carrying only a change of clothing and an alms bowl, and assuming the name of Darvísh Muḥammad-i-Írání, Bahá'u'lláh walked some two hundred miles into the remote regions of Kurdistán. He lived for many months on the mountain of Sar-Galú, which was three days' journey from the nearest settlement.*

His solitude was broken when a man sought Him out, having followed the directions given to him by the Prophet Muḥammad in a dream. Soon thereafter the leader of a religious order in the village of Sulaymáníyyih visited Bahá'u'lláh and persuaded Him, after repeated requests, to take up residence in a theological seminary in the village. Gradually the villagers began to realize that Darvísh Muḥammad possessed special gifts and powers, and the magnetism of His personality and the immensity of His knowledge made Him the object of the admiration of high and low, young and old, Kurds, Arabs, and Persians alike. "In a short time," *'Abdu'l-Bahá says,* "Kurdistán was magnetized with His love. . . . An atmosphere of majesty haloed Him as the sun at midday. Everywhere He was greatly revered and loved."

The fame of Darvísh Muḥammad quickly reached Baghdád. Bahá'u'lláh's family became convinced that Darvísh Muḥammad was Bahá'u'lláh. 'Abdu'l-Bahá, Bahá'u'lláh's twelve-year-old son, and Bahá'u'lláh's brother, Mírzá Músá, dispatched two men to implore Him to return. Mírzá Yaḥyá, whose true colors had by now been recognized by the remaining Bábís of prominence, also wrote to Bahá'u'lláh, begging Him to return.

THE WRONGS WHICH I SUFFER have blotted out the wrongs suffered by My First Name [the Báb] from the Tablet of creation. . . . From the Land of Ṭá [Ṭihrán], after countless afflictions, We reached ‘Iráq at the bidding of the Tyrant of Persia, where, after the fetters of Our foes, We were afflicted with the perfidy of Our friends. God knoweth what befell Me thereafter! At length I gave up My home and all therein, and renounced life and all that appertaineth unto it, and alone and friendless, chose to go into retirement. I roamed the wilderness of resignation, travelling in such wise that in My exile every eye wept sore over Me, and all created things shed tears of blood because of My anguish. The birds of the air were My companions and the beasts of the field My associates. . . . By the righteousness of God! I have borne what neither the oceans, nor the waves, nor the fruits, nor any created thing, whether of the past or of the future, hath borne or will be capable of bearing.

—BAHÁ’U’LLÁH 12

SOON AFTER OUR ARRIVAL,[5] We betook Ourself to the mountains of Kurdistán, where We led for a time a life of complete solitude. We sought shelter upon the summit of a remote mountain which lay at some three days’ distance from the nearest human habitation. The comforts of life were completely lacking. We remained entirely isolated from our

5. In Baghdád.

fellow men until a certain Shaykh Ismá'íl discovered Our abode and brought Us the food We needed.

—*BAHÁ'U'LLÁH 13*

IN THE EARLY DAYS OF OUR ARRIVAL in this land,[6] when We discerned the signs of impending events, We decided, ere they happened, to retire. We betook Ourselves to the wilderness, and there, separated and alone, led for two years a life of complete solitude. From Our eyes there rained tears of anguish, and in Our bleeding heart there surged an ocean of agonizing pain. Many a night We had no food for sustenance, and many a day Our body found no rest. By Him Who hath My being between His hands! notwithstanding these showers of afflictions and unceasing calamities, Our soul was wrapt in blissful joy, and Our whole being evinced an ineffable gladness. For in Our solitude We were unaware of the harm or benefit, the health or ailment, of any soul. Alone, We communed with Our spirit, oblivious of the world and all that is therein. We knew not, however, that the mesh of divine destiny exceedeth the vastest of mortal conceptions, and the dart of His decree transcendeth the boldest of human designs. None can escape the snares He setteth, and no soul can find release except through submission to His will. By the righteousness of God! Our withdrawal contemplated no return, and Our

6. 'Iráq.

separation hoped for no reunion. The one object of Our retirement was to avoid becoming a subject of discord among the faithful, a source of disturbance unto Our companions, the means of injury to any soul, or the cause of sorrow to any heart. Beyond these, We cherished no other intention, and apart from them, We had no end in view. And yet, each person schemed after his own desire, and pursued his own idle fancy, until the hour when, from the Mystic Source, there came the summons bidding Us return whence We came. Surrendering Our will to His, We submitted to His injunction.

—*BAHÁ'U'LLÁH* 14

FOR TWO YEARS OR RATHER LESS, I shunned all else but God, and closed Mine eyes to all except Him, that haply the fire of hatred may die down and the heat of jealousy abate.

—*BAHÁ'U'LLÁH* 15

Prayer from Kurdistán

PRAISE BE TO THEE, O LORD MY GOD, for the wondrous revelations of Thy inscrutable decree and the manifold woes and trials Thou hast destined for Myself. At one time Thou didst deliver Me into the hands of Nimrod; at another Thou hast allowed Pharaoh's rod to persecute Me. Thou, alone, canst estimate, through Thine all-encompassing knowledge and the operation of Thy Will, the incalculable afflictions I have suffered at their hands.

Again Thou didst cast Me into the prison-cell of the ungodly, for no reason except that I was moved to whisper into the ears of the well-favored denizens of Thy Kingdom an intimation of the vision with which Thou hadst, through Thy knowledge,inspired Me, and revealed to Me its meaning through the potency of Thy might. And again Thou didst decree that I be beheaded by the sword of the infidel. Again I was crucified for having unveiled to men's eyes the hidden gems of Thy glorious unity, for having revealed to them the wondrous signs of Thy sovereign and everlasting power. How bitter the humiliations heaped upon Me, in a subsequent age, on the plain of Karbilá! How lonely did I feel amidst Thy people! To what a state of helplessness I was reduced in that land! Unsatisfied with such indignities, My persecutors decapitated Me, and, carrying aloft My head from land to land paraded it before the gaze of the unbelieving multitude, and deposited it on the seats of the perverse and faithless. In a later age, I was suspended, and My breast was made a target to the darts of the malicious cruelty of My foes. My limbs were riddled with bullets, and My body was torn asunder. Finally, behold how, in this Day, My treacherous enemies have leagued themselves against Me, and are continually plotting to instill the venom of hate and malice into the souls of Thy servants. With all their might they are scheming to accomplish their purpose. . . . Grievous as is My plight, O God, My Well-Beloved, I render thanks unto Thee, and My Spirit is grateful for whatsoever hath befallen me in the path of Thy good-pleasure. I am well pleased with that which

Thou didst ordain for Me, and welcome, however calamitous, the pains and sorrows I am made to suffer.

—*BAHÁ'U'LLÁH 16*

Return from Kurdistán

BUT FOR MY RECOGNITION of the fact that the blessed Cause of the Primal Point was on the verge of being completely obliterated, and all the sacred blood poured out in the path of God would have been shed in vain, I would in no wise have consented to return to the people of the Bayán, and would have abandoned them to the worship of the idols their imaginations had fashioned.

—*BAHÁ'U'LLÁH 17*

WHAT PEN CAN RECOUNT THE THINGS We beheld upon Our return! Two years have elapsed during which Our enemies have ceaselessly and assiduously contrived to exterminate Us, whereunto all witness. Nevertheless, none amongst the faithful hath risen to render Us any assistance, nor did any one feel inclined to help in Our deliverance. Nay, instead of assisting Us, what showers of continuous sorrows, their words and deeds have caused to rain upon Our soul! Amidst them all, We stand, life in hand, wholly resigned to His will; that perchance, through God's loving kindness and His grace, this revealed and manifest Letter may lay down His life as a sacrifice in the path of the Primal Point, the most exalted Word. By Him at Whose bidding the Spirit hath spoken, but for this yearning of Our soul, We would not, for one moment, have tarried any longer in this city.

—BAHÁ'U'LLÁH 18

WE FOUND NO MORE THAN a handful of souls, faint and dispirited, nay utterly lost and dead. The Cause of God had ceased to be on any one's lips, nor was any heart receptive to its message.

—BAHÁ'U'LLÁH 19

UPON OUR RETURN TO BAGHDÁD, We found, to Our great astonishment, that the Cause of the Báb had been sorely neglected, that its influence had waned, that its very name had almost sunk into oblivion. We arose to revive His Cause and to save it from decay and corruption. At the time when fear and perplexity had taken fast hold of Our companions, We reasserted, with fearlessness and determination, its essential verities, and summoned all those who had become lukewarm to espouse with enthusiasm the Faith they had so grievously neglected. We sent forth Our appeal to the peoples of the world, and invited them to fix their gaze upon the light of His Revelation.

—BAHÁ'U'LLÁH 20

The return of Bahá'u'lláh from Sulaymáníyyih to Baghdád marks a turning point of the utmost significance in the history of the first Bahá'í century. The tide of the fortunes of the Faith, having reached its lowest ebb, was now beginning to surge back, and was destined to roll on, steadily and mightily, to a new high water-mark, associated this time with the Declaration of His Mission, on the eve of

His banishment to Constantinople. With His return to Baghdád a firm anchorage was now being established, an anchorage such as the Faith had never known in its history. . . .

Now at last . . . the Bábís found themselves able to center both their hopes and their movements round One Whom they believed (whatever their views as to His station) capable of insuring the stability and integrity of their Faith. The orientation which the Faith had thus acquired and the fixity of the center towards which it now gravitated continued, in one form or another, to be its outstanding features, of which it was never again to be deprived.

. . . .

During the seven years that elapsed between the resumption of His labors and the declaration of His prophetic mission . . . it would be no exaggeration to say that the Bahá'í community, under the name and in the shape of a re-arisen Bábí community was born and was slowly taking shape, though its Creator still appeared in the guise of, and continued to labor as, one of the foremost disciples of the Báb. It was a period during which the prestige of the community's nominal head steadily faded from the scene, paling before the rising splendor of Him Who was its actual Leader and Deliverer. It was a period in the course of which the first fruits of an exile, endowed with incalculable potentialities, ripened and were garnered. It was a period that will go down in history as one during which the prestige of a recreated community was immensely enhanced, its morals entirely reformed, its recognition of Him who rehabilitated its fortunes enthusiastically affirmed, its literature enormously enriched, and its victories over its new adversaries universally acknowledged.[7]

—*SHOGHI EFFENDI*

7. *God Passes By*, pp. 127–28.

The Divines of Baghdád

As the signs of the transformation Bahá'u'lláh effected in the Bábí community in Baghdád and throughout Persia became increasingly apparent, the Muslim clergy grew jealous. A leading divine, Shaykh 'Abdu'l-Ḥusayn, in league with the Persian consul, Mírzá Buzurg Khán, devised numerous schemes to undermine Bahá'u'lláh. Among them was the accusation that Bahá'u'lláh was plotting an insurrection against the Sháh and had 100,000 men ready to take up arms at His command. There was also an attempt to have Bahá'u'lláh extradited to Ṭihrán and placed in prison. For his part, the Persian consul commissioned Bahá'u'lláh's murder only to find that his agent twice lost his nerve completely when in Bahá'u'lláh's presence.

Having gained the Sháh's authorization to enlist the divines in the region in his campaign against Bahá'u'lláh, Shaykh 'Abdu'l-Ḥusayn convened a meeting of the clergy, who declared their desire to wage a holy war against the Bábís of Baghdád. However, the leading cleric among them, a man renowned for his tolerance and wisdom, refused to be a party to their plotting and would not approve the declaration. Hence they settled for submitting various questions for elucidation through an envoy to Bahá'u'lláh. When their representative returned with satisfactory answers, the divines sent him back to request that Bahá'u'lláh perform a miracle. "Although you have no right to ask this," *Bahá'u'lláh told the representative,* "for God should test His creatures, and they should not test God, still I allow and accept this request." *He then directed the divines to agree on one miracle and to vow that after it was performed they would one and all accept the truth of His Cause. The divines failed to arrive at a decision and dropped the matter. News of their conduct was widely circulated throughout Persia by the envoy, who even related it in person to the minister of foreign affairs.*

FOR TWELVE YEARS WE TARRIED in Baghdád.[8] Much as We desired that a large gathering of divines and fair-minded men be convened, so that truth might be distinguished from falsehood, and be fully demonstrated, no action was taken. . . . And likewise, while in 'Iráq, We wished to come together with the divines of Persia. No sooner did they hear of this, than they fled and said: "He indeed is a manifest sorcerer!" This is the word that proceeded aforetime out of the mouths of such as were like them. These [divines] objected to what they said, and yet, they themselves repeat, in this day, what was said before them, and understand not. By My life! They are even as ashes in the sight of thy Lord. If He be willing, tempestuous gales will blow over them, and make them as dust. Thy Lord, verily, doth what He pleaseth.

—BAHÁ'U'LLÁH 21

THE 'ULAMÁS MUST ASSEMBLE, and, with one accord, choose one miracle, and write that, after the performance of this miracle they will no longer entertain doubts about Me, and that all will acknowledge and confess the truth of My Cause. Let

---

8. Shoghi Effendi says, using Gregorian (solar calendar) dates, that Bahá'u'lláh arrived in Baghdád on 8 April 1853 and left on 3 May 1863. In this passage Bahá'u'lláh says He dwelt in 'Iráq twelve years, but in extract 24 (*Gleanings,* pp. 229–30) He says He lived there eleven years. The latter two references may refer to a calculation of this period based on the lunar, rather than the solar, calendar. According to the lunar calendar Bahá'u'lláh left Ṭihrán in 1269 and arrived in Constantinople in 1280.

them seal this paper, and bring it to Me. This must be the accepted criterion: if the miracle is performed, no doubt will remain for them; and if not, We shall be convicted of imposture.

—*BAHÁ'U'LLÁH 22*

TELL OUT TO THE NATIONS, O PEN of the Ancient of Days, the things that have happened in 'Iráq. Tell them of the messenger whom the congregation of the divines of that land had delegated to meet Us, who, when attaining Our presence, questioned Us concerning certain sciences, and whom We answered by virtue of the knowledge We inherently possess. Thy Lord is, verily, the Knower of things unseen. "We testify," said he, "that the knowledge Thou dost possess is such as none can rival. Such a knowledge, however, is insufficient to vindicate the exalted station which the people ascribe to Thee. Produce, if Thou speakest the truth, what the combined forces of the peoples of the earth are powerless to produce." Thus was it irrevocably decreed in the court of the presence of thy Lord, the All-Glorious, the Loving.

"Witness! What is it thou seest?" He was dumbfounded. And when he came to himself, he said: "I truly believe in God, the All-Glorious, the All-Praised." "Go thou to the people, and tell them: 'Ask whatsoever ye please. Powerful is He to do what He willeth. Nothing whatsoever, be it of the past or of the future, can frustrate His Will.' Say: 'O ye congregation of the divines! Choose any matter ye desire, and ask your Lord, the God of Mercy, to reveal it unto you. If He fulfil your wish, by virtue of His sovereignty, believe ye then in Him, and be not

of those that reject His truth.'" "The dawn of
understanding hath now broken," said he, "and the
testimony of the All-Merciful is fulfilled." He arose
and returned unto them that sent him, at the
bidding of God, the All-Glorious, the Well-Beloved.

Days passed and he failed to come back to Us.
Eventually, there came another messenger who
informed Us that the people had given up what they
originally had purposed. They are indeed a
contemptible people. This is what happened in 'Iráq,
and to what I reveal I Myself am witness. This
happening was noised abroad, yet none was found to
comprehend its meaning. Thus did We ordain it.
Would that ye knew this!

—BAHÁ'U'LLÁH 23

Banishment from Baghdád

*Bahá'u'lláh's ascendancy over the divines only increased the re-
solve of <u>Sh</u>ay<u>kh</u> 'Abdu'l-Ḥusayn and Mírzá Buzurg <u>Kh</u>án to rid
themselves of Him. After spending nine months trying to discredit
Bahá'u'lláh and incessantly urging the <u>Sh</u>áh and his ambassador
in Constantinople to remove Bahá'u'lláh from Ba<u>gh</u>dád, they finally achieved their goal. The <u>Sh</u>áh instructed his foreign minister
to appeal to Sulṭán 'Abdu'l-'Azíz of Turkey to banish Bahá'u'lláh
from Ba<u>gh</u>dád on the grounds that His continued presence in the
city constituted a threat to the Persian government's security.*

*After obtaining the Sulṭán's approval, the Turkish prime min-
ister, 'Álí Pá<u>sh</u>á, sent a letter to Namíq Pá<u>sh</u>á, the governor of
Ba<u>gh</u>dád, diplomatically inviting Bahá'u'lláh to transfer His residence to Constantinople as a guest of the Ottoman government.
Namíq Pá<u>sh</u>á, who admired Bahá'u'lláh greatly, was so disturbed
by the intrigues that it was only after three months had passed and*

five successive commands from 'Álí Pá<u>sh</u>á had arrived that he felt compelled to take up the matter with Bahá'u'lláh.

At Namíq Pá<u>sh</u>á's request, Bahá'u'lláh visited the mosque opposite the Government House. He was met there by the deputy-governor and, after being apprised of the Turkish government's invitation, gave His assent, although He refused to accept the sum of money offered to Him. When the deputy-governor urgently appealed to Him not to refuse the funds lest the authorities be offended, Bahá'u'lláh relented, but He distributed the money later that day to the poor.

FOR ELEVEN YEARS WE DWELT in that land, until the Minister representing thy government arrived, whose name Our pen is loth to mention, who was given to wine, who followed his lusts, and committed wickedness, and was corrupt and corrupted 'Iráq.[9] To this will bear witness most of the inhabitants of Ba<u>gh</u>dád, wert thou to inquire of them, and be of such as seek the truth. He it was who wrongfully seized the substance of his fellow-men, who forsook all the commandments of God, and perpetrated whatever God had forbidden. Eventually, he, following his desires, rose up against Us, and walked in the ways of the unjust. He accused Us, in his letter to thee, and thou didst believe him and followed in his way, without seeking any proof or trustworthy evidence from him. Thou didst ask for

---

9. This Tablet was addressed to Ḥájí Mírzá Ḥusayn <u>Kh</u>án-i-Qazvíní, the Persian ambassador in Constantinople. The Minister referred to is Mírzá Buzurg <u>Kh</u>án, the Persian consul-general in Ba<u>gh</u>dád.

no explanation, nor didst thou attempt either to investigate or ascertain the matter, that the truth might be distinguished from falsehood in thy sight, and that thou mightest be clear in thy discernment. Find out for thyself the sort of man he was by asking those Ministers who were, at that time, in 'Iráq, as well as the Governor of the City [Baghdád] and its high Counsellor, that the truth may be revealed to thee, and that thou mayest be of the well-informed.

God is Our witness! We have, under no circumstances, opposed either him, or others. We observed, under all conditions, the precepts of God, and were never one of those that wrought disorders. To this he himself doth testify. His intention was to lay hold on Us, and send Us back to Persia, that he might thereby exalt his fame and reputation.

—*BAHÁ'U'LLÁH 24*

I SAW[10] THE PROPHETS AND THE MESSENGERS gather and seat themselves around Me, moaning, weeping and loudly lamenting. Amazed, I inquired of them the reason, whereupon their lamentation and weeping waxed greater, and they said unto Me: "We weep for Thee, O Most Great Mystery, O Tabernacle of Immortality!" They wept with such a weeping that I too wept with them. Thereupon the Concourse on high addressed Me saying: ". . . Erelong shalt Thou behold with Thine own eyes what no Prophet hath

10. In a dream.

beheld. . . . Be patient, be patient." . . . They continued addressing Me the whole night until the approach of dawn.

—*BAHÁ'U'LLÁH* 25

THAT THE SPIRIT SHOULD DEPART out of the body of 'Iráq is indeed a wondrous sign unto all who are in heaven and all who are on earth. Erelong will ye behold this Divine Youth riding upon the steed of victory. Then will the hearts of the envious be seized with trembling.

—*BAHÁ'U'LLÁH* 26

Admonition to the Bábís upon Bahá'u'lláh's Departure from Baghdád

O MY COMPANIONS, I ENTRUST to your keeping this city of Baghdád, in the state ye now behold it, when from the eyes of friends and strangers alike, crowding its housetops, its streets and markets, tears like the rain of spring are flowing down, and I depart. With you it now rests to watch lest your deeds and conduct dim the flame of love that gloweth within the breasts of its inhabitants.

—*BAHÁ'U'LLÁH* 27

Bahá'u'lláh's Public Declaration of His Mission

Bahá'u'lláh's enemies intended that His banishment from Baghdád would result in His humiliation. However, the opposite occurred. News of His impending departure caused a tumult in the city. "A concourse of people of both sexes and of every age," Shoghi Effendi relates,

> *comprising friends and strangers, Arabs, Kurds, and Persians, notables and clerics, officials and merchants, as well as many of the lower classes, the poor, the orphaned, the outcast, some surprised, others heartbroken, many tearful and apprehensive, a few impelled by curiosity or secret satisfaction, thronged the approaches of His house, eager to catch a final glimpse of One Who, for a decade, had, through precept and example, exercised so potent an influence on so large a number of the heterogeneous inhabitants of their city.*

The acclaim accorded Bahá'u'lláh caused the joy of His enemies to be turned to chagrin and regret. The governor, Námiq Páshá, told Bahá'u'lláh: "'Formerly they insisted upon your departure. Now, however, they are even more insistent that you should remain.'"

On 22 April 1863, twenty-six days after receiving 'Álí Páshá's invitation to leave Baghdád, Bahá'u'lláh left His home and entered the Najíbíyyih Garden, where He stayed for twelve days. An indication of the divine authority He embodied was the finely embroidered táj *(crown) that He now wore. In successive waves, friends and companions attained His presence and bade Him farewell. Among them were Námiq Páshá and the muftí of Baghdád.*

Such were the circumstances surrounding the moment Bahá'u'lláh chose to announce publicly His prophetic mission. Shoghi Effendi describes the significance of the event:

The arrival of Bahá'u'lláh in the Najíbíyyih Garden, subsequently designated by His followers as the Garden of Riḍván, signalizes the commencement of what has come to be recognized as the holiest and most significant of all Bahá'í festivals, the festival commemorating the Declaration of His Mission to His companions. So momentous a Declaration may well be regarded both as the logical consummation of that revolutionizing process which was initiated by Himself upon His return from Sulaymáníyyih, and as a prelude to the final proclamation of that same Mission to the world and its rulers from Adrianople. . . .

. . . .

Of the exact circumstances attending that epoch-making Declaration, we, alas, are but scantily informed. The words Bahá'u'lláh actually uttered on that occasion, the manner of His Declaration, the reaction it produced, its impact on Mírzá Yaḥyá, the identity of those who were privileged to hear Him, are shrouded in an obscurity which future historians will find it difficult to penetrate.

What remains, however, are Tablets from the Supreme Pen that reveal the import of the announcement and convey a sense of the joy that filled the souls of those who were present.

THE DIVINE SPRINGTIME IS COME, O Most Exalted Pen, for the Festival of the All-Merciful is fast approaching. Bestir thyself, and magnify, before the entire creation, the name of God, and celebrate His praise, in such wise that all created things may be regenerated and made new. Speak, and hold not thy peace. The day star of blissfulness shineth above the horizon of Our name, the Blissful, inasmuch as the kingdom of the name of God hath been adorned with the ornament of the name of thy Lord, the

Creator of the heavens. Arise before the nations of the earth, and arm thyself with the power of this Most Great Name, and be not of those who tarry.

Methinks that thou hast halted and movest not upon My Tablet. Could the brightness of the Divine Countenance have bewildered thee, or the idle talk of the froward filled thee with grief and paralyzed thy movement? Take heed lest anything deter thee from extolling the greatness of this Day—the Day whereon the Finger of majesty and power hath opened the seal of the Wine of Reunion, and called all who are in the heavens and all who are on the earth. Preferrest thou to tarry when the breeze announcing the Day of God hath already breathed over thee, or art thou of them that are shut out as by a veil from Him?

No veil whatever have I allowed, O Lord of all names and Creator of the heavens, to shut me from the recognition of the glories of Thy Day—the Day which is the lamp of guidance unto the whole world, and the sign of the Ancient of Days unto all them that dwell therein. My silence is by reason of the veils that have blinded Thy creatures' eyes to Thee, and my muteness is because of the impediments that have hindered Thy people from recognizing Thy truth. Thou knowest what is in me, but I know not what is in Thee. Thou art the All-Knowing, the All-Informed. By Thy name that excelleth all other names! If Thy overruling and all-compelling behest should ever reach me, it would empower me to revive the souls of all men, through Thy most exalted Word, which I have heard uttered by Thy Tongue of power in Thy Kingdom of glory. It would enable me to announce the revelation of Thy effulgent countenance wherethrough that which lay hidden from the eyes of men hath been manifested in Thy name, the Perspicuous, the sovereign Protector, the Self-Subsisting.

Canst thou discover any one but Me, O Pen, in this Day? What hath become of the creation and the manifestations thereof? What of the names and their kingdom? Whither are gone all created things, whether seen or unseen? What of the hidden secrets of the universe and its revelations? Lo, the entire creation hath passed away! Nothing remaineth except My Face, the Ever-Abiding, the Resplendent, the All-Glorious.

This is the Day whereon naught can be seen except the splendors of the Light that shineth from the face of Thy Lord, the Gracious, the Most Bountiful. Verily, We have caused every soul to expire by virtue of Our irresistible and all-subduing sovereignty. We have, then, called into being a new creation, as a token of Our grace unto men. I am, verily, the All-Bountiful, the Ancient of Days.

This is the Day whereon the unseen world crieth out: "Great is thy blessedness, O earth, for thou hast been made the foot-stool of thy God, and been chosen as the seat of His mighty throne." The realm of glory exclaimeth: "Would that my life could be sacrificed for thee, for He Who is the Beloved of the All-Merciful hath established His sovereignty upon thee, through the power of His Name that hath been promised unto all things, whether of the past or of the future." This is the Day whereon every sweet smelling thing hath derived its fragrance from the smell of My garment—a garment that hath shed its perfume upon the whole of creation. This is the Day whereon the rushing waters of everlasting life have gushed out of the Will of the All-Merciful. Haste ye, with your hearts and souls, and quaff your fill, O Concourse of the realms above!

Say: He it is Who is the Manifestation of Him Who is the Unknowable, the Invisible of the Invisibles, could ye but perceive it. He it is Who hath laid bare before you the hidden and treasured Gem, were ye to seek it. He it is Who is the one Beloved of all things, whether of the past or of the future. Would that ye might set your hearts and hopes upon Him!

We have heard the voice of thy pleading, O Pen, and excuse thy silence. What is it that hath so sorely bewildered thee?

The inebriation of Thy presence, O Well-Beloved of all worlds, hath seized and possessed me.

Arise, and proclaim unto the entire creation the tidings that He Who is the All-Merciful hath directed His steps towards the Riḍván and entered it. Guide, then, the people unto the garden of delight which God hath made the Throne of His Paradise. We have chosen thee to be our most mighty Trumpet, whose blast is to signalize the resurrection of all mankind.

Say: This is the Paradise on whose foliage the wine of utterance hath imprinted the testimony: "He that was hidden from the eyes of men is revealed, girded with sovereignty and power!" This is the Paradise, the rustling of whose leaves proclaims: "O ye that inhabit the heavens and the earth! There hath appeared what hath never previously appeared. He Who, from everlasting, had concealed His Face from the sight of creation is now come." From the whispering breeze that wafteth amidst its branches there cometh the cry: "He Who is the sovereign Lord of all is made manifest. The Kingdom is God's," while from its streaming waters can be heard the murmur: "All eyes are gladdened, for He Whose secret no one hath discovered, hath lifted the veil of glory, and uncovered the countenance of Beauty."

Within this Paradise, and from the heights of its loftiest chambers, the Maids of Heaven have cried out and shouted: "Rejoice, ye dwellers of the realms above, for the fingers of Him Who is the Ancient of Days are ringing, in the name of the All-Glorious, the Most Great Bell, in the midmost heart of the heavens. The hands of bounty have borne round the cup of everlasting life. Approach, and quaff your fill. Drink with healthy relish, O ye that are the very incarnations of longing, ye who are the embodiments of vehement desire!"

This is the Day whereon He Who is the Revealer of the names of God hath stepped out of the Tabernacle of glory, and proclaimed unto all who are in the heavens and all who are on the earth: "Put away the cups of Paradise and all the life-giving waters they contain, for lo, the people of Bahá have entered the blissful abode of the Divine Presence, and quaffed the wine of reunion, from the chalice of the beauty of their Lord, the All-Possessing, the Most High."

Forget the world of creation, O Pen, and turn thou towards the face of thy Lord, the Lord of all names. Adorn, then, the world with the ornament of the favors of thy Lord, the King of everlasting days. For We perceive the fragrance of the Day whereon He Who is the Desire of all nations hath shed upon the kingdoms of the unseen and of the seen the splendor of the light of His most excellent names, and enveloped them with the radiance of the luminaries of His most gracious favors—favors which none can reckon except Him, Who is the omnipotent Protector of the entire creation.

Look not upon the creatures of God except with the eye of kindliness and of mercy, for Our loving providence hath pervaded all created things, and Our grace encompassed the earth and the heavens. This is the Day whereon the true servants of God partake of the life-giving waters of reunion, the Day whereon those that are nigh unto Him are able to drink of the soft-flowing river of immortality, and they who believe in His unity, the wine of His Presence, through their recognition of Him Who is the Highest and Last End of all, in Whom the Tongue of Majesty and Glory voiceth the call: "The Kingdom is Mine. I, Myself, am, of Mine own right, its Ruler."

Attract the hearts of men, through the call of Him, the one alone Beloved. Say: This is the Voice of God, if ye do but hearken. This is the Day Spring of the Revelation of God, did ye but know it. This is the Dawning-Place of the Cause of God, were ye to recognize it. This is the Source of the commandment of God, did ye but judge it fairly. This is the manifest and hidden Secret; would that ye might perceive it. O peoples of the world! Cast away, in My name that transcendeth all other names, the things ye possess, and immerse yourselves in this Ocean in whose depths lay hidden the pearls of wisdom and of utterance, an ocean that surgeth in My name, the All-Merciful. Thus instructeth you He with Whom is the Mother Book.

The Best-Beloved is come. In His right hand is the sealed Wine of His name. Happy is the man that turneth unto Him, and drinketh his fill, and exclaimeth: "Praise be to Thee, O Revealer of the signs of God!" By the righteousness of the Almighty! Every hidden thing hath been manifested through the power of truth. All the favors of God have been sent down, as a token of His grace. The waters of everlasting life have, in their fullness, been proffered unto men. Every single cup hath been borne round by the hand of the Well-Beloved. Draw near, and tarry not, though it be for one short moment.

Blessed are they that have soared on the wings of detachment and attained the station which, as ordained by God, overshadoweth the entire creation, whom neither the vain imaginations of the learned, nor the multitude of the hosts of the earth have succeeded in deflecting from His Cause. Who is there among you, O people, who will renounce the world, and draw nigh unto God, the Lord of all names? Where is he to be found who, through the power of My name that transcendeth all created things, will cast away the things that men possess, and cling, with all his might, to the things which God, the Knower of the unseen and of the seen, hath bidden him observe? Thus hath His bounty been sent down unto men, His testimony fulfilled, and His proof shone forth above the Horizon of mercy. Rich is the prize that shall be won by him who hath believed and exclaimed: "Lauded art Thou, O Beloved of all worlds! Magnified be Thy name, O Thou the Desire of every understanding heart!"

Rejoice with exceeding gladness, O people of Bahá, as ye call to remembrance the Day of supreme felicity, the Day whereon the Tongue of the Ancient of Days hath spoken, as He departed from His House, proceeding to the Spot from which He shed upon the whole of creation the splendors of His name, the All-Merciful. God is Our witness. Were We to reveal the hidden secrets of that Day, all they that dwell on earth and in the heavens would swoon away and die, except such as will be preserved by God, the Almighty, the All-Knowing, the All-Wise.

Such is the inebriating effect of the words of God upon Him Who is the Revealer of His undoubted proofs, that His Pen can move no longer. With these words He concludeth His Tablet: "No God is there but Me, the Most Exalted, the Most Powerful, the Most Excellent, the All-Knowing."

—*BAHÁ'U'LLÁH* 28

Chapter 7 / CONSTANTINOPLE

The Journey from Bag̲h̲dád to Constantinople

The same love and veneration shown to Bahá'u'lláh upon His departure from His house in Bag̲h̲dád for the Riḍván Garden was showered upon Him as He left the garden for Constantinople (now Istanbul) on 3 May 1863. Mounted on a magnificent red roan stallion, Bahá'u'lláh rode triumphantly through a throng of well-wishers who crowded around Him, some throwing themselves in His horse's path, others bowing before it, kissing its hooves, and embracing its stirrups. Similar acts of devotion were shown to Bahá'u'lláh in the villages and towns through which He passed on His journey. Local officials, responding to a written order issued by Námiq Pás̲h̲á, would meet Him on the outskirts of their town or village upon His arrival and escort Him out of town upon His departure. Nabíl writes that, "According to the unanimous testimony of those we met in the course of that journey, never before had they witnessed along this route, over which governors and mus̲h̲írs continually passed back and forth between Constantinople and Bag̲h̲dád, any one travel in such state, dispense such hospitality to all, and accord to each so great a share of his bounty."

Bahá'u'lláh was accompanied on His journey by fifty-four people, including members of His family, many companions, a mounted guard of soldiers, some fifty mules and horses, and seven howdahs. 'Abdu'l-Bahá, then a youth of nineteen, directed and supervised the entire operation. The travelers averaged a distance of twenty-five to thirty miles per day. After a three-day voyage on the Black Sea, Bahá'u'lláh and His entourage arrived at the port of Constantinople on 16 August 1863, where the Turkish authorities received Him with great honor. Carriages were waiting at the dock to take Bahá'u'lláh and His family to the home of Shamsí Big, the official assigned by the government to serve as His host.

I HAVE THROUGH THE GRACE OF GOD and His might besought the help of no one in the past, neither will I seek the help of any one in the future. He it is Who aided Me, through the power of truth, during the days of My banishment in 'Iráq. He it is Who overshadowed Me with His protection at a time when the kindreds of the earth were contending with Me. He it is Who enabled Me to depart out of the city,[1] clothed with such majesty as none, except the denier and the malicious, can fail to admit.

—*BAHÁ'U'LLÁH 1*

The Faithlessness of Mírzá Yaḥyá

The cowardice and deceit Mírzá Yaḥyá had demonstrated in Ṭihrán and Baghdád continued to characterize his behavior during the journey to Constantinople. When he learned of Bahá'u'lláh's banishment to that city, Mírzá Yaḥyá's first thoughts were to flee to India or Abyssinia (now Ethiopia). Bahá'u'lláh again advised him to go to Persia to disseminate the Báb's writings, but this also frightened him, for he knew that the Persian authorities

1. Baghdád.

were determined to eliminate the Bábís. He asked Bahá'u'lláh if he could stay behind in Baghdád but later proposed going to Mosul[2] *ahead of Bahá'u'lláh, fearing that once Bahá'u'lláh and His entourage left Baghdád, the authorities would turn on them and either kill them or hand them over to the Persian government. After procuring a false passport under an alias, he left Baghdád and joined Bahá'u'lláh's caravan in Mosul. Along the way he traveled separately by day and joined the caravan at night, pretending not to know Bahá'u'lláh or anyone else, keeping to himself, and maintaining his new identity. His only confidant in the caravan was Siyyid Muḥammad.*

On the day of Bahá'u'lláh's arrival in Constantinople, Nabíl overheard Mírzá Yaḥyá remarking to Siyyid Muḥammad, "Had I not chosen to hide myself, had I revealed my identity, the honor accorded to Him [Bahá'u'lláh] on this day would have been mine too."

WE ESPECIALLY APPOINTED CERTAIN ONES to collect the writings of the Primal Point. When this was accomplished, We summoned Mírzá Yaḥyá and Mírzá Vahháb-i-Khurásání, known as Mírzá Javád, to meet in a certain place. Conforming with Our instructions, they completed the task of transcribing two copies of the works of the Primal Point. I swear by God! This Wronged One, by reason of His constant association with men, hath not looked at these books, nor gazed with outward eyes on these writings. When We departed, these writings were in the possession of these two persons. It was agreed

2. A city in northwestern 'Iráq that lies on the route Bahá'u'lláh's caravan took to Constantinople.

that Mírzá Yaḥyá should be entrusted with them, and proceed to Persia, and disseminate them throughout that land. This Wronged One proceeded, at the request of the Ministers of the Ottoman Government to their capital. When We arrived in Mosul, We found that Mírzá Yaḥyá had left before Us for that city, and was awaiting Us there. Briefly, the books and writings were left in Bag͟hdád, while he himself proceeded to Constantinople and joined these servants. God beareth now witness unto the things which have touched this Wronged One, for after We had so arduously striven, he [Mírzá Yaḥyá] abandoned the writings and joined the exiles. This Wronged One was, for a long period, overwhelmed by infinite sorrows until such time when, in pursuance of measures of which none but the one true God is aware, We despatched the writings unto another place and another country, owing to the fact that in 'Iráq all documents must every month be carefully examined, lest they rot and perish. God, however, preserved them and sent them unto a place which He had previously ordained. He, verily, is the Protector, the Succorer.

—*BAHÁ'U'LLÁH* 2

Arrival in Constantinople

With the arrival of Bahá'u'lláh at Constantinople, the capital of the Ottoman Empire and seat of the Caliphate (acclaimed by the Muḥammadans as "the Dome of Islam," but stigmatized by Him as the spot whereon the "throne of tyranny" *had been established) the grimmest and most calamitous and yet the most glorious chapter in the history of the first Bahá'í century may be said to have opened. A period in which untold privations and unprecedented trials were mingled with the noblest spiritual triumphs was now commencing. The day-star of Bahá'u'lláh's ministry was about to reach its zenith. The most momentous years of the Heroic Age of His Dispensation were at hand. The catastrophic process, foreshadowed as far back as the year sixty by His Forerunner in the Qayyúmu'l-Asmá', was beginning to be set in motion.*[3]

—SHOGHI EFFENDI

UPON OUR ARRIVAL, there befell Us at the hands of the malicious that which the books of the world can never adequately recount. Thereupon the inmates of Paradise, and they that dwell within the retreats of holiness, lamented; and yet the people are wrapped in a thick veil!

—BAHÁ'U'LLÁH 3

NARRATE, O SERVANT, the things Thou didst behold at the time of Thine arrival in the City, that Thy testimony may endure amongst men, and serve as a warning unto them that believe. We found, upon Our arrival in the City, its governors and elders as children gathered about and disporting themselves with clay. We perceived no one sufficiently mature to acquire from Us the truths which God hath taught Us, nor ripe for Our wondrous words of wisdom. Our inner eye wept sore over them, and over their

3. *God Passes By*, p. 157.

transgressions and their total disregard of the thing for which they were created. This is what We observed in that City, and which We have chosen to note down in Our Book, that it may serve as a warning unto them, and unto the rest of mankind.

—*BAHÁ'U'LLÁH* 4

Dealings with Officials in Constantinople

The same fears that had motivated the Persian diplomats and divines in Baghdád to press for Bahá'u'lláh's removal were alive among the Persian diplomatic authorities in Constantinople. Fearing that the developments that had occurred in Baghdád would be repeated and that the sympathy or even the allegiance of influential Turkish government officials might be won, the Persian authorities sought to have Bahá'u'lláh banished to a remote part of the Turkish empire.

Upon Bahá'u'lláh's arrival in Constantinople, the Persian ambassador Mírzá Ḥusayn Khán, who had been instrumental in securing the Sulṭán's approval of the edict banishing Bahá'u'lláh to Constantinople, sent two high-ranking Persians to call on Bahá'u'lláh on his behalf. He expected Bahá'u'lláh to return the favor and call on him, but he soon found that Bahá'u'lláh had no intention of doing so. In those days it was customary for prominent visitors to Constantinople to call on high-ranking clerics, government ministers, and diplomats from other countries after arriving in the city. During such visits callers stated their needs, solicited favors, made deals, and presented gifts, all with the intention of winning the authorities' support to further their own positions. The Persians were particularly known for this. Bahá'u'lláh refused to be involved in such intrigues and exchanges of favors and maintained an upright and independent attitude. Kamál Páshá, a minister of the Sulṭán, and a few others were so forward as to remind Bahá'u'lláh of the custom.

His excellency, the late Mírzá Ḥusayn K͟hán, Mus͟híru'd-Dawlih,—may God forgive him—hath known this Wronged One, and he, no doubt, must have given to the Authorities a circumstantial account of the arrival of this Wronged One at the Sublime Porte, and of the things which He said and did. On the day of Our arrival the Government Official, whose duty it was to receive and entertain official visitors, met Us and escorted Us to the place he had been bidden to take Us. In truth, the Government showed these wronged ones the utmost kindness and consideration. The following day Prince S͟hujá'u'd-Dawlih, accompanied by Mírzá Ṣafá, acting as the representatives of the late Mus͟híru'd-Dawlih, the Minister (accredited to the Imperial Court) came to visit Us. Others, among whom were several Ministers of the Imperial Government, and including the late Kamál Pás͟há, likewise called on Us. Wholly reliant on God, and without any reference to any need He might have had, or to any other matter, this Wronged One sojourned for a period of four months in that city. His actions were known and evident unto all, and none can deny them except such as hate Him, and speak not the truth. He that hath recognized God, recognizeth none other but Him. We have never liked, nor like We, to make mention of such things.

Whenever high dignitaries of Persia came to that city [Constantinople] they would exert themselves to the utmost soliciting at every door such allowances and gifts as they might obtain. This Wronged One, however, if He hath done nothing that would redound to the glory of Persia, hath at least acted in a manner that could in no wise disgrace it. That which was done by his late Excellency [Mu<u>sh</u>íru'd-Dawlih]—may God exalt his station—was not actuated by his friendship towards this Wronged One, but rather was prompted by his own sagacious judgment, and by his desire to accomplish the service he secretly contemplated rendering his Government. I testify that he was so faithful in his service to his Government that dishonesty played no part, and was held in contempt, in the domain of his activities. It was he who was responsible for the arrival of these wronged ones in the Most Great Prison ['Akká]. As he was faithful, however, in the discharge of his duty, he deserveth Our commendation.

—BAHÁ'U'LLÁH 5

CALL THOU TO REMEMBRANCE Thine arrival in the City [Constantinople], how the Ministers of the Sulṭán thought Thee to be unacquainted with their laws and regulations, and believed Thee to be one of the ignorant. Say: Yes, by My Lord! I am ignorant of all things except what God hath, through His bountiful favor, been pleased to teach Me. To this We assuredly testify, and unhesitatingly confess it.

Say: If the laws and regulations to which ye cleave be of your own making, We will, in no wise, follow them. Thus have I been instructed by Him Who is the All-Wise, the All-Informed. Such hath been My way in the past, and such will it remain in the future, through the power of God and His might. This, indeed, is the true and right way. If they be ordained by God, bring forth, then, your proofs, if ye be of them that speak the truth. Say: We have written down in a Book which leaveth not unrecorded the work of any man, however insignificant, all that they have imputed to Thee, and all that they have done unto Thee.

Say: It behoveth you, O Ministers of State, to keep the precepts of God, and to forsake your own laws and regulations, and to be of them who are guided aright. Better is this for you than all ye possess, did ye but know it. If ye transgress the commandment of God, not one jot or one tittle of all your works shall be acceptable in His sight. Ye shall, erelong, discover the consequences of that which ye shall have done in this vain life, and shall be repaid for them. This, verily, is the truth, the undoubted truth.

—BAHÁ'U'LLÁH 6

ONE DAY, WHILE IN CONSTANTINOPLE, Kamál Pá<u>sh</u>á visited this Wronged One. Our conversation turned upon topics profitable unto man. He said that he had learned several languages. In reply We observed: "You have wasted your life. It beseemeth you and the other officials of the Government to convene a gathering and choose one of the divers languages, and likewise one of the existing scripts, or else to create a new language and a new script to be taught children in schools throughout the world. They would, in this way, be acquiring only two languages, one their own native tongue, the other the language in which all the peoples of the world would converse. Were men to take fast hold on that which hath been mentioned, the whole earth would come to be regarded as one country, and the people would be relieved and freed from the necessity of acquiring and teaching different languages." When in Our presence, he acquiesced, and even evinced great joy and complete satisfaction. We then told him to lay this matter before the officials and ministers of the Government, in order that it might be put into effect throughout the different countries. However, although he often returned to see Us after this, he never again referred to this subject, although that which had been suggested is conducive to the concord and the unity of the peoples of the world.

—BAHÁ'U'LLÁH 7

Banishment to Adrianople

Bahá'u'lláh's refusal to enter into the exchange of visits and favors with the Sulṭán's ministers gave Persian ambassador Mírzá Ḥusayn Khán the ammunition he needed to secure Bahá'u'lláh's banishment to a remote part of the Turkish empire. He portrayed Bahá'u'lláh as a proud and arrogant man Who was opposed to established authority and Who esteemed Himself above the law. It was this attitude, Mírzá Ḥusayn Khán alleged, that lay behind the differences that had arisen between Bahá'u'lláh and the Persian government. Mírzá Ḥusayn Khán presented this distorted picture of Bahá'u'lláh to the Sulṭán's ministers, to religious officials, and to other prominent people. Less than four months after Bahá'u'lláh arrived in the city, and just one day after a report from Mírzá Ḥusayn Khán calling for Bahá'u'lláh's removal was presented to the Sulṭán, the edict banishing Him to Adrianople (now Edirne) was issued.

The edict was delivered by the highly respected brother-in-law of 'Álí Páshá, the prime minister. But Bahá'u'lláh refused to receive the envoy and delegated 'Abdu'l-Bahá and Mírzá Músá to see him, promising to respond within three days. On the same day Bahá'u'lláh revealed a Tablet to Sulṭán 'Abdu'l-'Azíz that was delivered the next morning to 'Álí Páshá by Shamsí Big with the message that "it was sent down from God." "I know not what that letter contained," Shamsí Big reported, "for no sooner had the Grand Vizir perused it than he turned the color of a corpse, and remarked: 'It is as if the King of Kings were issuing his behest to his humblest vassal king and regulating his conduct.' So grievous was his condition that I backed out of his presence."

Bahá'u'lláh's Tablet to the Sulṭán opened the initial phase of His proclamation to the kings, which continued in Adrianople and concluded with the revelation of the Kitáb-i-Aqdas in 'Akká. Although the text of the Tablet is unknown, its tone and substance can be surmised from other Tablets Bahá'u'lláh revealed for Sulṭán 'Abdu'l-'Azíz and his ministers and for Ḥájí Mírzá Ḥusayn Khán, rebuking them for their immaturity and incompetence.

At first Bahá'u'lláh was angry and refused to comply with the Sulṭán's order. He reportedly said to His companions, "Do you wish to drain the cup of martyrdom? No better time can there be than now to offer your lives in the path of your Lord. Our innocence is manifestly evident, and they have no alternative but to declare their injustice." One of the companions wrote, "all of us, with the utmost joy, fidelity, unity and detachment, were eager to attain to that high station; and God is my witness that we were blissfully expecting martyrdom." However, Mírzá Yaḥyá and a few others wavered, and he, acting as their spokesman, asked Bahá'u'lláh to accept the edict. Perceiving the possibility of a rift developing among the Bábís, Bahá'u'lláh reluctantly consented to leave the capital. But He commented that a golden opportunity had been missed: "If we, few as we are, had stood our ground to fall as martyrs in the midmost heart of the world, the effect of that martyr-

dom would have been felt in all the worlds of God. And possibly nothing would have happened to us."

Once again Bahá'u'lláh and His family and companions set out on another journey to a place of exile. Having little time to prepare for their journey and lacking adequate clothing for the cold weather, the exiles departed on a snowy December morning in the midst of a cold spell of unprecedented severity. They rode in wagons and on pack animals, accompanied by Turkish officers, while their belongings were piled in oxcarts. Having become accustomed to 'Iráq's warm weather, the exiles found the severe cold especially difficult to bear. The only way they could obtain water along the way was by building a fire on a frozen river to melt the ice. One of the exiles recalls passing a number of people who had frozen to death.

BE FAIR IN YOUR JUDGMENT, O ye Ministers of State! What is it that We have committed that could justify Our banishment? What is the offense that hath warranted Our expulsion? It is We Who have sought you, and yet, behold how ye refused to receive Us! By God! This is a sore injustice that ye have perpetrated—an injustice with which no earthly injustice can measure. To this the Almighty is Himself a witness. . . .

Know ye that the world and its vanities and its embellishments shall pass away. Nothing will endure except God's Kingdom which pertaineth to none but Him, the Sovereign Lord of all, the Help in Peril, the All-Glorious, the Almighty. The days of your life shall roll away, and all the things with which ye are occupied and of which ye boast yourselves shall perish, and ye shall, most certainly, be summoned by a company of His angels to appear at the spot where the limbs of the entire creation shall be made to tremble, and the flesh of every oppressor to creep. Ye shall be asked of the things your hands have wrought in this, your vain life, and shall be repaid for your doings. This is the day that shall inevitably come upon you, the hour that none can put back. To this the Tongue of Him that speaketh the truth and is the Knower of all things hath testified.

—BAHÁ'U'LLÁH 8

WHAT DID IT PROFIT THEE,[4] and such as are like thee, to slay, year after year, so many of the oppressed, and to inflict upon them manifold afflictions, when they have increased a hundredfold, and ye find yourselves in complete bewilderment, knowing not how to relieve your minds of this oppressive thought. . . . His Cause transcends any and every plan ye devise. Know this much: Were all the governments on earth to unite and take My life and the lives of all who bear this Name, this Divine Fire would never be quenched. His Cause will rather encompass all the kings of the earth, nay all that hath been created from water and clay. . . . Whatever may yet befall Us, great shall be our gain, and manifest the loss wherewith they shall be afflicted.

—BAHÁ'U'LLÁH 9

4. Mírzá Ḥusayn Khán, the Persian ambassador in Constantinople.

THEY EXPELLED US FROM THY CITY [Constantinople] with an abasement with which no abasement on earth can compare. . . . Neither My family, nor those who accompanied Me had the necessary raiment to protect them from the cold in that freezing weather. . . . The eyes of Our enemies wept over Us, and beyond them those of every discerning person.

—BAHÁ'U'LLÁH 10

O SPOT THAT ART SITUATE ON THE SHORES of the two seas! The throne of tyranny hath, verily, been stablished upon thee, and the flame of hatred hath been kindled within thy bosom, in such wise that the Concourse on high and they who circle around the Exalted Throne have wailed and lamented. We behold in thee the foolish ruling over the wise, and darkness vaunting itself against the light. Thou art indeed filled with manifest pride. Hath thine outward splendor made thee vainglorious? By Him Who is the Lord of mankind! It shall soon perish, and thy daughters and thy widows and all the kindreds that dwell within thee shall lament. Thus informeth thee the All-Knowing, the All-Wise.

—BAHÁ'U'LLÁH 11

Chapter 8 / ADRIANOPLE

After twelve long days of arduous travel through snow, rain, and storm, Bahá'u'lláh and His companions arrived on 12 December 1863 in Adrianople (Edirne), a city Bahá'u'lláh designated in the Arabic Tablet of Aḥmad as the "remote prison."

After staying three nights in a caravansary, Bahá'u'lláh and His family were consigned to a house suitable only for summer living. Soon more spacious quarters were obtained. Those who had remained in the caravansary moved into the first house, while a house next door to Bahá'u'lláh's was rented for Mírzá Músá, Mírzá Yaḥyá, and their families. All of these houses, however, were too small and cold and were infested with vermin. The unusually cold weather, which continued for months with snow falling well into spring, made the dwellings even more uncomfortable. About ten months later a house that met Bahá'u'lláh's approval was found. It was a three-story house in the center of the city—a magnificent mansion with thirty rooms, known as the house of Amru'lláh (God's Command).

The orb of Bahá'u'lláh's revelation was rising. Tablets imbued with power and authority flowed unceasingly from His pen. However, before His ministry reached its zenith with the revelation of Tablets proclaiming His prophetic mission to the kings and leaders of the world, a crisis of unprecedented severity shook the foundations of the new Faith and temporarily eclipsed the brightness of its light. Shoghi Effendi describes this crisis as the "first major internal convulsion" that "threatened to cause an irreparable breach in the ranks" of "a newly rearisen community."

The crisis, brewing since the early days of Bahá'u'lláh's exile in Baghdád, was caused by the insatiable jealousy of Mírzá Yaḥyá and his scheming accomplice, Siyyid Muḥammad, who had followed Bahá'u'lláh to Adrianople. In Baghdád Mírzá Yaḥyá had witnessed with growing frustration the increasing admiration that officials and citizens showed toward Bahá'u'lláh. Now in Adrianople he again observed the same respect for and deference toward Bahá'u'lláh. He also saw the Bábí community's increasing acceptance of Bahá'u'lláh's prophetic office and the unrestrained veneration of pilgrims making their way to Adrianople. Such signs of Bahá'u'lláh's ascendancy drove Mírzá Yaḥyá to commit acts of treachery that brought inestimable sorrow to Bahá'u'lláh and constituted the heaviest blow leveled against Him in His lifetime.

Realizing that he now had no hope of fulfilling his desire for leadership, goaded by Siyyid Muḥammad, and emboldened by Bahá'u'lláh's consistent efforts to conceal his many transgressions and crimes, Mírzá Yaḥyá determined to take Bahá'u'lláh's life. Although Bahá'u'lláh tried to conceal the attempt from His companions, further acts of treachery and betrayal forced Him to sever all ties with His younger half-brother, whom He had served as guardian since their father's death when Mírzá Yaḥyá was a boy of nine. This "most great separation," *as Bahá'u'lláh referred to the severing of the relationship, perplexed and confused believers who were unfamiliar with Mírzá Yaḥyá's conduct, damaged the prestige of the Faith, and gratified and encouraged its enemies. The anguish it brought upon Bahá'u'lláh is reflected in the term He used to refer to this period—*Ayyám-i-Shidád, *the "Days of Stress."*

"Days of Stress"— The Rebellion of Mírzá Yaḥyá

ALAS, ALAS, FOR THE THINGS which have befallen Me! By God! There befell Me at the hands of him whom I have nurtured [Mírzá Yaḥyá], by day and by night, what hath caused the Holy Spirit, and the dwellers of the Tabernacle of the Grandeur of God, the Lord of this wondrous Day, to lament.

—*BAHÁ'U'LLÁH 1*

MY PEN, VERILY, LAMENTETH over Mine own Self, and My Tablet weepeth sore over what hath befallen Me at the hands of one [Mírzá Yaḥyá] over whom We watched for successive years, and who, day and night, served in My presence, until he was made to err by one of My servants, named Siyyid Muḥammad. . . . And there befell Me at the hands of both of them that which made every man of understanding to cry out, and he who is endued with insight to groan aloud, and the tears of the fair-minded to flow.

We pray to God to graciously assist them that have been led astray to be just and fair-minded, and to make them aware of that whereof they have been heedless. He, in truth, is the All-Bounteous, the Most Generous. Debar not Thy servants, O my Lord, from the door of Thy grace, and drive them not away from the court of Thy presence. Assist them to dispel the mists of idle fancy, and to tear away the veils of vain imaginings and hopes. Thou art, verily, the All-Possessing, the Most High. No God is there but Thee, the Almighty, the Gracious.

—BAHÁ'U'LLÁH 2

EVERY ONE OF THIS PEOPLE WELL KNOWETH that Siyyid Muḥammad was but one of Our servants. In the days when, as requested by the Imperial Ottoman Government, We proceeded to their Capital, he accompanied Us. Subsequently, he committed that which—I swear by God—hath caused the Pen of the Most High to weep and His Tablet to groan. We, therefore, cast him out; whereupon, he joined Mírzá Yaḥyá, and did what no tyrant hath ever done. We abandoned him, and said unto him: "Begone, O heedless one!"

—BAHÁ'U'LLÁH 3

A FEW BELIEVED IN HIM[1]; few of Our servants are the thankful. These He admonished, in all His Tablets—nay, in every passage of His wondrous writings—not to give themselves up in the Day of the promised Revelation to anything whatever, be it in the heaven or in the earth. "O people!" said He, "I have revealed Myself for His Manifestation, and have caused My Book, the Bayán, to descend upon you for no other purpose except to establish the truth of His Cause. Fear ye God, and contend not with Him as the people of the Qur'án have contended with Me. At

1. The Báb.

whatever time ye hear of Him, hasten ye towards Him, and cleave ye to whatsoever He may reveal unto you. Naught else besides Him can ever profit you, no, not though ye produce from first to last the testimonies of all those who were before you."

And when after the lapse of a few years the heaven of Divine decree was cleft asunder, and the Beauty of the Báb appeared in the clouds of the names of God, arrayed in a new raiment, these same people maliciously rose up against Him, Whose light embraceth all created things. They broke His Covenant, rejected His truth, contended with Him, caviled at His signs, treated His testimony as falsehood, and joined the company of the infidels. Eventually, they determined to take away His life. Such is the state of them who are in a far-gone error!

And when they realized their powerlessness to achieve their purpose, they arose to plot against Him. Witness how every moment they devise a fresh device to harm Him, that they may injure and dishonor the cause of God. Say: Woe be to you! By God! Your schemings cover you with shame. Your Lord, the God of mercy, can well dispense with all creatures. Nothing whatever can either increase or diminish the things He doth possess. If ye believe, to your own behoof will ye believe; and if ye believe not, ye yourselves will suffer. At no time can the hand of the infidel profane the hem of His Robe.

O My servant that believest in God! By the righteousness of the Almighty! Were I to recount to thee the tale of the things that have befallen Me, the souls and minds of men would be incapable of sustaining its weight. God Himself beareth Me witness. Watch over thyself, and follow not the footsteps of these people. Meditate diligently upon the Cause of thy Lord. Strive to know Him through His own Self and not through others. For no one else besides Him can ever profit thee. To this all created things will testify, couldst thou but perceive it.

—*BAHÁ'U'LLÁH* 4

I AM THE ONE, O LORD, whose heart and soul, whose limbs, whose inner and outer tongue testify to Thy unity and Thy oneness, and bear witness that Thou art God and that there is no God but Thee. Thou didst bring mankind into being to know Thee and to serve Thy Cause, that their station might thereby be elevated upon Thine earth and their souls be uplifted by virtue of the things Thou hast revealed in Thy Scriptures, Thy Books and Thy Tablets. Yet no sooner didst Thou manifest Thyself and reveal Thy signs than they turned away from Thee and repudiated Thee and rejected that which Thou didst unveil before their eyes through the potency of Thy might and Thy power. They rose up to inflict harm upon Thee, to extinguish Thy light and to put out the flame that blazeth in Thy Burning Bush. Their iniquity waxed so grievous that they conspired to shed Thy blood and to violate Thy honour. And likewise acted he whom Thou hadst nurtured with the hand of Thy loving-kindness, hadst protected from the mischief of the rebellious among Thy creatures and the froward amidst Thy servants, and whom Thou hadst set the task of writing Thy holy verses before Thy throne.[2]

Alas! Alas! for the things he perpetrated in Thy days to such an extent that he violated Thy Covenant and Thy Testament, rejected Thy holy Writ, rose up in rebellion and committed that which caused the denizens of Thy Kingdom to lament. Then no sooner had he found his hopes shattered and had perceived the odour of utter failure than he raised his voice and gave tongue to that which caused Thy chosen ones, who are nigh unto Thee, and the inmates of the pavilion of glory, to be lost in bewilderment.

Thou seest me, O my God, writhing in anguish upon the dust, like unto a fish. Deliver me, have mercy upon me, O Thou Whose aid is invoked by all men, O Thou within Whose grasp lie the reins of power over all men and women.

—BAHÁ'U'LLÁH 5

The Poisoning

Mírzá Yaḥyá had on previous occasions resorted to murder to eliminate people he perceived as rivals. During Bahá'u'lláh's withdrawal to Kurdistán, he had commissioned the assassination of Dayyán, one of the Báb's most outstanding followers, whom he both feared and envied. He had also brought about the assassination of Mírzá 'Alí-Akbar, the Báb's cousin, and had called for the murder of

2. Mírzá Yaḥyá.

other leading Bábís in an effort to eliminate all competition for leadership of the Bábí community. This time, however, the consequences of his actions were immediate and severe. Instead of resurrecting his defunct leadership, he sealed irretrievably his own doom.

Mírzá Yaḥyá began planning to murder Bahá'u'lláh about a year after their arrival in Adrianople. Under false pretexts he extracted from Mírzá Músá, one of Bahá'u'lláh's faithful brothers, knowledge about the effects of certain herbs and poisons. Then he began to invite Bahá'u'lláh to his home—though this was not his custom. One day he served Bahá'u'lláh tea in a cup that had been laced with poison. Bahá'u'lláh fell gravely ill. A doctor was called to treat Him, but His condition was so critical that the doctor pronounced His case hopeless, prostrated himself at Bahá'u'lláh's feet, and left without prescribing any remedy. Within a few days the doctor fell ill and died. However, before his death the doctor had said to Mírzá Áqá Ján, Bahá'u'lláh's amanuensis, that God had answered his prayers. Indeed, Bahá'u'lláh intimated that the doctor had sacrificed his life so that He might live.

Although Bahá'u'lláh's illness lasted an entire month and was accompanied by severe pains and high fever, He eventually recovered. However, the aftermath of this illness left Him with a shaking hand for the rest of His life.

HE WHO FOR MONTHS AND YEARS I REARED with the hand of loving-kindness hath risen to take My life.

—BAHÁ'U'LLÁH 6

THOU HAST PERPETRATED AGAINST THY BROTHER what no man hath perpetrated against another.

—BAHÁ'U'LLÁH 7

BY GOD! NO SPOT IS LEFT ON MY BODY that hath not been touched by the spears of thy machinations.

—BAHÁ'U'LLÁH 8

THE CRUELTIES INFLICTED BY MY OPPRESSORS have bowed Me down, and turned My hair white. Shouldst thou present thyself before My throne, thou wouldst fail to recognize the Ancient Beauty, for the freshness of His countenance is altered, and its brightness hath faded, by reason of the oppression of the infidels.

—*BAHÁ'U'LLÁH 9*

Acquainting Mírzá Yaḥyá with Bahá'u'lláh's Mission

When word of Mírzá Yaḥyá's attempt to murder Bahá'u'lláh became known despite Bahá'u'lláh's efforts to conceal it, Mírzá Yaḥyá alleged that Bahá'u'lláh had attempted to poison him but had mistakenly taken the poison Himself. Then he tried to induce an attendant to murder Bahá'u'lláh in the public bath. Although Bahá'u'lláh ordered the attendant not to speak about the incident to anyone, the attendant was so enraged that he could not contain himself. When the secret was revealed, Mírzá Yaḥyá disclaimed his intention and imputed the intended murder to the attendant.

The situation had reached a critical point. Bahá'u'lláh determined that the time had arrived to acquaint Mírzá Yaḥyá formally with His mission. Mírzá Áqá Ján was directed to deliver to Mírzá Yaḥyá the Súriy-i-Amr (the Tablet of the Command), which sets forth the nature of Bahá'u'lláh's station in clear terms, and to demand a conclusive reply. Mírzá Yaḥyá requested and was granted a day to prepare his response. He replied, Shoghi Effendi records, with "a counter-declaration, specifying the hour and the minute in which he had been made the recipient of an independent Revelation, necessitating the unqualified submission to him of the peoples of the earth in both the East and the West." Mírzá Yaḥyá's response, Shoghi Effendi says, signaled

> *the open and final rupture between Bahá'u'lláh and Mírzá Yaḥyá—a rupture that marks one of the darkest dates in Bahá'í history. Wishing to allay the fierce animosity that blazed in the bosom of His enemies, and to assure to each one of the exiles a complete freedom to choose between Him and them, Bahá'u'lláh withdrew with His family to the house of Riḍá Big (Shavvál 22, 1282* A.H.*),*[3] *which was rented by His order, and refused, for two months, to associate with either friend or stranger, including His own companions. He instructed Áqáy-i-Kalím*[4] *to divide all the furniture, bedding, clothing and utensils that were to be found in His home, and send half to the house of Mírzá Yaḥyá; to deliver to him certain relics he had long coveted, such as the seals, rings, and manuscripts in the handwriting of the Báb; and to insure that he received his full share of the allowance fixed by the government for the maintenance of the exiles and their families. He, moreover, directed Áqáy-i-Kalím to order to attend to Mírzá Yaḥyá's shopping, for several hours a day, any one of the companions whom he himself might select, and to assure him that whatever would henceforth be received in his name from Persia would be delivered into his own hands.*

SAY: O YAḤYÁ [AZAL][5], PRODUCE A SINGLE VERSE, if thou dost possess divinely-inspired knowledge. These words were formerly spoken by My Herald Who at

3. 10 March 1866.

4. Mírzá Músá, one of Bahá'u'lláh's faithful brothers.

5. When Bahá'u'lláh informed Mírzá Yaḥyá of His mission, Yaḥyá advanced his own claim to prophethood, using the title Ṣubḥ-i-Azal.

this hour proclaimeth: "Verily, verily, I am the first to adore Him." Be fair, O My brother. Art thou able to express thyself when brought face to face with the billowing ocean of Mine utterance? Canst thou unloose thy tongue when confronted with the shrill voice of My Pen? Hast thou any power before the revelations of Mine omnipotence? Judge thou fairly, I adjure thee by God, and call to mind when thou didst stand in the presence of this Wronged One and We dictated to thee the verses of God, the Help in Peril, the Self-Subsisting. Beware lest the source of falsehood withhold thee from the manifest Truth.

—BAHÁ'U'LLÁH 10

WHAT HATH PROCEEDED FROM THY PEN hath caused the Countenances of Glory to be prostrated upon the dust, hath rent in twain the Veil of Grandeur in the Sublime Paradise, and lacerated the hearts of the favored ones established upon the loftiest seats.

—BAHÁ'U'LLÁH 11

The "Most Great Idol"[6] *had at the bidding and through the power of Him Who is the Fountain-head of the Most Great Justice been cast out of the community of the Most Great Name, confounded, abhorred and broken. Cleansed from this pollution, delivered from this horrible possession, God's infant Faith could now forge ahead, and, despite the turmoil that had convulsed it, demonstrate its ca-*

6. Mírzá Yaḥyá.

pacity to fight further battles, capture loftier heights, and win mightier victories.[7]

—*SHOGHI EFFENDI*

Outpourings from Bahá'u'lláh's Pen

Shoghi Effendi explains that, although "a temporary breach had admittedly been made" in the infant Faith, "and its annals stained forever,"

> *its spirit was far from broken, nor could this so-called schism tear its fabric asunder. The Covenant of the Báb . . . with its immutable truths, incontrovertible prophecies, and repeated warnings, stood guard over that Faith, insuring its integrity, demonstrating its incorruptibility, and perpetuating its influence.*
>
> *Though He Himself was bent with sorrow, and still suffered from the effects of the attempt on His life, and though He was well aware a further banishment was probably impending, yet, undaunted by the blow which His Cause had sustained, and the perils with which it was encompassed, Bahá'u'lláh arose with matchless power, even before the ordeal was overpast, to proclaim the Mission with which He had been entrusted to those who, in East and West, had the reins of supreme temporal authority in their grasp. The day-star of His Revelation was, through this very Proclamation, destined to shine in its meridian glory, and His Faith manifest the plenitude of its divine power.*

The "most great separation" *was soon followed by a period of unparalleled revelation. "The Divine verses were raining down in*

7. *God Passes By,* p. 170.

such number," one of Bahá'u'lláh's companions noted, "that it was impossible to record them. Mírzá Áqá Ján wrote them as they were dictated, while the Most Great Branch[8] *was continually occupied in transcribing them. There was not a moment to spare." A number of secretaries were busy night and day recording the verses but could not keep up with the rapid pace at which they streamed forth.*

SUCH ARE THE OUTPOURINGS . . . from the clouds of Divine Bounty that within the space of an hour the equivalent of a thousand verses hath been revealed.

—BAHÁ'U'LLÁH 12

SO GREAT IS THE GRACE VOUCHSAFED IN THIS DAY that in a single day and night, were an amanuensis capable of accomplishing it to be found, the equivalent of the Persian Bayán would be sent down from the heaven of Divine holiness.

—BAHÁ'U'LLÁH 13

I SWEAR BY GOD! In those days the equivalent of all that hath been sent down aforetime unto the Prophets hath been revealed.

—BAHÁ'U'LLÁH 14

THAT WHICH HATH ALREADY BEEN REVEALED in this land [Adrianople] secretaries are incapable of transcribing. It has, therefore, remained for the most part untranscribed.

—BAHÁ'U'LLÁH 15

8. 'Abdu'l-Bahá.

Proclamation to the Kings and Leaders of the World

Bahá'u'lláh had already acquainted His companions with His prophetic mission in the Riḍván Garden on the eve of His departure from Baghdád and had announced His mission to the Bábís of Persia by dispatching Tablets and teachers from Adrianople. Now He returned to the announcement of His mission to the kings, rulers, and leaders of the world, a process He had begun in Constantinople with the revelation of a Tablet to Sulṭán 'Abdu'l-'Azíz after being informed of the decision of the Sulṭán and his chief ministers to banish Him to Adrianople. In the Súriy-i-Mulúk (Tablet of the Kings), revealed during September and October of 1867, Bahá'u'lláh addressed the kings of East and West, the Sulṭán of Turkey and his ministers, the kings of Christendom, the French and Persian ambassadors, the Muslim leaders and people of Constantinople, the people of Persia, and the philosophers of the world. Described by Shoghi Effendi as "the most momentous Tablet revealed by Bahá'u'lláh," the Súriy-i-Mulúk marked the culmination of the period of intense and prodigious activity immediately following the separation of Mírzá Yaḥyá from Bahá'u'lláh and was followed by the revelation of other weighty Tablets to individual monarchs and leaders.

O KINGS OF THE EARTH! Give ear unto the Voice of God, calling from this sublime, this fruit-laden Tree, that hath sprung out of the Crimson Hill, upon the holy Plain, intoning the words: "There is none other God but He, the Mighty, the All-Powerful, the All-Wise." . . . Fear God, O concourse of kings, and suffer not yourselves to be deprived of this most sublime grace. Fling away, then, the things ye possess, and take fast hold on the Handle of God, the Exalted, the Great. Set your hearts towards the Face of God, and abandon that which your desires have bidden you to follow, and be not of those who perish. Relate unto them, O servant, the story of 'Alí [the Báb], when He came unto them with truth, bearing His glorious and weighty Book, and holding in His hands a testimony and proof from God, and holy and blessed tokens from Him. Ye, however, O kings, have failed to heed the Remembrance of God in His days and to be guided by the lights which arose and shone forth above the horizon of a resplendent Heaven. Ye examined not His Cause when so to do would have been better for you than all that the sun shineth upon, could ye but perceive it. Ye remained careless until the divines of Persia—those cruel ones—pronounced judgment against Him, and unjustly slew Him. His spirit ascended unto God, and the eyes of the inmates of Paradise and the angels that are nigh unto Him wept sore by reason of this cruelty. Beware that ye be not careless henceforth as ye have been careless aforetime. Return, then, unto God, your Maker, and be not of the heedless. . . . My face hath come forth from the veils, and shed its radiance upon all that is in heaven and on earth; and yet, ye turned not towards Him, notwithstanding that ye were created for Him, O concourse of kings! Follow, therefore, that which I speak unto you, and hearken unto it with your hearts, and be not of such as have turned aside. For your glory consisteth not in your sovereignty, but rather in your nearness unto God and your observance of His command as sent down in His holy and preserved Tablets. Should any one of you rule over the whole earth, and over all that lieth within it and upon it, its seas, its lands, its mountains, and its plains, and yet be not remembered by God, all these would profit him not, could ye but know it. . . . Arise, then, and make steadfast your feet, and make ye amends for that which hath escaped you, and set then yourselves towards His holy Court, on the shore of His mighty Ocean, so that the pearls of knowledge and wisdom, which God hath stored up within the shell of His radiant heart, may be revealed unto you. . . . Beware lest ye hinder the breeze of God from blowing over your hearts, the breeze through which the hearts of such as have turned unto Him can be quickened. . . .

. . . .

If ye pay no heed unto the counsels which, in peerless and unequivocal language, We have revealed in this Tablet, Divine chastisement shall assail you from every direction, and the sentence of His justice shall be pronounced against you. On that day ye shall have no power to resist Him, and shall recognize your own impotence. Have mercy on yourselves and on those beneath you, and judge ye between them according to the precepts prescribed by God in His most holy and exalted Tablet, a Tablet wherein He hath assigned to each and every thing its settled measure, in which He hath given, with distinctness, an explanation of all things, and which is in itself a monition unto them that believe in Him.

Examine Our Cause, inquire into the things that have befallen Us, and decide justly between Us and

Our enemies, and be ye of them that act equitably towards their neighbors. . . .

Twenty years have passed, O kings, during which We have, each day, tasted the agony of a fresh tribulation. No one of them that were before Us hath endured the things We have endured. Would that ye could perceive it! They that rose up against Us, have put Us to death, have shed Our blood, have plundered Our property, and violated Our honor. Though aware of most of Our afflictions, ye, nevertheless, have failed to stay the hand of the aggressor. For is it not your clear duty to restrain the tyranny of the oppressor, and to deal equitably with your subjects, that your high sense of justice may be fully demonstrated to all mankind?

God hath committed into your hands the reins of the government of the people, that ye may rule with justice over them, safeguard the rights of the downtrodden, and punish the wrongdoers. If ye neglect the duty prescribed unto you by God in His Book, your names shall be numbered with those of the unjust in His sight. Grievous, indeed, will be your error. Cleave ye to that which your imaginations have devised, and cast behind your backs the commandments of God, the Most Exalted, the Inaccessible, the All-Compelling, the Almighty? Cast away the things ye possess, and cling to that which God hath bidden you observe. Seek ye His grace, for he that seeketh it treadeth His straight Path.

Consider the state in which We are, and behold ye the ills and troubles that have tried Us. Neglect Us not, though it be for a moment, and judge ye between Us and Our enemies with equity. This will, surely, be a manifest advantage unto you. Thus do We relate to you Our tale, and recount the things that have befallen Us, that ye might take off Our ills and ease Our burden. Let him who will, relieve Us from Our trouble; and as to him that willeth not, my Lord is assuredly the best of Helpers.

—*BAHÁ'U'LLÁH 16*

HEARKEN, O KING,[9] TO THE SPEECH of Him that speaketh the truth, Him that doth not ask thee to recompense Him with the things God hath chosen to bestow upon thee, Him Who unerringly treadeth the straight Path. He it is Who summoneth thee unto God, thy Lord, Who showeth thee the right course, the way that leadeth to true felicity, that haply thou mayest be of them with whom it shall be well.

Beware, O King, that thou gather not around thee such ministers as follow the desires of a corrupt inclination, as have cast behind their backs that which hath been committed into their hands and manifestly betrayed their trust. Be bounteous to others as God hath been bounteous to thee, and abandon not the interests of thy people to the mercy of such ministers as these. Lay not aside the fear of God, and be thou of them that act uprightly. Gather around thee those ministers from whom thou canst perceive the fragrance of faith and of justice, and

9. Sulṭán 'Abdu'l-'Azíz.

take thou counsel with them, and choose whatever is best in thy sight, and be of them that act generously.

. . . .

Wert thou to incline thine ear unto My speech and observe My counsel, God would exalt thee to so eminent a position that the designs of no man on the whole earth could ever touch or hurt thee. Observe, O King, with thine inmost heart and with thy whole being, the precepts of God, and walk not in the paths of the oppressor. Seize thou, and hold firmly within the grasp of thy might, the reins of the affairs of thy people, and examine in person whatever pertaineth unto them. Let nothing escape thee, for therein lieth the highest good.

. . . .

Allow not the abject to rule over and dominate them who are noble and worthy of honour, and suffer not the high-minded to be at the mercy of the contemptible and worthless, for this is what We observed upon Our arrival in the City [Constantinople], and to it We bear witness. We found among its inhabitants some who were possessed of an affluent fortune and lived in the midst of excessive riches, whilst others were in dire want and abject poverty. This ill beseemeth thy sovereignty, and is unworthy of thy rank.

Let My counsel be acceptable to thee, and strive thou to rule with equity among men, that God may exalt thy name and spread abroad the fame of thy justice in all the world. Beware lest thou aggrandize thy ministers at the expense of thy subjects. Fear the sighs of the poor and of the upright in heart who, at every break of day, bewail their plight, and be unto them a benignant sovereign. They, verily, are thy treasures on earth. It behoveth thee, therefore, to safeguard thy treasures from the assaults of them who wish to rob thee. Inquire into their affairs, and ascertain, every year, nay every month, their condition, and be not of them that are careless of their duty.

. . . .

Have a care not to entrust thine affairs of state entirely into another's hands. None can discharge thy functions better than thine own self. Thus do We make clear unto thee Our words of wisdom, and send down upon thee that which can enable thee to pass over from the left hand of oppression to the right hand of justice, and approach the resplendent ocean of His favours. Such is the path which the kings that were before thee have trodden, they that have acted equitably towards their subjects, and walked in the ways of undeviating justice.

. . . .

Let thine ear be attentive, O King, to the words We have addressed to thee. Let the oppressor desist from his tyranny, and cut off the perpetrators of injustice from among them that profess thy faith. By the righteousness of God! The tribulations We have sustained are such that any pen that recounteth them cannot but be overwhelmed with anguish. No one of them that truly believe and uphold the unity of God can bear the burden of their recital. So great have been Our sufferings that even the eyes of Our enemies have wept over Us, and beyond them those of every discerning person. And to all these trials have We been subjected, in spite of Our action in approaching thee, and in bidding the people to enter beneath thy shadow, that thou mightest be a stronghold unto them that believe in and uphold the unity of God.

Have I, O King, ever disobeyed thee? Have I, at any time, transgressed any of thy laws? Can any of thy ministers that represented thee in ‘Iráq produce any proof that can establish my disloyalty to thee? No, by Him Who is the Lord of all worlds! Not for one short moment did We rebel against thee, or against any of thy ministers. Never, God willing, shall We revolt against thee, though We be exposed to trials more severe than any We suffered in the past.

In the day-time and in the night season, at even and at morn, We pray to God on thy behalf, that He may graciously aid thee to be obedient to Him and to observe His commandment, that He may shield thee from the hosts of the evil ones. Do, therefore, as it pleaseth thee, and treat Us as befitteth thy station and beseemeth thy sovereignty. Be not forgetful of the law of God in whatever thou desirest to achieve, now or in the days to come. Say: Praise be to God, the Lord of all worlds!

—BAHÁ’U’LLÁH 17

DOST THOU IMAGINE, O MINISTER of the Sháh[10] in the City [Constantinople], that I hold within My grasp

10. Mírzá Ḥusayn Khán, the Persian ambassador in Constantinople.

the ultimate destiny of the Cause of God? Thinkest thou that My imprisonment, or the shame I have been made to suffer, or even My death and utter annihilation, can deflect its course? Wretched is what thou hast imagined in thine heart! Thou art indeed of them that walk after the vain imaginings which their hearts devise. No God is there but Him. Powerful is He to manifest His Cause, and to exalt His testimony, and to establish whatsoever is His Will, and to elevate it to so eminent a position that neither thine own hands, nor the hands of them that have turned away from Him, can ever touch or harm it.

Dost thou believe thou hast the power to frustrate His Will, to hinder Him from executing His judgment, or to deter Him from exercising His sovereignty? Pretendest thou that aught in the heavens or in the earth can resist His Faith? No, by Him Who is the Eternal Truth! Nothing whatsoever in the whole of creation can thwart His Purpose. Cast away, therefore, the mere conceit thou dost follow, for mere conceit can never take the place of truth. Be thou of them that have truly repented and returned to God, the God Who hath created thee, Who hath nourished thee, and made thee a minister among them that profess thy faith.

. . . .

Pause for but a little while and reflect, O Minister, and be fair in thy judgment. What is it that We have committed that could justify thee in having slandered Us unto the King's Ministers, in following thy desires, in perverting the truth, and in uttering thy calumnies against Us? We have never met each other except when We met thee in thy father's house, in the days when the martyrdom of the Imám Ḥusayn was being commemorated. On those occasions no one could have the chance of making known to others his views and beliefs in conversation or in discourse. Thou wilt bear witness to the truth of My words, if thou be of the truthful. I have frequented no other gatherings in which thou couldst have learned My mind or in which any other could have done so. How, then, didst thou pronounce thy verdict against Me, when thou hadst not heard My testimony from Mine own lips? Hast thou not heard what God, exalted be His glory, hath said: "Say not to every one who meeteth you with a greeting, 'Thou art not a believer.'" "Thrust not away those who cry to their Lord at morn and even, craving to behold His face." Thou hast indeed forsaken what the Book of God hath prescribed, and yet thou deemest thyself to be a believer!

Despite what thou hast done I entertain—and to this God is My witness—no ill-will against thee, nor against any one, though from thee and others We receive such hurt as no believer in the unity of God can sustain. My cause is in the hand of none except God, and My trust is in no one else but Him. Erelong shall your days pass away, as shall pass away the days of those who now, with flagrant pride, vaunt themselves over their neighbor. Soon shall ye be gathered together in the presence of God, and shall be asked of your doings, and shall be repaid for what your hands have wrought, and wretched the abode of the wicked doers!

By God! Wert thou to realize what thou hast done, thou wouldst surely weep sore over thyself, and wouldst flee for refuge to God, and wouldst pine away and mourn all the days of thy life, till God will have forgiven thee, for He, verily, is the Most Generous, the All-Bountiful. Thou wilt, however, persist, till the hour of thy death, in thy heedlessness, inasmuch as thou hast, with all thine heart, thy soul and inmost being, busied thyself with the vanities of the world. Thou shalt, after thy departure, discover what We have revealed unto thee, and shalt find all thy doings recorded in the Book wherein the works of all them that dwell on earth, be they greater or less than the weight of an atom, are noted down. Heed, therefore, My counsel, and hearken thou, with the hearing of thine heart, unto My speech, and be not careless of My words, nor be of them that reject My truth. . . .

. . . .

It is not Our purpose in addressing to thee these words to lighten the burden of Our woe, or to induce thee to intercede for Us with any one. No, by Him Who is the Lord of all worlds! We have set forth the whole matter before thee, that perchance thou might realize what thou hast done, might desist from inflicting on others the hurt thou hast inflicted on Us, and might be of them that have truly repented to God, Who created thee and created all things, and might act with discernment in the future.

—*BAHÁ'U'LLÁH 18*

O YE DIVINES OF THE CITY![11] We came to you with the truth, whilst ye were heedless of it. Methinks ye are as dead, wrapt in the coverings of your own selves. Ye sought not Our presence, when so to do would have been better for you than all your doings. . . . Know ye, that had your leaders, to whom ye owe allegiance, and on whom ye pride yourselves, and whom ye mention by day and by night, and from whose traces ye seek guidance—had they lived in these days, they would have circled around Me, and would not have separated themselves from Me, whether at eventide or at morn. Ye, however, did not turn your faces towards My face, for even less than a moment, and waxed proud, and were careless of this Wronged One, Who hath been so afflicted by men that they dealt with Him as they pleased. Ye failed to inquire about My condition, nor did ye inform yourselves of the things which befell Me. Thereby have ye withheld from yourselves the winds of holiness, and the breezes of bounty, that blow from this luminous and perspicuous Spot. Methinks ye have clung to outward things, and forgotten the inner things, and say that which ye do not. Ye are lovers of names, and appear to have given yourselves up to them. For this reason make ye mention of the names of your leaders. And should any one like them, or superior unto them, come unto you, ye would flee him. Through their names ye have exalted yourselves, and have secured your positions,

11. Constantinople.

and live and prosper. And were your leaders to reappear, ye would not renounce your leadership, nor would ye turn in their direction, nor set your faces towards them. We found you, as We found most men, worshipping names which they mention during the days of their life, and with which they occupy themselves. No sooner do the Bearers of these names appear, however, than they repudiate them, and turn upon their heels. . . . Know ye that God will not, in this day, accept your thoughts, nor your remembrance of Him, nor your devotions, nor your vigilance, unless ye be made new in the estimation of this Servant, could ye but perceive it.

—BAHÁ'U'LLÁH 19

WARN AND ACQUAINT THE PEOPLE, O Servant,[12] with the things We have sent down unto Thee, and let the fear of no one dismay Thee, and be Thou not of them that waver. The day is approaching when God will have exalted His Cause and magnified His testimony in the eyes of all who are in the heavens and all who are on the earth. Place, in all circumstances, Thy whole trust in Thy Lord, and fix Thy gaze upon Him, and turn away from all them that repudiate His truth. Let God, Thy Lord, be Thy sufficing Succorer and Helper. We have pledged Ourself to secure Thy triumph upon earth and to exalt Our Cause above all men, though no king be found who would turn his face towards Thee. . . .

—BAHÁ'U'LLÁH 20

12. Here the voice of God is addressing Bahá'u'lláh.

Banishment to 'Akká

Following the revelation of the Súriy-i-Mulúk and other Tablets to individual kings and leaders, Bahá'u'lláh revealed the prayers for fasting and the Tablet of the Branch, which foreshadowed 'Abdu'l-Bahá's future station as the Center of Bahá'u'lláh's Covenant. Other significant developments during the concluding years of Bahá'u'lláh's sojourn in Adrianople were the adoption of the term "Bahá'í" in place of "Bábí" and "people of Bahá" in place of "people of the Bayán," a term that was used henceforth to refer to the followers of Mírzá Yaḥyá. Similarly, the greeting "Alláh-u-Abhá" (God is Most Glorious) replaced "Alláh-u-Akbar" (God is Most Great). Moreover, Nabíl-i-A'ẓam, bearing gifts for the wife of the Báb, made a pilgrimage on Bahá'u'lláh's behalf to Shíráz and Baghdád, reciting two newly revealed Tablets of Pilgrimage at the Houses of the Báb and Bahá'u'lláh in those cities, acts that marked the inception of one of the holiest Bahá'í observances.

The internal developments in the new religion were paralleled by the growing acclaim the citizens of Adrianople exhibited toward Bahá'u'lláh. So great was their veneration that when He walked through the streets and bazaars or entered a gathering, they would fall silent and bow before Him. One Friday when He walked to the mosque, throngs of people lined the way, raising their voices in acclamation, prostrating themselves at His feet and bringing traffic to a halt. When He entered the mosque, the preacher, addressing the congregation from his pulpit, stopped in midsentence, awestruck, unable to remember what he wanted to say.

The foreign consuls stationed in Adrianople and local officials also held Bahá'u'lláh in high esteem, foremost among them being three successive governors posted to Adrianople—one of them a former prime minister. The unrestrained veneration of the people of Adrianople, combined with an increasing stream of pilgrims, the challenging tone of Bahá'u'lláh's Tablets to the Sulṭán and his ministers, an exaggerated report made by the foreign minister fol-

lowing a visit to Adrianople, and allegations by Mírzá Yaḥyá and his supporters that Bahá'u'lláh was conspiring with Bulgarian leaders and certain European ministers to conquer Constantinople led the Sulṭán to take drastic action to isolate Bahá'u'lláh in an attempt to destroy His Faith.

One morning Bahá'u'lláh's house was surrounded by soldiers, and sentinels were posted at its gates. His followers were interrogated by the authorities and told to prepare for their departure. The governor was so embarrassed by the actions of the government that he left the city and instructed a subordinate to present Bahá'u'lláh with the Sulṭán's edict, which called for Bahá'u'lláh, His two brothers Mírzá Músá and Mírzá Muḥammad-Qulí, and one servant, to be sent to 'Akká, and for everyone else to go to Constantinople. The prospect of separation filled the members of Bahá'u'lláh's family and His companions with extreme anxiety. One Bahá'í was so disturbed that he attempted to end his life by cutting his throat with a razor.

Foreign consuls, alarmed by the government's decision, gathered at Bahá'u'lláh's home and offered to intervene, but He declined all offers of assistance. On 12 August 1868, Bahá'u'lláh and His family, accompanied by soldiers assigned by the local government, left Adrianople in carriages on a four-day journey to Gallipoli, leaving behind a city gripped in sorrow.

On the way to Gallipoli Bahá'u'lláh revealed the Súriy-i-Ra'ís, addressed to 'Álí Pás͟há, the Turkish prime minister. The Tablet upbraids 'Álí Pás͟há for his abusive behavior, predicts the collapse of the Ottoman Empire, and prophesies that Bahá'u'lláh's Faith will encompass the world.

At one point on the journey Bahá'u'lláh directed 'Umar Effendi, a major assigned the task of enforcing Bahá'u'lláh's banishment to 'Akká, to arrange a meeting with the Sulṭán so that He could demonstrate whatever proof of the truth of His faith the Sulṭán might require. 'Umar Effendi assured Bahá'u'lláh that he would deliver the message, but no response was forthcoming.

In Gallipoli rumors were rife. No one knew where Bahá'u'lláh would be sent, and some believed that the exiles would be separated, dispersed, or even executed. The fear of separation from Bahá'u'lláh provoked scenes of extreme distress. At Bahá'u'lláh's insistence, and through 'Umar Effendi's intercession, the Sulṭán's edict was revoked, and a new order was issued. About seventy exiles, including twenty-three women, Siyyid Muḥammad, and one of His confederates, were to go with Bahá'u'lláh and His brothers to 'Akká. Four of the exiles were to go to Cyprus with Mírzá Yaḥyá. "So grievous were the dangers and trials confronting Bahá'u'lláh at the hour of His departure from Gallipoli," Shoghi Effendi relates, "that He warned His companions that 'this journey will be unlike any of the previous journeys,' *and that whoever did not feel himself* 'man enough to face the future' *had best* 'depart to whatever place he pleaseth, and be preserved from tests, for hereafter he will find himself unable to leave'*—a warning which His companions unanimously chose to disregard."*

THE CONSULS OF THAT CITY [ADRIANOPLE] gathered in the presence of this Youth at the hour of His departure and expressed their desire to aid Him. They, verily, evinced towards Us manifest affection.

—BAHÁ'U'LLÁH 21

SAY, THIS YOUTH HATH DEPARTED out of this country and deposited beneath every tree and every stone a trust, which God will erelong bring forth through the power of truth.

—BAHÁ'U'LLÁH 22

THE LOVED ONES OF GOD and His kindred were left on the first night without food . . . The people surrounded the house, and Muslims and Christians wept over Us . . . We perceived that the weeping of the people of the Son [Christians] exceeded the weeping of others—a sign for such as ponder.

—BAHÁ'U'LLÁH 23

THERE IS A MATTER, which, if thou[13] findest it possible, I request thee to submit to His Majesty the Sulṭán, that for ten minutes this Youth be enabled to meet him so that he may demand whatsoever he deemeth as a sufficient testimony and regardeth as proof of the veracity of Him Who is the Truth. Should God enable Him to produce it, let him, then, release these wronged ones, and leave them to themselves.

—BAHÁ'U'LLÁH 24

HE[14] PROMISED TO TRANSMIT THIS MESSAGE, and to give Us his reply. We received, however, no news from him. Although it becometh not Him Who is the Truth to present Himself before any person, inasmuch as all have been created to obey Him, yet in view of the condition of these little children and the large number of women so far removed from their friends and countries, We have acquiesced in this matter. In spite of this nothing hath resulted. 'Umar himself is alive and accessible. Inquire from him, that the truth may be made known unto you.

—BAHÁ'U'LLÁH 25

---

13. 'Umar Effendi.
14. 'Umar Effendi.

KNOW YE THAT TRIALS AND TRIBULATIONS have, from time immemorial, been the lot of the chosen Ones of God and His beloved, and such of His servants as are detached from all else but Him, they whom neither merchandise nor traffic beguile from the remembrance of the Almighty, they that speak not till He hath spoken, and act according to His commandment. Such is God's method carried into effect of old, and such will it remain in the future. Blessed are the steadfastly enduring, they that are patient under ills and hardships, who lament not over anything that befalleth them, and who tread the path of resignation. . . .

The day is approaching when God will have raised up a people who will call to remembrance Our days, who will tell the tale of Our trials, who will demand the restitution of Our rights from them that, without a tittle of evidence, have treated Us with manifest injustice. God, assuredly, dominateth the lives of them that wronged Us, and is well aware of their doings. He will, most certainly, lay hold on them for their sins. He, verily, is the fiercest of avengers.

—*BAHÁ'U'LLÁH 26*

HEARKEN, O CHIEF[15] . . . to the Voice of God, the Sovereign, the Help in Peril, the Self-Subsisting . . . Thou hast, O Chief, committed that which hath made Muḥammad, the Apostle of God,

15. 'Álí Pá<u>sh</u>á.

groan in the Most Exalted Paradise. The world hath made thee proud, so much so that thou hast turned away from the Face through Whose brightness the Concourse on high hath been illumined. Soon thou shalt find thyself in evident loss . . . The day is approaching when the Land of Mystery [Adrianople] and what is beside it shall be changed, and shall pass out of the hands of the King, and commotions shall appear, and the voice of lamentation shall be raised, and the evidences of mischief shall be revealed on all sides, and confusion shall spread by reason of that which hath befallen these captives at the hands of the hosts of oppression. The course of things shall be altered, and conditions shall wax so grievous, that the very sands on the desolate hills will moan, and the trees on the mountain will weep, and blood will flow out of all things. Then wilt thou behold the people in sore distress.

—BAHÁ'U'LLÁH 27

ERELONG WILL GOD RAISE UP from among the kings one who will aid His loved ones. He, verily, encompasseth all things. He will instill in the hearts the love of His loved ones. This, indeed, is irrevocably decreed by One Who is the Almighty, the Beneficent.

—BAHÁ'U'LLÁH 28

AFTER OUR DEPARTURE FROM ADRIANOPLE, a discussion arose among the government officials in Constantinople as to whether We and Our companions should not be thrown into the sea. The report of such a discussion reached Persia, and gave

> rise to a rumour that We had actually suffered that fate. In Khurasán particularly, Our friends were greatly perturbed. Mírzá Aḥmad-i-Azghandí, as soon as he was informed of this news, was reported to have asserted that under no circumstances could he credit such a rumour. "The Revelation of the Báb," he said, "must, if this be true, be regarded as utterly devoid of foundation." The news of Our safe arrival in the prison-city of 'Akká rejoiced the hearts of Our friends, deepened the admiration of the believers of Khurasán for the faith of Mírzá Aḥmad, and increased their confidence in him.
>
> —*BAHÁ'U'LLÁH 29*

On 21 August 1868, Bahá'u'lláh and His family and companions left Gallipoli by steamer for Alexandria, stopping en route for two days at Smyrna, where one of the companions who had fallen ill was taken to a hospital. In Alexandria the exiles were transferred to another steamer. After stops at Port Said and Jaffa, they landed in Haifa on 31 August 1868. As Bahá'u'lláh stepped into the boat that would take Him to the dock, one of the four companions condemned to go to Cyprus with Mírzá Yaḥyá became so distraught that, shouting "Yá Bahá'u'l-Abhá,"[16] *he threw himself into the sea. After he was rescued and revived with great difficulty, officials forced him to continue his journey to Cyprus.*

The prisoners spent a few hours in Haifa, where they were counted and handed over to government officials. Then they boarded a sailing vessel to cross the bay to 'Akká. There was no wind, and it took eight hours to cross the bay. In misery from ex-

16. "O Thou the Glory of the Most Glorious!" An invocation derived from the name of Bahá'u'lláh.

posure to the hot August sun, the exiles arrived at the sea gate. There being no dock, the men were ordered to wade ashore and carry the women on their backs. 'Abdu'l-Bahá objected and, finding a chair, insisted that the women be carried ashore one at a time. Having been led to believe that Bahá'u'lláh and His followers were criminals of the worst sort, the citizens and officials of 'Akká gathered at the sea gate to jeer and curse at the exiles. Such was the reception that the people of 'Akká had prepared for the Lord of the Age.

Chapter 9 / 'AKKÁ

Bahá'u'lláh's arrival in 'Akká opened the last and longest phase of His ministry—a stage that spanned a third of His life and over half of the period of His prophetic mission. His first banishment to Baghdád had placed Him in close proximity to the holy cities of Najaf and Karbilá and had brought Him in contact with the leading proponents of Shí'ah Islám. His removal to Constantinople had taken Him to the capital of the Ottoman Empire, where He proclaimed His message to the Sulṭán and to the leaders of Sunní Islám. Bahá'u'lláh's final exile took Him to the Holy Land, a Land sanctified by the Prophets of Judaism and Christianity and associated with Muḥammad's night journey through the seven heavens to the throne of God. "It is difficult to understand," *'Abdu'l-Bahá declares,* "how Bahá'u'lláh could have been obliged to leave Persia, and to pitch His tent in this Holy Land, but for the persecution of His enemies, His banishment and exile."

Arrival in 'Akká

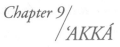

Known today as Acre or 'Akko, 'Akká lies on the eastern end of the Mediterranean Sea, on the northern tip of the Bay of Haifa across from the city of Haifa, Israel. 'Akká is an ancient city founded some four thousand years ago. Having been the capital of the Crusader kingdom in the thirteenth century, a port for French merchants in the sixteenth century, and a provincial capital of the Ottoman Empire in the latter part of the eighteenth century, 'Akká

fell upon hard times in the late eighteenth and nineteenth centuries, suffering damaging attacks by Napoleon in 1799, the Egyptians in 1832, and the British in 1840.

By the time Bahá'u'lláh arrived in 1868, 'Akká was in serious decline. It had been relegated to the status of a penal colony—the "Bastille of the Middle East"—to which the most dangerous criminals and political enemies of the Turkish government were consigned. Surrounded by a double system of ramparts and accessible only by a land gate and a sea gate, the city had no source of fresh water. It was damp, infested with fleas, and rife with disease.

After the exiles had disembarked from the vessel that had brought them across the bay from Haifa, they were led through the dirty, dark, and winding streets to the barracks. Overcome by the cruel conditions, the stench, and the heat of the August afternoon, Bahíyyih Khánum, the saintly daughter of Bahá'u'lláh, fainted as she entered the prison.

Bahá'u'lláh was placed in a barren, filthy room, while His followers were crowded into another, the floor of which was covered with mud. Ten soldiers were posted to stand guard over them. To add further to their misery, the exiles, parched from a long day in the hot sun, soon found that the only water available to them was unfit for consumption. Mothers were unable to feed their babies, and infants cried for hours. 'Abdu'l-Bahá appealed repeatedly to the guards and the governor for mercy, but to no avail. The next morning the exiles were given their first daily ration of water and three inedible loaves of salty, coarse, black bread, which they were later allowed to exchange in the market for two loaves of better quality.

Under these conditions, all but 'Abdu'l-Bahá and one other fell ill. Within a matter of days three men died. The officials denied the prisoners permission to leave the citadel to bury them, and the guards demanded payment before removing the bodies. Bahá'u'lláh ordered that His prayer rug, the only item of any value that He possessed, be sold to cover the cost of the burial. The guards pocketed the money and buried the men in the clothes in which they died, without coffins and without washing or wrapping the bodies in shrouds.

Three days after the exiles' arrival, the Sulṭán's edict was read aloud in the mosque. It sentenced Bahá'u'lláh, His family, and His companions to life imprisonment and expressly forbade the exiles to associate with one another or with local inhabitants. Harsh, indeed, were the terms and conditions that Bahá'u'lláh faced upon His internment in the "afflictive prison" of 'Akká—an internment that marked the culmination of His sufferings.

UPON OUR ARRIVAL, We were welcomed with banners of light, where upon the Voice of the Spirit cried out saying: "Soon will all that dwell on earth be enlisted under these banners."

—BAHÁ'U'LLÁH 1

KNOW THOU THAT UPON OUR ARRIVAL at this Spot, We chose to designate it as the "Most Great Prison." Though previously subjected in another land [Ṭihrán] to chains and fetters, We yet refused to call it by that name. Say: Ponder thereon, O ye endued with understanding!

—BAHÁ'U'LLÁH 2

ACCORDING TO WHAT THEY SAY, it is the most desolate of the cities of the world, the most unsightly of them in appearance, the most detestable in climate, and the foulest in water. It is as though it were the metropolis of the owl.

—BAHÁ'U'LLÁH 3

THE FIRST NIGHT ALL WERE DEPRIVED of either food or drink . . . They even begged for water, and were refused.

—BAHÁ'U'LLÁH 4

NONE KNOWETH WHAT BEFELL US, except God, the Almighty, the All-Knowing . . . From the foundation of the world until the present day a cruelty such as this hath neither been seen nor heard of.

—BAHÁ'U'LLÁH 5

The Object of Bahá'u'lláh's Imprisonment

MORE GRIEVOUS BECAME OUR PLIGHT from day to day, nay, from hour to hour, until they took Us forth from Our prison and made Us, with glaring injustice, enter the Most Great Prison. And if anyone ask them: "For what crime were they imprisoned?" they would answer and say: "They, verily, sought to supplant the Faith with a new religion!" If that which is ancient be what ye prefer, wherefore, then, have ye discarded that which hath been set down in the Torah and the Evangel? Clear it up, O men! By My life! There is no place for you to flee to in this day. If this be My crime, then Muḥammad, the Apostle of God, committed it before Me, and before Him He Who was the Spirit of God [Jesus Christ], and yet earlier He Who conversed with God [Moses]. And if My sin be this, that I have exalted the Word of God and revealed His Cause, then indeed am I the greatest of sinners! Such a sin I will not barter for the kingdoms of earth and heaven.

—BAHÁ'U'LLÁH 6

THE ANCIENT BEAUTY HATH CONSENTED to be bound with chains that mankind may be released from its bondage, and hath accepted to be made a prisoner within this most mighty Stronghold that the whole world may attain unto true liberty. He hath drained to its dregs the cup of sorrow, that all the peoples of the earth may attain unto abiding joy, and be filled with gladness. This is of the mercy of your Lord, the Compassionate, the Most Merciful. We have accepted to be abased, O believers in the Unity of God, that ye may be exalted, and have suffered manifold afflictions, that ye might prosper and flourish. He Who hath come to build anew the whole world, behold, how they that have joined partners with God have forced Him to dwell within the most desolate of cities!

—BAHÁ'U'LLÁH 7

MEDITATE ON THE WORLD and the state of its people. He, for Whose sake the world was called into being, hath been imprisoned in the most desolate of cities ['Akká], by reason of that which the hands of the wayward have wrought. From the horizon of His prison-city He summoneth mankind unto the Dayspring of God, the Exalted, the Great.

—BAHÁ'U'LLÁH 8

EVERY UNBIASED OBSERVER will readily admit that, ever since the dawn of His Revelation, this wronged One hath invited all mankind to turn their faces towards the Day Spring of Glory, and hath forbidden corruption, hatred, oppression, and wickedness. And yet, behold what the hand of the oppressor hath wrought! No pen dare describe his tyranny. Though the purpose of Him Who is the Eternal Truth hath been to confer everlasting life upon all men, and ensure their security and peace, yet witness how they have arisen to shed the blood of His loved ones, and have pronounced on Him the sentence of death.

The instigators of this oppression are those very persons who, though so foolish, are reputed the wisest of the wise. Such is their blindness that, with unfeigned severity, they have cast into this fortified and afflictive Prison Him, for the servants of Whose Threshold the world hath been created. The Almighty, however, in spite of them and those that have repudiated the truth of this "Great Announcement," hath transformed this Prison House into the Most Exalted Paradise, the Heaven of Heavens.

—BAHÁ'U'LLÁH 9

Prayers and Meditations from the Most Great Prison

O THOU WHO ART THE RULER OF EARTH and heaven and the Author of all names! Thou hearest the voice of my lamentation which from the fortress-town of 'Akká ascendeth towards Thee, and beholdest how my captive friends have fallen into the hands of the workers of iniquity.

We render Thee thanks, O our Lord, for all the troubles which have touched us in Thy path. Oh, that the span of my earthly life could be so extended as to embrace the lives of the former and the latter generations, or could even be so lengthened that no man on the face of the earth could measure it, and be afflicted every day and every moment with a fresh tribulation for love of Thee and for Thy pleasure's sake!

Thou well knowest, however, O my God, that my wish is wholly dissolved in Thy wish, and that Thou hast irrevocably decreed that my soul should ascend unto the loftiest mansions of Thy Kingdom, and pass into the presence of my all-glorious Companion.

Hasten, by Thy grace and bounty, my passing, O my Lord, and pour forth upon all them that are dear to Thee what will preserve them from fear and trembling after me. Powerful art Thou to do whatsoever may please Thee. No God is there except Thee, the All-Glorious, the All-Wise.

Thou seest, O my Lord, how Thy servants have left their homes in their longing to meet Thee, and how they have been hindered by the ungodly from looking upon Thy face, and from circumambulating the sanctuary of Thy grandeur.[1] Pour out Thy steadfastness and send down Thy calm upon them, O my Lord! Thou art, in truth, the Ever-Forgiving, the Most Compassionate.

—BAHÁ'U'LLÁH 10

GLORIFIED ART THOU, O MY GOD! Thou knowest that my sole aim in revealing Thy Cause hath been to reveal Thee and not my self, and to manifest Thy glory rather than my glory. In Thy path, and to attain Thy pleasure, I have scorned rest, joy, delight. At all times and under all conditions my gaze hath been fixed on Thy precepts, and mine eyes bent upon the things Thou hast bidden me observe in Thy Tablets. I have wakened every morning to the light of Thy praise and Thy remembrance, and reached every evening inhaling the fragrances of Thy mercy.

---

1. During the first few months of Bahá'u'lláh's imprisonment, pilgrims who traveled to 'Akká to visit Him had to be satisfied with standing beyond the second moat and glimpsing His face in the window of His cell, while those who managed to enter the city had to leave without seeing Him at all. One pilgrim who stood beyond the moat for hours, hoping to catch a glimpse of Him, was prevented from attaining the object of his quest because of his poor eyesight—an event that brought tears to the eyes of members of Bahá'u'lláh's family who watched from within the prison.

And when the entire creation was stirred up, and the whole earth was convulsed, and the sweet savors of Thy name, the All-Praised, had almost ceased to breathe over Thy realms, and the winds of Thy mercy had well-nigh been stilled throughout Thy dominions, Thou didst, through the power of Thy might, raise me up among Thy servants, and bid me to show forth Thy sovereignty amidst Thy people. Thereupon I arose before all Thy creatures, strengthened by Thy help and Thy power, and summoned all the multitudes unto Thee, and announced unto all Thy servants Thy favors and Thy gifts, and invited them to turn towards this Ocean, every drop of the waters of which crieth out, proclaiming unto all that are in heaven and on earth that He is, in truth, the Fountain of all life, and the Quickener of the entire creation, and the Object of the adoration of all worlds, and the Best-Beloved of every understanding heart, and the Desire of all them that are nigh unto Thee.

Though the fierce winds of the hatred of the wicked doers blew and beat on this Lamp, He was, at no time, in His love for Thy beauty, hindered from shedding the fragrance of His light. As the transgressions committed against Thee waxed greater and greater, my eagerness to reveal Thy Cause correspondingly increased, and as the tribulations deepened—and to this Thy glory beareth me witness—a fuller measure of Thy sovereignty and of Thy power was vouchsafed by me unto Thy creatures.

And finally, I was cast by the transgressors into the prison-city of 'Akká, and my kindred were made captives in Baghdád.[2] The power of Thy might beareth me witness, O my God! Every trouble that hath touched me in Thy path hath added to my joy and increased my gladness. I swear by Thee, O Thou Who art the King of Kings! None of the kings of the earth hath power to hinder me from remembering Thee or from extolling Thy virtues. Were they to be leagued—as they have been leagued—against me, and to brandish their sharpest swords and most afflictive spears against me, I would not hesitate to magnify Thy name before all them that are in Thy heaven and on Thy earth. Nay rather, I would cry out and say: "This, O my Beloved, is my face which I have offered up for Thy face, and this is my spirit which I have sacrificed for Thy spirit, and this is my blood that seetheth in my veins, in its longing to be shed for love of Thee and in Thy path."

Though—as Thou beholdest me, O my God—I be dwelling in a place within whose walls no voice can be heard except the sound of the echo, though all the gates of ease and comfort be shut against us, and thick darkness appear to have compassed us on every side, yet my soul hath been so inflamed by its love for Thee, that nothing whatsoever can either quench the fire of its love or abate the consuming flame of its desire. Lifting up its voice, it crieth aloud

---

2. A reference to the arrest in Karbilá of three Bahá'ís who were brought to Baghdád in chains and to the banishment of seventy Bahá'ís from Baghdád to Mosul shortly before Bahá'u'lláh left Adrianople.

amidst Thy servants, and calleth them, at all times and under all conditions, unto Thee.

I beseech Thee, by Thy Most Great Name, to open the eyes of Thy servants, that they may behold Thee shining above the horizon of Thy majesty and glory, and that they may not be hindered by the croaking of the raven from hearkening to the voice of the Dove of Thy sublime oneness, nor be prevented by the corrupt waters from partaking of the pure wine of Thy bounty and the everlasting streams of Thy gifts.

Gather them, then, together around this Divine Law, the covenant of which Thou hast established with all Thy Prophets and Thy Messengers, and Whose ordinances Thou hast written down in Thy Tablets and Thy Scriptures. Raise them up, moreover, to such heights as will enable them to perceive Thy Call.

Potent art Thou to do what pleaseth Thee. Thou art, verily, the Inaccessible, the All-Glorious.

—BAHÁ’U’LLÁH 11

PRAISED BE THOU, O MY GOD! Thou seest me shut up in this Prison, and art well aware that I have entered it solely for Thy sake and for the sake of the glorification of Thy word and the proclamation of Thy Cause. I cry out to Thee, this very moment, O Thou Who art the Lord of all worlds, beseeching Thee, by Thine undoubted Name, to attract the hearts of Thy servants unto the Day-Spring of Thy most excellent titles and the Dawning-Place of Thy most resplendent signs.

But for the troubles that touch me in Thy path, O my God, how else could my heart rejoice in Thy days; and were it not for the blood which is shed for love of Thee, what else could tinge the faces of Thy chosen ones before the eyes of Thy creatures? I swear by Thy might! The ornament that adorneth the countenance of Thy dear ones is the blood which, in their love for Thee, floweth out of their foreheads over their faces.

Thou beholdest, O my God, how every bone in my body soundeth like a pipe with the music of Thine inspiration, revealing the signs of Thy oneness and the clear tokens of Thy unity. I entreat Thee, O my God, by Thy Name which irradiateth all things, to raise up such servants as shall incline their ears to the voice of the melodies that hath ascended from the right hand of the throne of Thy glory. Make them, then, to quaff from the hand of Thy grace the wine of Thy mercy, that it may assure their hearts, and cause them to turn away from the left hand of idle fancies and vain imaginings to the right hand of confidence and certitude.

Now that Thou hast guided them unto the door of Thy grace, O my Lord, cast them not away, by Thy bounty; and now that Thou hast summoned them unto the horizon of Thy Cause, keep them not back from Thee, by Thy graciousness and favor. Powerful art Thou to do as Thou pleasest. No God is there but Thee, the Omniscient, the All-Informed.

—*BAHÁ'U'LLÁH 12*

O MY GOD! THOU BEHOLDEST THE LORD of all mankind confined in His Most Great Prison, calling aloud Thy Name, gazing upon Thy face, proclaiming that which hath enraptured the denizens of Thy kingdoms of revelation and of creation. O my God! I behold Mine own Self captive in the hands of Thy servants, yet the light of Thy sovereignty and the revelations of Thine invincible power shine resplendent from His face, enabling all to know of a certainty that Thou art God, and that there is none other God but Thee. Neither can the power of the powerful frustrate Thee, nor the ascendancy of the rulers prevail against Thee. Thou doest whatsoever Thou willest by virtue of Thy sovereignty which encompasseth all created things, and ordainest that which Thou pleasest through the potency of Thy behest which pervadeth the entire creation.

I implore Thee by the glory of Thy Manifestation and by the power of Thy might, Thy sovereignty and Thine exaltation to render victorious those who have arisen to serve Thee, who have aided Thy Cause and humbled themselves before the splendour of the light of Thy face. Make them then, O my God, triumphant over Thine enemies and cause them to be steadfast in Thy service, that through them the evidences of Thy dominion may be established throughout Thy realms and the tokens of Thine indomitable power be manifested in Thy lands. Verily Thou art potent to do what Thou willest; no God is there but Thee, the Help in Peril, the Self-Subsisting.

—BAHÁ'U'LLÁH 13

The Martyrdom of Mírzá Mihdí, the Purest Branch

To the many tribulations Bahá'u'lláh suffered during the first two years of His imprisonment in 'Akká, Shoghi Effendi says, was added

> *the bitter grief of a sudden tragedy—the premature loss of the noble, the pious Mírzá Mihdí, the Purest Branch, 'Abdu'l-Bahá's twenty-two year old brother, an amanuensis of Bahá'u'lláh and a companion of His exile from the days when, as a child, he was brought from Ṭihrán to Baghdád to join His Father after His return from Sulaymáníyyih. He was pacing the roof of the barracks in the twilight, one evening, wrapped in his customary devotions, when he fell through the unguarded skylight onto a wooden crate, standing on the floor beneath, which pierced his ribs, and caused, twenty-two hours later, his death, on the 23rd of Rabí'u'l-Avval 1287 A.H. (June 23, 1870). His dying supplication to a grieving Father was that his life might be accepted as a ransom for those who were prevented from attaining the presence of their Beloved. . . .*
>
> . . . .
>
> *After he had been washed in the presence of Bahá'u'lláh, he* "that was created of the light of Bahá," *to whose* "meekness" *the Supreme Pen had testified, and of the* "mysteries" *of whose ascension that same Pen had made mention, was borne forth, escorted by the fortress guards, and laid to rest, beyond the city walls, in a spot adjacent to the shrine of Nabí Ṣáliḥ, from whence, seventy years later, his remains, simultaneously with those of his illustrious mother, were to be translated to the slopes of Mt. Carmel, in the precincts of the grave of his sister, and under the shadow of the Báb's holy sepulcher.*[3]

---

3. Mírzá Mihdí's remains were moved to Mount Carmel in 1939. Ásíyih Khánum, entitled Navváb, was his mother; Bahíyyih Khánum, entitled the Greatest Holy Leaf, his sister.

As those who had buried the body of the Purest Branch returned to the prison, an earthquake lasting about three minutes struck the area, an event that they took as the effect of the interment of that holy being. Bahá'u'lláh refers to the earthquake in a Tablet that pays tribute to the Purest Branch (see extract 17).

In His prayers and Tablets Bahá'u'lláh terms the death of the Purest Branch an act of martyrdom, describes it as a sacrifice He Himself has made, and exalts it, Shoghi Effendi explains, "to the rank of those great acts of atonement associated with Abraham's intended sacrifice of His son, with the crucifixion of Jesus Christ and the martyrdom of the Imám Ḥusayn."

Although we do not know what words passed between Bahá'u'lláh and His beloved son as Mírzá Mihdí lay dying before Him, we do know that Bahá'u'lláh, holding in His hands the power of life and death, asked Mírzá Mihdí whether he wished to live and that He accepted His son's request to offer his life that the gates of the prison would be opened to pilgrims who longed to enter His Father's presence.

Four months later the mobilization of Turkish troops required the authorities to reclaim the barracks for military purposes. Bahá'u'lláh and His family were moved to a house in the western quarter of the city, and over the next ten months lived in three different houses until they settled in what later became known as the House of 'Abbúd, where they resided for seven years. From the date of their removal from the prison barracks, the terms of their confinement progressively relaxed until eventually Bahá'u'lláh was able to leave the prison-city and live outside its walls in freedom and majesty.

The mysterious forces released by the sacrifice of the Purest Branch continue to exercise their influence on the world. Through his sacrifice, Shoghi Effendi explains, the unity of the nations and the oneness of humanity will be realized.

LAUDED BE THY NAME, O LORD MY GOD! Thou seest me in this day shut up in my prison, and fallen into the hands of Thine adversaries, and beholdest my son [The Purest Branch] lying on the dust before Thy face. He is Thy servant, O my Lord, whom Thou hast caused to be related to Him Who is the Manifestation of Thyself and the Day-Spring of Thy Cause.

At his birth he was afflicted through his separation from Thee, according to what had been ordained for him through Thine irrevocable decree. And when he had quaffed the cup of reunion with Thee, he was cast into prison for having believed in Thee and in Thy signs. He continued to serve Thy Beauty until he entered into this Most Great Prison. Thereupon I offered him up, O my God, as a sacrifice in Thy path. Thou well knowest what they who love Thee have endured through this trial that hath caused the kindreds of the earth to wail, and beyond them the Concourse on high to lament.

I beseech Thee, O my Lord, by him and by his exile and his imprisonment, to send down upon such as loved him what will quiet their hearts and bless their works. Potent art Thou to do as Thou willest. No God is there but Thee, the Almighty, the Most Powerful.

—BAHÁ'U'LLÁH 14

AT THIS VERY MOMENT MY SON is being washed before My face, after Our having sacrificed him in the Most Great Prison. Thereat have the dwellers of the Abhá Tabernacle wept with a great weeping, and such as have suffered imprisonment with this Youth in the path of God, the Lord of the promised Day, lamented. Under such conditions My Pen hath not been prevented from remembering its Lord, the Lord of all nations. It summoneth the people unto God, the Almighty, the All-Bountiful. This is the day whereon he that was created by the light of Bahá has suffered martyrdom, at a time when he lay imprisoned at the hands of his enemies.

Upon thee, O Branch of God! be the remembrance of God and His praise, and the praise of all that dwell in the Realm of Immortality, and of all the denizens of the Kingdom of Names. Happy art thou in that thou hast been faithful to the Covenant of God and His Testament, until Thou didst sacrifice thyself before the face of thy Lord, the Almighty, the Unconstrained. Thou, in truth, hast been wronged, and to this testifieth the Beauty of Him, the Self-Subsisting. Thou didst, in the first days of thy life, bear that which hath caused all things to groan, and made every pillar to tremble. Happy is the one that remembereth thee, and draweth nigh, through thee, unto God, the Creator of the Morn.

—BAHÁ'U'LLÁH 15

GLORIFIED ART THOU, O LORD, MY GOD! Thou seest me in the hands of Mine enemies, and My son bloodstained before Thy face, O Thou in Whose hands is the kingdom of all names. I have, O my Lord, offered up that which Thou hast given Me, that Thy servants may be quickened and all that dwell on earth be united.

—BAHÁ'U'LLÁH 16

> BLESSED ART THOU AND BLESSED HE that turneth unto thee, and visiteth thy grave, and draweth nigh, through thee, unto God, the Lord of all that was and shall be. . . . I testify that thou didst return in meekness unto thine abode. Great is thy blessedness and the blessedness of them that hold fast unto the hem of thy outspread robe. . . . Thou art, verily, the trust of God and His treasure in this land. Erelong will God reveal through thee that which He hath desired. He, verily, is the Truth, the Knower of things unseen. When thou wast laid to rest in the earth, the earth itself trembled in its longing to meet thee. Thus hath it been decreed, and yet the people perceive not. . . . Were We to recount the mysteries of thine ascension, they that are asleep would waken, and all beings would be set ablaze with the fire of the remembrance of My Name, the Mighty, the Loving.
>
> —*BAHÁ'U'LLÁH* 17

The Murder of Siyyid Muḥammad and Two of His Companions

About a year and a half after the death of the Purest Branch and shortly after Bahá'u'lláh and His family had moved into the House of 'Abbúd, a crisis that had been brewing for years erupted.

Ever since the exiles had entered 'Akká, Siyyid Muḥammad and a companion named Áqá Ján-i-Kaj-Kuláh had sought to misrepresent Bahá'u'lláh's motives and to subvert the Bahá'í community. When Bahá'u'lláh expelled Mírzá Riḍá-Qulíy-i-Tafrishí from the community because of his disreputable behavior, he and his sister, Badrí-Ján, an estranged wife of Mírzá Yaḥyá, joined forces with Siyyid Muḥammad and Áqá Ján, adding impetus to their campaign. By spreading lies and falsified writings of Bahá'u'lláh, the three men succeeded in poisoning the public against the exiles to such an extent that the Bahá'ís became objects of open hostility.

Although Bahá'u'lláh had repeatedly warned the Bahá'ís not to retaliate and had disciplined those who had appealed to Him for permission to deal with the plotters in their own way, seven Bahá'ís could no longer contain themselves and on 22 January 1872 shot Siyyid Muḥammad, Áqá Ján-i-Kaj-Kuláh, and Mírzá Riḍá-Qulíy-i-Tafrishí in their lodgings.

Badrí-Ján went to the governorate and accused Bahá'u'lláh of ordering the death of her brother and his friends, knowing that Bahá'u'lláh had expressly forbidden His followers from taking any action against them.

Soon a contingent of troops with drawn swords, led by the governor, surrounded Bahá'u'lláh's house. A noisy crowd of onlookers also gathered. Bahá'u'lláh was summoned to the governorate, where the commandant of the city asked, "Is it proper that some of your followers should act in such a manner?" Bahá'u'lláh replied, "If one of your soldiers were to commit a reprehensible act, would you be held responsible, and punished in his place?"

Bahá'u'lláh was held in custody for three nights. 'Abdu'l-Bahá was imprisoned in chains the first night, after which He was allowed to join Bahá'u'lláh, while twenty-five of the exiles were cast into another prison and held for six months. The murderers were imprisoned for several years.

After the third night, Bahá'u'lláh was brought to the governorate for interrogation. Shoghi Effendi relates that

> *He was asked to state His name and that of the country from which He came.* "It is more manifest than the sun," *He answered. The same question was put to Him again, to which He gave the following reply:* "I deem it not proper to mention it. Refer to the farmán of the government which is in your possession." *Once again they, with marked deference, reiterated their request, whereupon Bahá'u'lláh spoke with majesty and power these words:* "My name is Bahá'u'lláh

(Light of God), and My country is Núr *(Light).* Be ye apprised of it." *Turning then, to the Muftí, He addressed him words of veiled rebuke, after which He spoke to the entire gathering, in such vehement and exalted language that none made bold to answer Him. Having quoted verses from the Súriy-i-Mulúk, He, afterwards, arose and left the gathering. The Governor, soon after, sent word that He was at liberty to return to His home, and apologized for what had occurred.*

The murders enkindled an outpouring of animosity toward the Bahá'ís, who were accused of terrorism, heresy, and atheism and who became the object of ostracism and ridicule. The situation aroused Bahá'u'lláh's indignation, brought Him acute humiliation and distress, and eroded the goodwill that 'Abdu'l-Bahá had won from the officials and citizens of 'Akká through years of patient effort.

WERE WE TO MAKE MENTION of what befell Us, the heavens would be rent asunder and the mountains would crumble.

—*BAHÁ'U'LLÁH* 18

MY IMPRISONMENT DOETH ME NO HARM, neither the tribulations I suffer, nor the things that have befallen Me at the hands of My oppressors. That which harmeth Me is the conduct of those who, though they bear My name, yet commit that which maketh My heart and My pen to lament.

—*BAHÁ'U'LLÁH* 19

MY CAPTIVITY CAN BRING ON ME NO SHAME. Nay, by My life, it conferreth on Me glory. That which can make Me ashamed is the conduct of such of My followers as profess to love Me, yet in fact follow the Evil One.

—*BAHÁ'U'LLÁH* 20

I SORROW NOT FOR THE BURDEN of My imprisonment. Neither do I grieve over My abasement, or the tribulation I suffer at the hands of Mine enemies. By My life! They are My glory, a glory wherewith God hath adorned His own Self. Would that ye know it!

The shame I was made to bear hath uncovered the glory with which the whole of creation had been invested, and through the cruelties I have endured, the Day Star of Justice hath manifested itself, and shed its splendor upon men.

My sorrows are for those who have involved themselves in their corrupt passions, and claim to be associated with the Faith of God, the Gracious, the All-Praised.

It behoveth the people of Bahá to die to the world and all that is therein, to be so detached from all earthly things that the inmates of Paradise may inhale from their garment the sweet smelling savor of sanctity, that all the peoples of the earth may recognize in their faces the brightness of the All-Merciful, and that through them may be spread abroad the signs and tokens of God, the Almighty, the All-Wise. They that have tarnished the fair name of the Cause of God, by following the things of the flesh—these are in palpable error!

—BAHÁ'U'LLÁH 21

Bahíyyih Khánum, the Greatest Holy Leaf

A source of solace to Bahá'u'lláh during the dark days of the Adrianople and 'Akká periods was the consecrated service of His daughter, Bahíyyih Khánum. First as a child in Ṭihrán during Bahá'u'lláh's incarceration in the Síyáh-Chál and later in Baghdád during the anxious years of His withdrawal to Kurdistán, she had demonstrated, Shoghi Effendi recounts, a "tender solicitude" and the ability to both share the burden and make the sacrifices "which her high birth demanded." In her teens she had been entrusted by her Father with grave and delicate missions and had withstood the calamities of the years spent in Adrianople with exemplary calm and grace. At the age of twenty-two, when faced with imprisonment within the walls of 'Akká, she had displayed "in the plenitude of her power and in the full abundance of her love" for her Father the qualities that single her out among the members of the Holy Family as, next to 'Abdu'l-Bahá, "the brightest embodiment of that love which is born of God and of that human sympathy which few mortals are capable of evincing."

Turning her back on all earthly attachments and renouncing marriage, Bahíyyih Khánum stood resolutely by 'Abdu'l-Bahá's side and dedicated her life to the service of her Father's Cause, earning, in Bahá'u'lláh's words, "a station such as none other woman hath surpassed."

HE IS THE ETERNAL! This is My testimony for her who hath heard My voice and drawn nigh unto Me. Verily, she is a leaf that hath sprung from this preexistent Root. She hath revealed herself in My name and tasted of the sweet savours of My holy, My wondrous pleasure. At one time We gave her to drink from My honeyed Mouth, at another caused her to partake of My mighty, My luminous Kawthar.[4] Upon her rest the glory of My name and the fragrance of My shining robe.

4. Abundance. Cf. Qur'án 108:1–3; traditionally, the lake or river in Paradise that Anas says Muḥammad saw on the night of His mystic vision (Mi'ráj) in which He was transported from Mecca to Jerusalem and shown the signs of God.

Let these exalted words be thy love-song on the tree of Bahá, O thou most holy and resplendent Leaf: "God, besides Whom is none other God, the Lord of this world and the next!" Verily, We have elevated thee to the rank of one of the most distinguished among thy sex, and granted thee, in My court, a station such as none other woman hath surpassed. Thus have We preferred thee and raised thee above the rest, as a sign of grace from Him Who is the Lord of the throne on high and earth below. We have created thine eyes to behold the light of My countenance, thine ears to hearken unto the melody of My words, thy body to pay homage before My throne. Do thou render thanks unto God, thy Lord, the Lord of all the world.

How high is the testimony of the Sadratu'l-Muntahá for its leaf; how exalted the witness of the Tree of Life unto its fruit! Through My remembrance of her a fragrance laden with the perfume of musk hath been diffused; well is it with him that hath inhaled it and exclaimed: "All praise be to Thee, O God, my Lord the most glorious!" How sweet thy presence before Me; how sweet to gaze upon thy face to bestow upon thee My loving-kindness, to favour thee with My tender care, to make mention of thee in this, My Tablet—a Tablet which I have ordained as a token of My hidden and manifest grace unto thee.

—BAHÁ'U'LLÁH 22

O MY LEAF! HEARKEN THOU UNTO MY VOICE: Verily there is none other God but Me, the Almighty, the All-Wise. I can well inhale from thee the fragrance of

My love and the sweet-smelling savour wafting from the raiment of My Name, the Most Holy, the Most Luminous. Be astir upon God's Tree in conformity with thy pleasure and unloose thy tongue in praise of thy Lord amidst all mankind. Let not the things of the world grieve thee. Cling fast unto this divine Lote-Tree from which God hath graciously caused thee to spring forth. I swear by My life! It behoveth the lover to be closely joined to the loved one, and here indeed is the Best-Beloved of the world.

—*BAHÁ'U'LLÁH* 23

Proclamation to the Kings

Having initiated the proclamation of His prophetic mission to the kings and rulers of the world in Constantinople with a Tablet addressed to Sulṭán 'Abdu'l-'Azíz and in Adrianople with the revelation of the Súriy-i-Mulúk, Bahá'u'lláh continued to reveal Tablets proclaiming His mission to the world's leaders during His incarceration in the prison-barracks of 'Akká.

In addition to revealing the Súriy-i-Mulúk in Adrianople, Bahá'u'lláh had also addressed a Tablet to Napoleon III. Shortly after arriving in 'Akká in 1868, Bahá'u'lláh received a report through one of Napoleon's ministers that no response to the Tablet would be forthcoming. In fact, the emperor is reported to have flung down the Tablet, saying, "If this man is God, I am two gods!" In 1868 Bahá'u'lláh revealed a second Tablet to Napoleon. In powerful and majestic language He rebuked the emperor for rejecting the first Tablet and upbraided him for his arrogance and insincerity, prophesying that his empire would soon be "thrown into confusion" and would pass from his hands.

Before leaving Adrianople, Bahá'u'lláh had also addressed a Tablet to Náṣiri'd-Dín Shāh. However, that Tablet was not dispatched until 1869, for Bahá'u'lláh was waiting to find someone with the wisdom to ensure its safe delivery and the courage and forbearance to withstand the torture he would undoubtedly undergo. The assignment was given to Áqá Buzurg, a youth of seventeen, who had walked from Mosul to 'Akká to enter Bahá'u'lláh's presence. In two private interviews with Bahá'u'lláh the youth had been created anew and had been given the name Badí' (Wonderful). Badí' begged to be allowed to carry out the important mission, knowing fully that whoever delivered the Tablet to the Sháh would face certain death. After walking from 'Akká to Ṭihrán, Badí' succeeded in presenting Bahá'u'lláh's Tablet to the Sháh, who ordered Badí''s immediate arrest. For three days he endured brutal torture without showing any sign of pain. On the fourth day his guards became so exasperated that they beat him to death.

During the early years of Bahá'u'lláh's incarceration in 'Akká He also revealed Tablets to Pope Pius IX, Czar Alexander II, and Queen Victoria. These Tablets disclose Bahá'u'lláh's station, summon their recipients to recognize His Cause and arise to promote its triumph, and impart various counsels, warnings, and prophecies tailored to each recipient. The process concluded in 1873 with the revelation of the Kitáb-i-Aqdas, which includes further summons and counsels to secular and religious leaders. "Never since the beginning of the world," *Bahá'u'lláh asserts,* "hath the Message been so openly proclaimed."

UPON OUR ARRIVAL AT THIS PRISON, We purposed to transmit to the kings the messages of their Lord, the Mighty, the All-Praised. Though We have transmitted to them, in several Tablets, that which We were commanded, yet We do it once again, as a token of God's grace.

—*BAHÁ'U'LLÁH 24*

FROM OUR MOST GREAT PRISON We were moved to address to the several rulers and crowned heads of the world Epistles in which We summoned them to arise and embrace the Cause of God. To the Sháh of Persia We sent Our messenger Badí', into whose hands We entrusted the Tablet. It was he who raised it aloft before the eyes of the multitude and, with uplifted voice, appealed to his sovereign to heed the words that Tablet contained. The rest of the Epistles likewise reached their destination. To the Tablet We addressed to the Emperor of France, an answer was received from his minister, the original of which is now in the possession of the Most Great Branch.[5] To him We addressed these words: "Bid the high priest, O Monarch of France, to cease ringing his bells, for, lo! the Most Great Bell, which the hands of the will of the Lord thy God are ringing, is made manifest in the person of His chosen One." The Epistle We addressed to the Czar of Russia, alone failed to reach its destination. Other Tablets, however, have reached him, and that Epistle will eventually be delivered into his hands.

—BAHÁ'U'LLÁH 25

O KINGS OF THE EARTH! He Who is the sovereign Lord of all is come. The Kingdom is God's, the omnipotent Protector, the Self-Subsisting. Worship none but God, and, with radiant hearts, lift up your faces unto your Lord, the Lord of all names. This is a Revelation to which whatever ye possess can never be

5. 'Abdu'l-Bahá.

compared, could ye but know it. We see you rejoicing in that which ye have amassed for others, and shutting out yourselves from the worlds which naught except My Guarded Tablet can reckon. The treasures ye have laid up have drawn you far away from your ultimate objective. This ill beseemeth you, could ye but understand it. Wash your hearts from all earthly defilements, and hasten to enter the Kingdom of your Lord, the Creator of earth and heaven, Who caused the world to tremble, and all its peoples to wail, except them that have renounced all things and clung to that which the Hidden Tablet hath ordained. . . .

O Kings of the earth! The Most Great Law hath been revealed in this Spot,[6] this Scene of transcendent splendour. Every hidden thing hath been brought to light, by virtue of the Will of the Supreme Ordainer, He Who hath ushered in the Last Hour, through Whom the Moon hath been cleft, and every irrevocable decree expounded.

Ye are but vassals, O Kings of the earth! He Who is the King of kings hath appeared, arrayed in His most wondrous glory, and is summoning you unto Himself, the Help in Peril, the Self-Subsisting. Take heed lest pride deter you from recognizing the Source of Revelation; lest the things of this world shut you out as by a veil from Him Who is the Creator of heaven. Arise, and serve Him Who is the Desire of all nations, Who hath created you through

6. 'Akká.

a word from Him, and ordained you to be, for all time, the emblems of His sovereignty.

By the righteousness of God! It is not Our wish to lay hands on your kingdoms. Our mission is to seize and possess the hearts of men. Upon them the eyes of Bahá are fastened. To this testifieth the Kingdom of Names, could ye but comprehend it. . . .

How great is the blessedness that awaiteth the king who will arise to aid My Cause in My Kingdom, who will detach himself from all else but Me! Such a king is numbered with the companions of the Crimson Ark, the Ark which God hath prepared for the people of Bahá. All must glorify his name, must reverence his station, and aid him to unlock the cities with the keys of My Name, the omnipotent Protector of all that inhabit the visible and invisible kingdoms. Such a king is the very eye of mankind, the luminous ornament on the brow of creation, the fountainhead of blessings unto the whole world. Offer up, O people of Bahá, your substance, nay your very lives, for his assistance.

We have asked nothing from you. For the sake of God We, verily, exhort you, and will be patient as We have been patient in that which hath befallen Us at your hands, O concourse of kings!

—BAHÁ'U'LLÁH 26

O KING OF PARIS! TELL THE PRIEST to ring the bells no longer. By God, the True One! The Most Mighty Bell hath appeared in the form of Him Who is the Most Great Name, and the fingers of the will of Thy

Lord, the Most Exalted, the Most High, toll it out in the heaven of Immortality, in His name, the All-Glorious. Thus have the mighty verses of Thy Lord been again sent down unto thee, that thou mayest arise to remember God, the Creator of earth and heaven, in these days when all the tribes of the earth have mourned, and the foundations of the cities have trembled, and the dust of irreligion hath enwrapped all men, except such as God, the All-Knowing, the All-Wise, was pleased to spare. . . .

. . . .

O King! We heard the words thou didst utter in answer to the Czar of Russia, concerning the decision made regarding the war [Crimean War]. Thy Lord, verily, knoweth, is informed of all. Thou didst say: "I lay asleep upon my couch, when the cry of the oppressed, who were drowned in the Black Sea, wakened me." This is what we heard thee say, and, verily, the Lord is witness unto what I say. We testify that that which wakened thee was not their cry but the promptings of thine own passions, for We tested thee, and found thee wanting.[7] Comprehend the meaning of My words, and be thou of the discerning. It is not Our wish to address thee words of condemnation, out of regard for the dignity We conferred upon thee in this mortal life. We, verily, have chosen courtesy, and made it the true mark of such as are nigh unto Him. Courtesy, is, in

7. An allusion to Napoleon's contemptuous response to Bahá'u'lláh's first Tablet to him.

truth, a raiment which fitteth all men, whether young or old. Well is it with him that adorneth his temple therewith, and woe unto him who is deprived of this great bounty. Hadst thou been sincere in thy words, thou wouldst have not cast behind thy back the Book of God, when it was sent unto thee by Him Who is the Almighty, the All-Wise. We have proved thee through it, and found thee other than that which thou didst profess. Arise, and make amends for that which escaped thee. Ere long the world and all that thou possessest will perish, and the kingdom will remain unto God, thy Lord and the Lord of thy fathers of old. It behoveth thee not to conduct thine affairs according to the dictates of thy desires. Fear the sighs of this Wronged One, and shield Him from the darts of such as act unjustly.

For what thou hast done, thy kingdom shall be thrown into confusion, and thine empire shall pass from thine hands, as a punishment for that which thou hast wrought. Then wilt thou know how thou hast plainly erred. Commotions shall seize all the people in that land, unless thou arisest to help this Cause, and followest Him Who is the Spirit of God [Jesus Christ] in this, the Straight Path. Hath thy pomp made thee proud? By My Life! It shall not endure; nay, it shall soon pass away, unless thou holdest fast by this firm Cord. We see abasement hastening after thee, whilst thou art of the heedless. It behoveth thee when thou hearest His Voice calling from the seat of glory to cast away all that thou possessest, and cry out: "Here am I, O Lord of all that is in heaven and all that is on earth!"

—BAHÁ'U'LLÁH 27

O CZAR OF RUSSIA! INCLINE THINE EAR unto the voice of God, the King, the Holy, and turn thou unto Paradise, the Spot wherein abideth He Who, among the Concourse on high, beareth the most excellent titles, and Who, in the kingdom of creation, is called by the name of God, the Effulgent, the All-Glorious. Beware lest thy desire deter thee from turning towards the face of thy Lord, the Compassionate, the Most Merciful. We, verily, have heard the thing for which thou didst supplicate thy Lord, whilst secretly communing with Him. Wherefore, the breeze of My loving-kindness wafted forth, and the sea of My mercy surged, and We answered thee in truth.[8] Thy Lord, verily, is the All-Knowing, the All-Wise. Whilst I lay chained and fettered in the prison, one of thy ministers extended Me his aid. Wherefore hath God ordained for thee a station which the knowledge of none can comprehend except His knowledge. Beware lest thou barter away this sublime station . . . Beware lest thy sovereignty withhold thee from Him Who is the Supreme Sovereign. He, verily, is come with His Kingdom, and all the atoms cry aloud: "Lo! The Lord is come in His great majesty!" He Who is the Father is come, and the Son [Jesus], in the holy vale, crieth out:

8. Bahá'u'lláh later confirmed that the thing for which the Czar prayed was for God to make him victorious in battle against the Turks. In 1877–78 Russian troops defeated the Ottomans, occupied Adrianople, and came up to the gates of Constantinople, triggering a chain of events that led to the disintegration of the Ottoman Empire some thirty years later.

"Here am I, here am I, O Lord, My God!" whilst Sinai circleth round the House, and the Burning Bush calleth aloud: "The All-Bounteous is come mounted upon the clouds! Blessed is he that draweth nigh unto Him, and woe betide them that are far away."

Arise thou amongst men in the name of this all-compelling Cause, and summon, then, the nations unto God, the Exalted, the Great. Be thou not of them who called upon God by one of His names, but who, when He Who is the Object of all names appeared, denied Him and turned aside from Him, and, in the end, pronounced sentence against Him with manifest injustice. Consider and call thou to mind the days whereon the Spirit of God [Jesus] appeared, and Herod gave judgment against Him. God, however, aided Him with the hosts of the unseen, and protected Him with truth, and sent Him down unto another land, according to His promise. He, verily, ordaineth what He pleaseth. Thy Lord truly preserveth whom He willeth, be he in the midst of the seas, or in the maw of the serpent, or beneath the sword of the oppressor. . . .

Again I say: Hearken unto My Voice that calleth from My prison that it may acquaint thee with the things that have befallen My Beauty, at the hands of them that are the manifestations of My glory, and that thou mayest perceive how great hath been My patience, notwithstanding My might, and how immense My forbearance, notwithstanding My power. By My Life! Couldst thou but know the things sent down by My Pen, and discover the treasures of My Cause, and the pearls of My mysteries which lie hid in the seas of My names and in the goblets of My words, thou wouldst, in thy love for My name, and in thy longing for My glorious and sublime Kingdom, lay down thy life in My path.

—BAHÁ'U'LLÁH 28

O QUEEN IN LONDON! INCLINE THINE EAR unto the voice of thy Lord, the Lord of all mankind, calling from the Divine Lote-Tree: Verily, no God is there but Me, the Almighty, the All-Wise! Cast away all that is on earth, and attire the head of thy kingdom with the crown of the remembrance of thy Lord, the All-Glorious. He, in truth, hath come unto the world in His most great glory, and all that hath been mentioned in the Gospel hath been fulfilled. . . .

Lay aside thy desire, and set then thine heart towards thy Lord, the Ancient of Days. We make mention of thee for the sake of God, and desire that thy name may be exalted through thy remembrance of God, the Creator of earth and heaven. He, verily, is witness unto that which I say. We have been informed that thou hast forbidden the trading in slaves, both men and women. This, verily, is what God hath enjoined in this wondrous Revelation. God hath, truly, destined a reward for thee, because of this. He, verily, will pay the doer of good his due recompense, wert thou to follow what hath been sent unto thee by Him Who is the All-Knowing, the All-Informed. . . .

We have also heard that thou hast entrusted the reins of counsel into the hands of the representatives of the people. Thou, indeed, hast done well, for thereby the foundations of the edifice of thine affairs will be strengthened, and the hearts of all that are beneath thy shadow, whether high or low, will be tranquilized. It behoveth them, however, to be trustworthy among His servants, and to regard themselves as the representatives of all that dwell on earth. . . .

Turn thou unto God and say: O my Sovereign Lord! I am but a vassal of Thine, and Thou art, in truth, the King of Kings. I have lifted my suppliant hands unto the heaven of Thy grace and Thy bounties. Send down, then, upon me from the clouds of Thy generosity that which will rid me of all save Thee, and draw me nigh unto Thyself. I beseech Thee, O my Lord, by Thy name, which Thou hast made the king of names, and the manifestation of Thyself to all who are in heaven and on earth, to rend asunder the veils that have intervened between me and my recognition of the Dawning-Place of Thy signs and the Day Spring of Thy Revelation. Thou art, verily, the Almighty, the All-Powerful, the All-Bounteous.

—*BAHÁ'U'LLÁH 29*

O POPE! REND THE VEILS ASUNDER. He Who is the Lord of Lords is come overshadowed with clouds, and the decree hath been fulfilled by God, the Almighty, the Unrestrained . . . He, verily, hath again come down from Heaven even as He came down from it the first time. Beware that thou dispute not with Him even as the Pharisees disputed with Him [Jesus] without a clear token or proof. On His right hand flow the living waters of grace, and on His left the choice Wine of justice, whilst before Him march the angels of Paradise, bearing the banners of His signs. . . .

. . . .

The Word which the Son concealed is made manifest. It hath been sent down in the form of the human temple in this day. Blessed be the Lord Who is the Father! He, verily, is come unto the nations in His most great majesty. Turn your faces towards Him, O concourse of the righteous . . . This is the day whereon the Rock [Peter] crieth out and shouteth, and celebrateth the praise of its Lord, the All-Possessing, the Most High, saying: "Lo! The Father is come, and that which ye were promised in the Kingdom is fulfilled! . . ." My body longeth for the cross, and Mine head waiteth the thrust of the spear, in the path of the All-Merciful, that the world may be purged from its transgressions. . . .

O Supreme Pontiff! Incline thine ear unto that which the Fashioner of mouldering bones counselleth thee, as voiced by Him Who is His Most Great Name. Sell all the embellished ornaments thou dost possess, and expend them in the path of God, Who causeth the night to return upon the day, and the day to return upon the night. Abandon thy kingdom unto the kings, and emerge from thy habitation, with thy face set towards the Kingdom, and, detached from the world, then speak forth the praises of thy Lord betwixt earth and heaven. Thus hath bidden thee He Who is the Possessor of Names, on the part of thy Lord, the Almighty, the All-Knowing.

—BAHÁ'U'LLÁH 30

Revelation of the Kitáb-i-Aqdas

"Unique and stupendous" as was Bahá'u'lláh's proclamation to the kings, rulers, and religious leaders of the world, Shoghi Effendi explains,

> *it proved to be but a prelude to a still mightier revelation of the creative power of its Author, and to what may well rank as the most signal act of His ministry—the promulgation of the Kitáb-i-Aqdas. Alluded to in the Kitáb-i-Íqán; the principal repository of that Law which the Prophet Isaiah had anticipated, and which the writer of the Apocalypse had described as the* "new heaven" *and the* "new earth," *as* "the Tabernacle of God," *as the* "Holy City," *as the* "Bride," *the* "New Jerusalem coming down from God," *this* "Most Holy Book," *whose provisions must remain inviolate for no less than a thousand years, and whose system will embrace the entire planet, may well be regarded as the brightest emanation of the mind of Bahá'u'lláh, as the Mother Book of His Dispensation, and the Charter of His New World Order.*
>
> *Revealed soon after Bahá'u'lláh had been transferred to the house of 'Údí Khammár*[9] *(circa 1873), at a time when He was still encompassed by the tribulations that had afflicted Him, through the acts committed by His enemies and the professed adherents of His Faith, this Book, this treasury enshrining the priceless gems of His Revelation, stands out, by virtue of the principles it inculcates, the administrative institutions it ordains and the function with which it invests the appointed Successor of its Author, unique and incomparable among the world's sacred Scriptures. For, unlike the Old Testament and the Holy Books which preceded it, in which the actual pre-*

9. Adjacent to and later joined with the House of 'Abbúd in 'Akká.

cepts uttered by the Prophet Himself are non-existent; unlike the Gospels, in which the few sayings attributed to Jesus Christ afford no clear guidance regarding the future administration of the affairs of His Faith; unlike even the Qur'án which, though explicit in the laws and ordinances formulated by the Apostle of God, is silent on the all-important subject of the succession, the Kitáb-i-Aqdas, revealed from first to last by the Author of the Dispensation Himself, not only preserves for posterity the basic laws and ordinances on which the fabric of His future World Order must rest, but ordains, in addition to the function of interpretation which it confers upon His Successor, the necessary institutions through which the integrity and unity of His Faith can alone be safeguarded.

WHILE IN PRISON WE HAVE REVEALED A BOOK which We have entitled "The Most Holy Book." We have enacted laws therein and adorned it with the commandments of thy Lord, Who exerciseth authority over all that are in the heavens and on the earth. Say: Take hold of it, O people, and observe that which hath been sent down in it of the wondrous precepts of your Lord, the Forgiving, the Bountiful. It will truly prosper you both in this world and in the next and will purge you of whatsoever ill beseemeth you. He is indeed the Ordainer, the Expounder, the Giver, the Generous, the Gracious, the All-Praised.

—*BAHÁ'U'LLÁH 31*

IN SUCH MANNER HATH the *Kitáb-i-Aqdas* been revealed that it attracteth and embraceth all the divinely appointed Dispensations. Blessed those who peruse it. Blessed those who apprehend it. Blessed those who meditate upon it. Blessed those who ponder its meaning. So vast is its range that it hath encompassed all men ere their recognition of it. Ere long will its sovereign power, its pervasive influence and the greatness of its might be manifested on earth. Verily, thy God is the All-Knowing, the All-Informed.

—BAHÁ'U'LLÁH 32

BY MY LIFE, IF YOU KNEW what We have desired for you in revealing Our holy laws, you would offer up your souls for this sacred, mighty and lofty Cause.

—BAHÁ'U'LLÁH 33

THIS BOOK IS NONE OTHER than the ancient Lamp of God for the whole world and His undeviating Path amongst men. Say, it is verily the Dayspring of divine knowledge, did ye but know it, and the Dawning-place of the commandments of God, could ye but comprehend it.

—BAHÁ'U'LLÁH 34

SAY, THIS IS THE SPIRIT OF THE SCRIPTURES breathed into the Pen of Glory, causing all creation to be dumbfounded, except those who are stirred by the vitalizing fragrance of My tender mercy and the sweet savours of My bounty which pervade all created things.

—BAHÁ'U'LLÁH 35

THIS BOOK IS A HEAVEN which We have adorned with the stars of Our commandments and prohibitions.

—BAHÁ'U'LLÁH 36

BLESSED THE MAN WHO WILL READ IT, and ponder the verses sent down in it by God, the Lord of Power, the Almighty. Say, O men! Take hold of it with the hand of resignation . . . By My life! It hath been sent down in a manner that amazeth the minds of men. Verily, it is My weightiest testimony unto all people, and the proof of the All-Merciful unto all who are in heaven and all who are on earth.

—*BAHÁ'U'LLÁH 37*

BLESSED THE PALATE THAT SAVORETH its sweetness, and the perceiving eye that recognizeth that which is treasured therein, and the understanding heart that comprehendeth its allusions and mysteries. By God! Such is the majesty of what hath been revealed therein, and so tremendous the revelation of its veiled allusions that the loins of utterance shake when attempting their description.

—*BAHÁ'U'LLÁH 38*

Prayers Revealed for the Bahá'ís

UNTO THEE BE PRAISE, O LORD MY GOD! I beseech Thee by Thy Most Great Name Who hath been shut up in the prison-town of 'Akká, and Who—as Thou beholdest, O my God—hath fallen into the hands of His enemies, and is threatened by the swords of the wicked doers, to make me steadfast in His Cause, and to direct mine eyes continually towards His court, in such wise that nothing whatsoever will have the power to turn me back from Him.

I testify, O my Lord, that He hath surrendered His life in Thy path, and hath wished for Himself nothing but tribulation in the love He beareth to Thee. He hath endured all manner of vexations that He may manifest Thy sovereignty unto Thy servants, and exalt Thy word amidst Thy creatures. As the adversities deepened, and the troubles sent down by Thee compassed Him on every side, He became so impassioned by His thought of Thee, that the hosts of all them that had disbelieved in Thee and repudiated Thy signs ceased to affright Him.

I implore Thee, O my Lord, by Him and by whatsoever pertaineth unto Him, to set my affections upon Him even as He hath set His own affections upon Thyself. I testify that His love is Thy love, and His self Thy self, and His beauty Thy beauty, and His Cause Thy Cause.

Deny me not, O my Lord, what is with Thee, and suffer me not to be forgetful of what Thou didst desire in Thy days. Thou art, verily, the Almighty, the Most Exalted, the All-Glorious, the All-Wise.

—BAHÁ'U'LLÁH 39

THOU SEEST, O MY GOD, how Thy servants have been cleaving fast to Thy names, and have been calling on them in the daytime and in the night season. No sooner, however, had He been made manifest through Whose word the kingdom of names and the heaven of eternity were created, than they broke away from Him and disbelieved in the greatest of Thy signs. They finally banished Him from the land of His birth, and caused Him to dwell within the most desolate of Thy cities, though all the world had been built up by Thee for His sake. Within this, the Most Great Prison, He hath established His seat. Though sore tried by trials, the like of which the eye of creation hath not seen, He summoneth the people unto Thee, O Thou Who art the Fashioner of the universe!

I beseech Thee, O Thou the Shaper of all the nations and the Quickener of every moldering bone, to graciously enable Thy servants to recognize Him Who is the Manifestation of Thy Self and the Revealer of Thy transcendent might, that they may cut down, by Thy power, all the idols of their corrupt inclinations, and enter beneath the shadow of Thine all-encompassing mercy, which, by virtue of Thy name, the Most Exalted, the All-Glorious, hath surpassed the entire creation.

—BAHÁ'U'LLÁH 40

Chapter 10 / MAZRA'IH AND BAHJÍ

In the years following the revelation of the Kitáb-i-Aqdas the attitude of the authorities and the public toward Bahá'u'lláh, His family, and His followers underwent a gradual but dramatic transformation. Several governors of 'Akká began to demonstrate openly their respect for 'Abdu'l-Bahá and to seek His counsel, and increasing numbers of pilgrims were permitted to enter the prison-city. Numerous men of influence traveled to 'Akká to visit Bahá'u'lláh, including a European general and 'Azíz Pá<u>sh</u>á, the governor-general of Beirut, who had been the deputy governor of Adrianople during Bahá'u'lláh's exile there. One governor intimated that Bahá'u'lláh was free to leave 'Akká whenever He pleased. For their part, the citizens of 'Akká expressed their veneration for Bahá'u'lláh by referring to Him as the " 'august leader' " and " 'his highness.' " They attributed the noticeable improvement in the city's climate and water to His presence among them.[1]

Despite the improved conditions, Bahá'u'lláh longed for the beauty of the countryside He had enjoyed in His youth. One day He remarked, "I have not gazed on verdure for nine years. The country is the world of the soul, the city is the world of bodies." When 'Abdu'l-Bahá learned of this, He determined to arrange a home for His Father in the countryside and soon rented the Mansion of Mazra'ih, a large home north of 'Akká. He had it repaired

1. At Bahá'u'lláh's suggestion, Governor Aḥmad Big Tawfíq initiated restoration of an aqueduct that for thirty years had fallen into disuse.

and refurbished and arranged for a carriage to take Bahá'u'lláh there. At first Bahá'u'lláh flatly refused to go, because He was still officially a prisoner. 'Abdu'l-Bahá then asked the muftí of 'Akká, who loved Bahá'u'lláh greatly and was very much favored by Him, to go to Bahá'u'lláh, hold His hands, and beg Him to leave the city. After an hour of the muftí's entreaties, Bahá'u'lláh finally consented. On a June day in 1877 'Abdu'l-Bahá took Bahá'u'lláh out through the gates of the prison-city to the Mansion of Mazra'ih.

Set amid charming gardens, Mazra'ih lies half a mile from the Mediterranean Sea and offers a splendid view of the hills of Galilee to the east. Mazra'ih provided Bahá'u'lláh with a quiet and comfortable retreat. He resided there for two years and made periodic visits to the garden of Na'mayn, which He called the Garden of Riḍván, recalling the blissful joy of the days when He announced His prophetic mission to His companions in the Riḍván Garden of Baghdád some fifteen years earlier. Bahá'u'lláh also referred to the garden as the "'New Jerusalem,'" "'Our Verdant Isle,'" *and* "Our Green Island."

Although the two years spent at Mazra'ih were pleasant, the mansion was too small to serve the needs of Bahá'u'lláh, His family, and the growing number of exiles and expatriates settled in 'Akká. Thus it was timely and fortunate when in 1879 'Abdu'l-Bahá was able to rent the palace of 'Údí Khammár, which lay about two miles north of 'Akká. The owner and his family had abruptly abandoned the home due to the outbreak of an epidemic disease. This dwelling place Bahá'u'lláh named Bahjí (Delight) and characterized as the "'lofty mansion,' *the spot which* 'God hath ordained as the most sublime vision of mankind.'" *Here Bahá'u'lláh lived the remaining days of His earthly life in a manner that was majestic yet simple, noble, and modest. Although the harsh farmán of Sulṭán 'Abdu'l-'Azíz remained officially unrepealed, it had become a dead letter. Bahá'u'lláh was still nominally a prisoner, but "'the doors of majesty and true sovereignty were,' in the words of 'Abdu'l-Bahá, 'flung wide open.'"*

The Garden of Riḍván—
"Our Green Island"

HE IS GOD, GLORIFIED BE HE,
Grandeur and Might are His!

On the morning of the blessed Friday we proceeded from the Mansion and entered the Garden. Every tree uttered a word, and every leaf sang a melody. The trees proclaimed: "Behold the evidences of God's Mercy" and the twin streams recited in the eloquent tongue the sacred verse "From us all things were made alive." Glorified be God! Mysteries were voiced by them, which provoked wonderment. Methought: in which school were they educated, and from whose presence had they acquired their learning? Yea! This Wronged One knoweth and He saith: "From God, the All-Encompassing, the Self-Subsistent."

Upon Our being seated, Ráḍíyih, upon her be My glory, attained Our presence on thy behalf, laid the table of God's bounty and in thy name extended hospitality to all present.[2] In truth, all that which stimulateth the appetite and pleaseth the eye was offered, and indeed that which delighteth the ear could also be heard as the leaves were stirred by the Will of God, and from this movement a refreshing

---

2. Ráḍíyih was a sister of Munírih Khánum, the wife of 'Abdu'l-Bahá. She served the dinner on behalf of her husband, Siyyid 'Alí, to whom this Tablet is addressed.

voice was raised, as if uttering a blissful call inviting the absent to this Feast. God's power and the perfection of His handiwork could enjoyably be seen in the blossoms, the fruits, the trees, the leaves and the streams. Praised be God Who hath thus confirmed thee and her.

In brief, all in the Garden were recipients of the choicest bounties and in the end expressed their thanksgiving unto their Lord. O that all God's beloved would have been present on this day!

We beseech God, exalted be He, to cause to descend upon thee at every moment, a blessing and a mercy and a measure of divine grace from His presence. He is the Forgiving, the All-Glorious.

We send greetings to His loved ones, and supplicate for each one of them that which is worthy of mention and is acceptable in His presence. Peace be upon thee, and upon God's sincere servants. Praise be to Him, the Lord of all mankind.

—BAHÁ'U'LLÁH 1

ONE DAY OF DAYS WE REPAIRED unto Our Green Island. Upon Our arrival, We beheld its streams flowing, and its trees luxuriant, and the sunlight playing in their midst. Turning Our face to the right, We beheld what the pen is powerless to describe; nor can it set forth that which the eye of the Lord of Mankind witnessed in that most sanctified, that most sublime, that blest, and most exalted Spot. Turning, then, to the left We gazed on one of the Beauties of the Most Sublime Paradise, standing on a pillar of light, and calling aloud saying: "O inmates of earth and heaven! Behold ye My beauty, and My radiance, and My revelation, and My effulgence. By God, the True One! I am Trustworthiness and the revelation thereof, and the beauty thereof. I will recompense whosoever will cleave unto Me, and recognize My rank and station, and hold fast unto My hem. I am the most great ornament of the people of Bahá, and the vesture of glory unto all who are in the kingdom of creation. I am the supreme instrument for the prosperity of the world, and the horizon of assurance unto all beings." Thus have We sent down for thee that which will draw men nigh unto the Lord of creation.

—BAHÁ'U'LLÁH, 2

Navváb, the Most Exalted Leaf

In 1886 Ásíyih Khánum, the saintly, selfless, and long-suffering wife of Bahá'u'lláh, died, bringing great sorrow to the members of the Holy Family, the Bahá'í community, and the people of 'Akká. Given by Bahá'u'lláh the titles the Most Exalted Leaf and Navváb (an honorific implying grace or highness), she passed away in her room in the House of 'Abbúd in 'Akka after an illness. One of her granddaughters reported that while she lay dying Bahá'u'lláh entered her room and was with her when she passed away.

For fifty-one years Ásíyih Khánum had been Bahá'u'lláh's constant companion. After a brief period of prosperity, she had endured nearly forty years of destitution, persecution, exile, and imprisonment.

Ásíyih Khánum's funeral cortege was led by muezzins and reciters of the Qur'án, followed by dignitaries of 'Akka, Muslim and Christian clergymen, and school children chanting poems and verses expressing their grief. She was buried in a cemetery outside of 'Akká until Shoghi Effendi transferred her remains in 1939 to the Monument Gardens in Haifa. There the twin monuments commemorating her and her son Mírzá Mihdí, the Purest Branch—together with the shrine of her daughter, Bahíyyih Khánum, the Greatest Holy Leaf, and the tomb of 'Abdu'l-Bahá's wife, Munírih Khánum—form the focal point of the Bahá'í Faith's world administrative center.

Bahíyyih Khánum recalled that her mother was "queenly in her dignity and loveliness, full of consideration for everybody, gentle, of a marvellous unselfishness" and that "no action of hers ever failed to show the loving-kindness of her pure heart; her very presence seemed to make an atmosphere of love and happiness wherever she came, enfolding all comers in the fragrance of gentle courtesy." Throughout her life, Shoghi Effendi says, she evinced "a fortitude, a piety, a devotion and a nobility of soul which earned her from the pen of her Lord the posthumous and unrivalled tribute of having been made His 'perpetual consort in all the worlds of God.'"

THE FIRST SPIRIT through which all spirits were revealed, and the first Light by which all lights shone forth, rest upon thee, O Most Exalted Leaf, thou who hast been mentioned in the Crimson Book! Thou art the one whom God created to arise and serve His own Self, and the Manifestation of His Cause, and the Day-Spring of His Revelation, and the Dawning-Place of His signs, and the Source of His commandments; and Who so aided thee that thou didst turn with thy whole being unto Him, at a time when His servants and handmaidens had turned away from His Face. . . . Happy art thou, O My handmaiden, and My Leaf, and the one mentioned in My Book, and inscribed by My Pen of

Glory in My Scrolls and Tablets. . . . Rejoice thou, at this moment, in the most exalted Station and the All-highest Paradise, and the Abhá Horizon, inasmuch as He Who is the Lord of Names hath remembered thee. We bear witness that thou didst attain unto all good, and that God hath so exalted thee, that all honor and glory circled around thee.

—BAHÁ'U'LLÁH 3

O NAVVÁB! O LEAF THAT HATH SPRUNG from My Tree, and been My companion! My glory be upon thee, and My loving-kindness, and My mercy that hath surpassed all beings. We announce unto thee that which will gladden thine eye, and assure thy soul, and rejoice thine heart. Verily, thy Lord is the Compassionate, the All-Bountiful. God hath been and will be pleased with thee, and hath singled thee out for His own Self, and chosen thee from among His handmaidens to serve Him, and hath made thee the companion of His Person in the daytime and in the night-season.

—BAHÁ'U'LLÁH 4

HEAR THOU ME ONCE AGAIN, God is well-pleased with thee, as a token of His grace and a sign of His mercy. He hath made thee to be His companion in every one of His worlds, and hath nourished thee with His meeting and presence, so long as His Name, and His Remembrance, and His Kingdom, and His Empire shall endure. Happy is the handmaid that hath mentioned thee, and sought thy good-pleasure, and humbled herself before thee, and held fast unto the cord of thy love. Woe betide him that denieth thy exalted station, and the things ordained for thee from God, the Lord of all names, and him that hath turned away from thee, and rejected thy station before God, the Lord of the mighty throne.

—BAHÁ'U'LLÁH 5

O FAITHFUL ONES! Should ye visit the resting-place of the Most Exalted Leaf, who hath ascended unto the Glorious Companion, stand ye and say: "Salutation and blessing and glory upon thee, O Holy Leaf that hath sprung from the Divine Lote-Tree! I bear witness that thou hast believed in God and in His signs, and answered His Call, and turned unto Him, and held fast unto His cord, and clung to the hem of His grace, and fled thy home in His path, and chosen to live as a stranger, out of love for His presence and in thy longing to serve Him. May God have mercy upon him that draweth nigh unto thee, and remembereth thee through the things which My Pen hath voiced in this, the most great station. We pray God that He may forgive us, and forgive them that have turned unto thee, and grant their desires, and bestow upon them, through His wondrous grace, whatever be their wish. He, verily, is the Bountiful, the Generous. Praise be to God, He Who is the Desire of all worlds; and the Beloved of all who recognize Him.

—BAHÁ'U'LLÁH 6

A Decade of Persecution and Libelous Accusations

Despite the newfound tranquillity and freedom that surrounded Bahá’u’lláh at Mazra‘ih and Bahjí, tribulations continued to rain upon Him and His infant Faith.

In Persia Bahá’ís were again under pressure. In 1877 Káẓim, a former mullá who had become a Bahá’í, was beheaded in Iṣfahán before a crowd in a public square. After being subjected to barbarous indignities for three days, his body was burned, and its charred remains were thrown into an abandoned well. In 1879 in the same city a Muslim divine who was bitterly opposed to the Faith stirred up anti-Bahá’í sentiments, leading to the execution of two highly respected Bahá’í brothers and the confiscation of their wealth and property. Bahá’u’lláh titled the brothers the King of Martyrs and the Beloved of Martyrs. Throughout the 1880s Bahá’ís were imprisoned and executed in Persia. In Mázindarán in 1883 ‘Alí-Ján, a former Islamic priest, was arrested, taken to Ṭihrán, and executed. In Rasht in 1888 Ḥájí Naṣír was arrested and died a martyr’s death in prison. In Ṭihrán in 1891 the Hands of the Cause of God Ḥájí Mullá ‘Alí-Akbar-i-Shahmírzádí and Ibn-i-Abhar together with Ḥájí Amín were arrested and imprisoned. In Yazd seven Bahá’ís were savagely murdered by a mob—an event that brought such sorrow to Bahá’u’lláh that for nine days He withheld revelation and allowed no one to be admitted into His presence.

Opposition of a different sort was being fomented in Constantinople, where a group of Mírzá Yaḥyá’s followers, by then known as Azalís—a name derived from Mírzá Yaḥyá’s title Ṣubḥ-i-Azal (Morning of Eternity)—had begun to gather in the 1880s. Two of them ran a Persian reformist newspaper called Akhtar *(Star) and were allied with a well-known political agitator named Jamálu’d-Dín-i-Afghání, who advocated the Sháh’s overthrow. Although Jamálu’d-Dín opposed the Bahá’í Faith, the Azalís allied themselves with him because they, too, were determined to depose the Sháh. Another Azalí had close ties to the Persian consul-general, who was also an ally of Jamálu'd-Dín. This group spared no effort in attacking the Bahá'ís and in spreading false accusations to discredit them and Bahá'u'lláh. The Azalís' reach was wide, and their articles against the Faith appeared in several places, including a Persian newspaper published in Paris named* 'Urvatu'l-Vuthqá *(The Sure Handle), a Beirut encyclopedia, and an Egyptian newspaper.*

In 1880 members of the Báb's family, known as Afnán, decided to establish a trading company in Constantinople for which they sought and obtained Bahá'u'lláh's permission. To run the business they invited an experienced merchant from Qazvín and a devoted Bahá'í, Shaykh Muḥammad-'Alí, whom Bahá'u'lláh named Nabíl ibn-i-Nabíl (Nabíl, son of Nabíl); his father had been one of the earliest Bábís. The business began in 1882 and was soon very successful. Nabíl became known as one of the most trustworthy merchants in the city, a fact that aroused the jealousy of the Azalís, who instituted a villainous campaign of slander against him within the city's higher circles.

Nabíl ibn-i-Nabíl was also the victim of false accusations made by Muḥammad-'Alíy-i-Iṣfahání, a troublemaker whom Bahá'u'lláh had sent away from 'Akká to Constantinople. There Muḥammad-'Alíy-i-Iṣfahání set himself up as a small trader and began causing difficulty for the Afnán's trading establishment. To counter the damaging effects of Muḥammad-'Alí's behavior, Nabíl proposed to the Afnán that they make him a partner in the business. For years things went smoothly, and Muḥammad-'Alí profited handsomely. Unbeknown to Nabíl, however, Muḥammad-'Alí joined forces with the Azalís, and the campaign of defamation grew stronger. Foremost among the objects of their venom was the distinguished brother of the wife of the Báb, Ḥájí Mírzá Siyyid Ḥasan, known as Afnán-i-Kabír (the Great Afnán). Damaging articles about him appeared in Akhtar.

Eventually the abuse drove Nabíl to attempt suicide by throwing himself into the sea, but he was rescued by boatmen. Hearing of Nabíl's plight, Bahá'u'lláh invited him to make a pilgrimage to 'Akká. While Nabíl was away, Muḥammad-'Alí stole four hundred pounds from the trading company and accused another Bahá'í passing through Constantinople of the theft. The accusation was circulated widely throughout the city and was brought to the attention of the Persian ambassador, who investigated the incident and exonerated the Bahá'í. Muḥammad-'Alí, spurred on by the Azalís, then took the case to the Turkish courts, which again exonerated the Bahá'í.

Stung by their defeat in the courts, Muḥammad-'Alí and his accomplices increased their attacks on the Bahá'ís in Akhtar, *publishing libelous falsehoods about the trading house and the Bahá'ís. Nabíl returned to Constantinople in 1889 to refute the attacks and won the case in court. Moreover, prominent merchants in Constantinople signed a document testifying to the perfidy of Muḥammad-'Alí. Again, however, defeat only emboldened the Azalís further, and they initiated an even more outrageous campaign of slander. Nabíl could endure it no longer and killed himself by taking poison.*

Bahá'u'lláh comments on the persecutions, libelous accusations, and other events in numerous Tablets revealed toward the end of His life. One such Tablet, Epistle to the Son of the Wolf, *is addressed to Shaykh Muḥammad Taqíy-i-Najafí, (the Son of the Wolf), an opponent of the Faith who was responsible for the deaths of the King of Martyrs and the Beloved of Martyrs and who volunteered to serve as their executioner. Throughout the Tablet Bahá'u'lláh repeatedly calls upon the Shaykh to ponder and reflect on these events and to make amends for his misdeeds.*

O SHAYKH! WHILE HEMMED IN BY TRIBULATIONS this Wronged One is occupied in setting down these words. On every side the flame of oppression and tyranny can be discerned. On the one hand, tidings have reached Us that Our loved ones have been arrested in the land of Ṭá [Ṭihrán] and this notwithstanding that the sun, and the moon, and the land, and the sea all testify that this people are adorned with the adornment of fidelity, and have clung and will cling to naught except that which can ensure the exaltation of the government, and the maintenance of order within the nation, and the tranquillity of the people.

O Shaykh! We have time and again stated that for a number of years We have extended Our aid unto His Majesty the Sháh. For years no untoward incident hath occurred in Persia. The reins of the stirrers of sedition among various sects were held firmly in the grasp of power. None hath transgressed his limits. By God! This people have never been, nor are they now, inclined to mischief. Their hearts are illumined with the light of the fear of God, and adorned with the adornment of His love. Their concern hath ever been and now is for the betterment of the world. Their purpose is to obliterate differences, and quench the flame of hatred and enmity, so that the whole earth may come to be viewed as one country.

On the other hand, the officials of the Persian Embassy in the Great City [Constantinople] are energetically and assiduously seeking to exterminate these wronged ones. They desire one thing, and God desireth another. Consider now what hath befallen the trusted ones of God in every land. At one time they have been accused of theft and larceny; at another they have been calumniated in a manner without parallel in this world. Answer thou fairly. What could be the results and consequences, in foreign countries, of the accusation of theft brought by the Persian Embassy against its own subjects? If this Wronged One was ashamed, it was not because of the humiliation it brought this servant, but rather because of the shame of its becoming known to the Ambassadors of foreign countries how incompetent and lacking in understanding are several eminent officials of the Persian Embassy. . . . Briefly, instead of seeking, as they should, through Him Who occupieth this sublime station, to attain unto the most exalted ranks, and to obtain His advice, they have exerted themselves and are striving their utmost to put out His light. However, according to what hath been reported, His Excellency the Ambassador Mu'ínu'l-Mulk, Mírzá Muḥsin Khán—may God assist him—was, at that time, absent from Constantinople. Such things have happened because it was believed that His Majesty the Sháh of Persia—may the All-Merciful assist him—was angry with them that have attained and revolve round the Sanctuary of Wisdom. God well knoweth and testifieth that this Wronged One hath, at all times, been cleaving fast unto whatever would be conducive to the glory of both the government and the people. God, verily, is sufficient Witness.

—BAHÁ'U'LLÁH 7

O SHAYKH! TIME AND AGAIN HAVE I DECLARED, and now yet again I affirm, that for two score years We have, through the grace of God and by His irresistible and potent will, extended such aid to His Majesty the Sháh—may God assist him—as the exponents of justice and of equity would regard as incontestable and absolute. None can deny it, unless he be a transgressor and sinner, or one who would hate Us or doubt Our truth. How very strange that until now the Ministers of State and the representatives of the people have alike remained unaware of such conspicuous and undeniable service, and, if apprized of it, have, for reasons of their own, chosen to ignore it! Previous to these forty years controversies and conflicts continually prevailed and agitated the servants of God. But since then, aided by the hosts of wisdom, of utterance, of exhortations and understanding, they have all seized and taken fast hold of the firm cord of patience and of the shining hem of fortitude, in such wise that this wronged people endured steadfastly whatever befell them, and committed everything unto God, and this notwithstanding that in Mázindarán and at Rasht a great many have been most hideously tormented. Among them was his honor, Ḥájí Naṣír, who, unquestionably, was a brilliant light that shone forth above the horizon of resignation. After he had suffered martyrdom, they plucked out his eyes and cut off his nose, and inflicted on him such indignities that strangers wept and lamented, and secretly raised funds to support his wife and children.

O Shaykh! My Pen is abashed to recount what actually took place. In the land of Ṣád [Iṣfahán] the fire of tyranny burned with such a hot flame that every fair-minded person groaned aloud. By thy life! The cities of knowledge and of understanding wept with such a weeping that the souls of the pious and of the God-fearing were melted. The twin shining lights, Ḥasan and Ḥusayn [The King of Martyrs and the Beloved of Martyrs] offered up spontaneously their lives in that city. Neither fortune, nor wealth, nor glory, could deter them! God knoweth the things which befell them and yet the people are, for the most part, unaware!

Before them one named Káẓim and they who were with him, and after them, his honor Ashraf,[3] all quaffed the draught of martyrdom with the utmost fervor and longing, and hastened unto the Supreme Companion. In like manner, at the time of Sardár 'Azíz Khán,[4] that godly man, Mírzá Muṣṭafá, and his fellow-martyrs, were arrested, and despatched unto the Supreme Friend in the All-Glorious Horizon. Briefly, in every city the evidences of a tyranny, beyond like or equal, were unmistakably clear and manifest, and yet none arose in self-defence! Call thou to mind his honor Badí', who was the bearer of the Tablet to His Majesty the Sháh, and reflect how he laid down his life. That knight, who spurred on his charger in the arena of renunciation, threw down the precious crown of life for the sake of Him Who is the Incomparable Friend.

O Shaykh! If things such as these are to be denied, what shall, then, be deemed worthy of credence? Set forth the truth, for the sake of God, and be not of them that hold their peace. They arrested his honor Najaf-'Alí, who hastened, with rapture and great longing, unto the field of

3. Mírzá Ashraf-i-Ábádí.
4. The governor of Ádhirbáyján.

martyrdom, uttering these words: "We have kept both Bahá and the khún-bahá (bloodmoney)!"[5] With these words he yielded up his spirit. Meditate on the splendor and glory which the light of renunciation, shining from the upper chamber of the heart of Mullá 'Alí-Ján, hath shed. He was so carried away by the breezes of the Most Sublime Word and by the power of the Pen of Glory that to him the field of martyrdom equalled, nay outrivalled, the haunts of earthly delights. Ponder upon the conduct of 'Abá-Baṣír and Siyyid Ashraf-i-Zanjání. They sent for the mother of Ashraf to dissuade her son from his purpose. But she spurred him on until he suffered a most glorious martyrdom.

O Shaykh! This people have passed beyond the narrow straits of names, and pitched their tents upon the shores of the sea of renunciation. They would willingly lay down a myriad lives, rather than breathe the word desired by their enemies. They have clung to that which pleaseth God, and are wholly detached and freed from the things which pertain unto men. They have preferred to have their heads cut off rather than utter one unseemly word. Ponder this in thine heart. Methinks they have quaffed their fill of the ocean of renunciation. The life of the present world

5. A play on words. *Khún* means "blood." *Bahá* in Arabic means "glory" and in Persian, "value." "Bloodmoney" refers to the reward Najáf-'Alí will receive for sacrificing his life in the path of God. By ransoming his life as a martyr, the true value of the bloodmoney is realized.

hath failed to withhold them from suffering martyrdom in the path of God.

—*BAHÁ'U'LLÁH 8*

GRACIOUS GOD! This is the day whereon the wise should seek the advice of this Wronged One, and ask Him Who is the Truth what things are conducive to the glory and tranquillity of men. And yet, all are earnestly striving to put out this glorious and shining light, and are diligently seeking either to establish Our guilt, or to voice their protest against Us. Matters have come to such a pass, that the conduct of this Wronged One hath, in every way, been grossly misrepresented, and in a manner which it would be unseemly to mention. One of Our friends hath reported that among the residents of the Great City [Constantinople] he had heard with the greatest regret someone state that, each year, a sum of fifty thousand túmáns was being despatched from his native land to 'Akká! It hath not, however, been made clear who had disbursed the sum, nor through whose hands it had passed!

Briefly, this Wronged One hath, in the face of all that hath befallen Him at their hands, and all that hath been said of Him, endured patiently, and held His peace, inasmuch as it is Our purpose, through the loving providence of God—exalted be His glory—and His surpassing mercy, to abolish, through the force of Our utterance, all disputes, war, and bloodshed, from the face of the earth. Under all conditions We have, in spite of what they have said, endured with seemly patience, and have left them to God. In answer to this particular imputation, however, We have replied, that if that which he affirmeth be true, it behooveth him to be thankful to Him Who is the Lord of all being, and the King of the seen and unseen, for having raised up in Persia One Who, though a prisoner and with none to help and assist Him, hath succeeded in establishing His ascendency over that land, and in drawing from it a yearly revenue. Such an achievement should be praised rather than censured, if he be of them that judge equitably. Should anyone seek to be acquainted with the condition of this Wronged One, let him be told that these captives whom the world hath persecuted and the nations wronged have, for days and nights, been entirely denied the barest means of subsistence. We are loth to mention such things, neither have We had, nor do We have now, any desire to complain against Our accuser. Within the walls of this prison a highly-esteemed man was for some time obliged to break stones that he might earn a living, whilst others had, at times, to nourish themselves with that Divine sustenance which is hunger! We entreat God—exalted and glorified be He—to aid all men to be just and fair-minded, and to graciously assist them to repent and return unto Him. He, verily, heareth, and is ready to answer.

Glorified art Thou, O Lord my God! Thou seest what hath befallen this Wronged One at the hands of them that have not associated with Me, and who have arisen to harm and abase Me, in a manner which no pen can describe, nor tongue recount, nor can any Tablet sustain its weight. Thou hearest the cry of Mine heart, and the groaning of Mine inmost being, and the things that have befallen Thy trusted ones in Thy cities and Thy chosen ones in Thy land, at the hands of such as have broken Thy Covenant and Thy Testament. I beseech Thee, O my Lord, by the sighs of Thy lovers throughout the world, and by their lamentation in their remoteness from the court of Thy presence, and by the blood that hath been shed for love of Thee, and by the hearts that have melted in Thy path, to protect Thy loved ones from the cruelty of such as have remained unaware of the mysteries of Thy Name, the Unconstrained. Assist them, O my Lord, by Thy power that hath prevailed over all things, and aid them to be patient and long-suffering. Thou art the All-Powerful, the Almighty, the All-Bountiful. No God is there but Thee, the Generous, the Lord of grace abounding.

In these days there are some who, far from being just and fair-minded, have assaulted Me with the sword of hatred and the spear of enmity, forgetting that it behooveth every fair-minded person to succor Him Whom the world hath cast away and the nations abandoned, and to lay hold on piety and righteousness. Most men have until now failed to discover the purpose of this Wronged One, nor have they known the reason for which He hath been willing to endure countless afflictions. Meanwhile, the voice of Mine heart crieth out these words: "O that My people knew!" This Wronged One, rid of attachment unto all things, uttereth these exalted words: "Waves have encompassed the Ark of God, the Help in Peril, the Self-Subsisting. Fear not the tempestuous gales, O Mariner! He Who causeth the dawn to appear is, verily, with Thee in this darkness that hath struck terror into the hearts of all men, except such as God, the Almighty, the Unconstrained, hath been pleased to spare."

—*BAHÁ'U'LLÁH 9*

O SHAYKH! WE HAD SEIZED THE REINS of authority by the power of God and His Divine might, as He alone can seize, Who is the Mighty, the Strong. None had the power to stir up mischief or sedition. Now, however, as they have failed to appreciate this loving-kindness and these bounties, they have been, and will be, afflicted with the retribution which their acts must entail. The State officials, considering the secret progress of the Extended Cord have, from every direction, incited and aided Mine adversaries. In the Great City [Constantinople] they have roused a considerable number of people to oppose this Wronged One. Things have come to such a pass that the officials in that city have acted in a manner which hath brought shame to both the government and the people. A distinguished siyyid,[6] whose well-known integrity, acceptable conduct, and commercial reputation, were recognized by the majority of fair-minded men, and who was regarded by all as a highly honored merchant, once visited Beirut. In view of his friendship for this Wronged One they telegraphed the Persian Dragoman[7] informing him that this siyyid, assisted by his

6. The brother of the wife of the Báb, Ḥájí Mírzá Siyyid Ḥasan, known as Afnán-i-Kabir (the Great Afnán).

7. Interpreter.

servant, had stolen a sum of money and other things and gone to 'Akká. Their design in this matter was to dishonor this Wronged One. And yet, far be it from the people of this country to allow themselves to be deflected, by these unseemly tales, from the straight path of uprightness and truth. Briefly, they have assaulted Me from every side, and are reinforcing Mine adversaries. This Wronged One, however, beseecheth the one true God to graciously assist every one in that which beseemeth these days. Day and night I fix My gaze on these perspicuous words, and recite: "O God, my God! I beseech Thee by the sun of Thy grace, and the sea of Thy knowledge, and the heaven of Thy justice, to aid them that have denied Thee to confess, and such as have turned aside from Thee to return, and those who have calumniated Thee to be just and fair-minded. Assist them, O my Lord, to return unto Thee, and to repent before the door of Thy grace. Powerful art Thou to do what Thou willest, and in Thy grasp are the reins of all that is in the heavens and all that is on earth. Praise be unto God, the Lord of the worlds."

—*BAHÁ'U'LLÁH 10*

CONCERNING THIS WRONGED ONE, most of the things reported in the newspapers are devoid of truth. Fair speech and truthfulness, by reason of their lofty rank and position, are regarded as a sun shining above the horizon of knowledge. The waves rising from this Ocean are apparent before the eyes of the peoples of the world and the effusions of the Pen of wisdom and utterance are manifest everywhere.

It is reported in the press that this Servant hath fled from the land of Ṭá [Ṭihrán] and gone to 'Iráq. Gracious God! Not even for a single moment hath this Wronged One ever concealed Himself. Rather hath He at all times remained steadfast and conspicuous before the eyes of all men. Never have We retreated, nor shall We ever seek flight. In truth it is the foolish people who flee from Our presence. We left Our home country accompanied by two mounted escorts, representing the two honoured governments of Persia and Russia until We arrived in 'Iráq in the plenitude of glory and power. Praise be to God! The Cause whereof this Wronged One is the Bearer standeth as high as heaven and shineth resplendent as the sun. Concealment hath no access unto this station, nor is there any occasion for fear or silence.

—*BAHÁ'U'LLÁH 11*

GOD ALONE—EXALTED BE HIS GLORY—is cognizant of the things which befell this Wronged One. Every day bringeth a fresh report of stories current against Us at the Embassy in Constantinople. Gracious God! The sole aim of their machinations is to bring about the extermination of this servant. They are, however, oblivious of the fact that abasement in the path of God is My true glory. In the newspapers the following hath been recorded: "Touching the fraudulent dealings of some of the exiles of 'Akká, and the excesses committed by them against several people, etc. . . ." Unto them who are the exponents of justice and the daysprings of equity the intention of the writer is evident and his purpose clear. Briefly, he arose and inflicted upon Me divers tribulations, and treated Me with injustice and cruelty. By God! This Wronged One would not barter this place of exile for the Most Sublime Habitation. In the estimation of men of insight whatsoever befalleth in the path of God is manifest glory and a supreme attainment.

—*BAHÁ'U'LLÁH 12*

GRACIOUS GOD! A thing hath recently happened which caused great astonishment. It is reported that a certain person[8] went to the seat of the imperial throne in Persia and succeeded in winning the good graces of some of the nobility by his ingratiating behaviour. How pitiful indeed, how deplorable! One wondereth why those who have been the symbols of highest glory should now stoop to boundless shame. What is become of their high resolve? Whither is gone the sense of dignity and honour? The sun of glory and wisdom hath unceasingly been shining above the horizon of Persia, but nowadays it hath sunk to such a low level that certain dignitaries have allowed themselves to be treated as playthings in the hands of the foolish. The aforesaid person hath written such things concerning this people in the Egyptian press and in the Beirut Encyclopedia that the well-informed and the learned were astonished. He proceeded then to Paris where he published a newspaper entitled *'Urvatu'l-Vuthqá* [The Sure Handle] and sent copies thereof to all parts of the

8. Jamálu'd-Dín-i-Afghání.

world. He also sent a copy to the Prison of 'Akká, and by so doing he meant to show affection and to make amends for his past actions. In short, this Wronged One hath observed silence in regard to him. We entreat God, the True One, to protect him and to shed upon him the light of justice and fairness.

—BAHÁ'U'LLÁH 13

O THOU WHO HAST TURNED THY GAZE towards My face! In these days there occurred that which hath plunged Me into dire sadness. Certain wrong-doers who profess allegiance to the Cause of God committed such deeds as have caused the limbs of sincerity, of honesty, of justice, of equity to quake. One known individual[9] to whom the utmost kindness and favour had been extended perpetrated such acts as have brought tears to the eye of God. Formerly We uttered words of warning and premonition, then for a number of years We kept the matter secret that haply he might take heed and repent. But all to no purpose. In the end he bent his energies upon vilifying the Cause of God before the eyes of all men. He tore the veil of fairness asunder and felt sympathy neither for himself nor for the Cause of God. Now, however, the deeds of certain individuals have brought sorrows far more grievous than those which the deeds of the former had caused. Beseech thou God, the True One, that He

9. Muḥammad-'Alíy-i-Iṣfahání.

> may graciously enable the heedless to retract and repent. Verily He is the Forgiving, the Bountiful, the Most Generous.
>
> —*BAHÁ'U'LLÁH* 14

The Azalís in Persia

Another source of suffering for Bahá'u'lláh was the behavior of a few Azalís who sullied the Faith's reputation. Two such persons were Ṣadru'l-'Ulamá and Mírzá Hádíy-i-Dawlat-Ábádí. Ṣadru'l-'Ulamá was a divine who had become a Bábí but had fallen under the influence of Siyyid Muḥammad, Mírzá Yaḥyá's ally from the time of Bahá'u'lláh's exile in Ba<u>gh</u>dád until his death in 1872. Mírzá Hádíy-i-Dawlat-Ábádí was Mírzá Yaḥyá's representative in Persia who later became his successor. Years before, Mírzá Hádí had become a Bábí and had followed Mírzá Yaḥyá when he advanced his claim to be the one foretold by the Báb. Mírzá Hádí had rallied other Bábís to Mírzá Yaḥyá's side and had spread many misunderstandings and falsehoods about Bahá'u'lláh and His Cause.

In 1888, when the clergy was clamoring for the arrest and execution of prominent Bahá'í teachers, <u>Sh</u>ay<u>kh</u> Muḥammad-Taqíy-i-Najafí (the Son of the Wolf) called for the execution of Mírzá A<u>sh</u>raf-i-Ábádí in Iṣfahán. Denounced as a Bahá'í and imprisoned, Mírzá A<u>sh</u>raf was interrogated by the divines, including <u>Sh</u>ay<u>kh</u> Muḥammad Taqíy-i-Najafí. After strongly and eloquently refuting their arguments, Mírzá A<u>sh</u>raf was sentenced to death and hung in the public square, whereupon his body was savagely mutilated. Soon thereafter <u>Sh</u>ay<u>kh</u> Muḥammad Taqí called for the death of Hádí, who publicly recanted his faith from the pulpit, cursing and reviling the Báb and Bahá'u'lláh in the foulest language. He was promptly absolved of the charge of being a Bahá'í, and his life was spared. Seizing their opportunity, en-

emies of the Faith publicized Hádí's recantation throughout the country. Despite his shameful behavior, Hádí carried on as leader of the Azalís in Persia. Although the Azalís were few in number, Bahá'u'lláh continued to admonish Hádí and his handful of followers, hoping to lead them away from the oblivion toward which they were headed.

IT BEHOOVETH THEE NOW TO REFLECT upon the state of Mírzá Hádí Dawlat-Ábádí and of Ṣád-i-Iṣfahání (Ṣadru'l-'Ulamá), who reside in the Land of Ṭá [Ṭihrán].[10] No sooner had the former heard that he had been called a Bábí than he became so perturbed that his poise and dignity forsook him. He ascended the pulpits and spoke words which ill befitted him. From time immemorial the clay clods of the world have, wholly by reason of their love of leadership, perpetrated such acts as have caused men to err. Thou must not, however, imagine that all the faithful are such as these two. We have described unto thee the constancy, the firmness, the steadfastness, the certitude, the imperturbability and the dignity of the martyrs of this Revelation, that thou mayest be well-informed. . . . Certain faint-hearted ones, however, such as Hádí and others, have tampered with the Cause of God and have, in their concern for this fleeting life, said and done that which caused the eye of justice to weep and the Pen of Glory to groan, notwithstanding their ignorance

10. This passage is addressed to Shaykh Muḥammad Taqíy-i-Najafí.

of the essentials of this Cause; whereas this Wronged One hath revealed it for the sake of God.

O Hádí! Thou hast gone unto My brother and hast seen him. Set now thy face towards the court of this Wronged One, that haply the breezes of Revelation and the breaths of inspiration may assist thee and enable thee to attain thy goal. Whoever gazeth this day on My signs will distinguish truth from falsehood as the sun from shadow, and will be made cognizant of the goal. God is aware and beareth Me witness that whatever hath been mentioned was for the sake of God, that haply thou mayest be the cause of the guidance of men, and mayest deliver the peoples of the world from idle fancies and vain imaginings.

—*BAHÁ'U'LLÁH* 15

O HÁDÍ! GIVE EAR UNTO THE VOICE of this trustworthy Counsellor: direct thy steps from the left unto the right, that is turn away from idle fancy unto certitude. Lead not the people into error. The divine Luminary shineth, His Cause is manifest and His signs are all-embracing. Set thy face towards God, the Help in Peril, the Self-Subsisting. Renounce thy leadership for the sake of God and leave the people unto themselves. Thou art ignorant of the essential truth, thou art not acquainted therewith.

O Hádí! Be thou of one face in the path of God. When in company with the infidels, thou art an infidel and with the pious, thou art pious. Reflect thou upon such souls as offered up their lives and their substance in that land, that haply thou mayest be admonished and roused from slumber. Consider:

who is to be preferred, he who preserveth his body, his life and his possessions or the one who surrendereth his all in the path of God? Judge thou fairly and be not of the unjust. Take fast hold of justice and adhere unto equity that perchance thou mayest not, for selfish motives, use religion as a snare, nor disregard the truth for the sake of gold. Indeed thine iniquity and the iniquity of such people as thyself have waxed so grievous that the Pen of Glory was moved to make such observations. Fear thou God. He Who heralded this Revelation hath declared: "He shall proclaim under all conditions: 'Verily, verily, I am God, no God is there but Me, the Help in Peril, the Self-Subsisting.'"

. . . .

O Hádí! Thou hast not been in Our company, thou art therefore ignorant of the Cause. Act not according to thine idle imaginings. Aside from these things, scrutinize the Writings with thine own eyes and ponder upon that which hath come to pass. Have pity upon thyself and upon the servants of God and be not the cause of waywardness like unto the people aforetime. The path is unmistakable and the proof is evident. Change injustice into justice and inequity into equity. We cherish the hope that the breaths of divine inspiration may strengthen thee and that thine inner ear may be enabled to hear the blessed words: "Say, it is God, then leave them to entertain themselves with their cavillings." Thou hast been there [Cyprus] and hast seen him [Mírzá Yaḥyá]. Now speak forth with fairness. Do not misrepresent the matter, neither to thyself nor to the people. Thou art both ignorant and uninformed.

Give ear unto the Voice of this Wronged One and hasten towards the ocean of divine knowledge that perchance thou mayest be adorned with the ornament of comprehension and mayest renounce all else but God. Hearken unto the Voice of this benevolent Counsellor, calling aloud, unveiled and manifest, before the faces of kings and their subjects, and summon the people of the world, one and all, unto Him Who is the Lord of Eternity.

—BAHÁ'U'LLÁH 16

Meditations and Prayers on Bahá'u'lláh's Tribulations

AS MY TRIBULATIONS MULTIPLIED, so did My love for God and for His Cause increase, in such wise that all that befell Me from the hosts of the wayward was powerless to deter Me from My purpose. Should they hide Me away in the depths of the earth, yet would they find Me riding aloft on the clouds, and calling out unto God, the Lord of strength and of might. I have offered Myself up in the way of God, and I yearn after tribulations in My love for Him, and for the sake of His good-pleasure. Unto this bear witness the woes which now afflict Me, the like of which no other man hath suffered. Every single hair of Mine head calleth out that which the Burning Bush uttered on Sinai, and each vein of My body invoketh God and saith: "O would I had been severed in Thy path, so that the world might be quickened, and all its peoples be united!" Thus hath it been decreed by Him Who is the All-Knowing, the All-Informed.

—*BAHÁ'U'LLÁH 17*

THE ONE TRUE GOD WELL KNOWETH, and all the company of His trusted ones testify, that this Wronged One hath, at all times, been faced with dire peril. But for the tribulations that have touched Me in the path of God, life would have held no sweetness for Me, and My existence would have profited Me nothing. For them who are endued with discernment, and whose eyes are fixed upon the Sublime Vision, it is no secret that I have been, most of the days of My life, even as a slave, sitting under a sword hanging on a thread, knowing not whether it would fall soon or late upon him. And yet, notwithstanding all this We render thanks unto God, the Lord of the worlds. Mine inner tongue reciteth, in the day-time and in the night-season, this prayer: "Glory to Thee, O my God! But for the tribulations which are sustained in Thy path, how could Thy true lovers be recognized; and were it not for the trials which are borne for love of Thee, how could the station of such as yearn for Thee be revealed? Thy might beareth Me witness! The companions of all who adore Thee are the tears they shed, and the comforters of such as seek Thee are the groans they utter, and the food of them who haste to meet Thee is the fragments of their broken hearts. How sweet to my taste is the bitterness of death suffered in Thy path, and how precious in my estimation are the shafts of Thine enemies when encountered for the sake of the exaltation of Thy Word! Let me quaff in

Thy Cause, O my God and my Master, whatsoever Thou didst desire, and send down upon me in Thy love all Thou didst ordain. By Thy glory! I wish only what Thou wishest, and cherish what Thou cherishest. In Thee have I, at all times, placed My whole trust and confidence. Thou art verily the All-Possessing, the Most High. Raise up, I implore Thee, O my God, as helpers to this Revelation such as shall be counted worthy of Thy Name and of Thy sovereignty, that they may remember Thee among Thy creatures, and hoist the ensigns of Thy victory in Thy land, and adorn them with Thy virtues and Thy commandments. No God is there but Thee, the Help in Peril, the Self-Subsisting."

—BAHÁ'U'LLÁH 18

I GIVE THEE THANKS, O MY GOD, for that Thou hast made me to be a target for the darts of Thine adversaries in Thy path. I offer Thee most high praise, O Thou Who art the Knower of the seen and unseen and the Lord of all being, that Thou hast suffered me to be cast into prison for love of Thee, and caused me to quaff the cup of woe, that I may reveal Thy Cause and glorify Thy word.

Which of my tribulations am I to recount before Thy face, O my Lord? Am I to recite before Thee what in days of old befell me at the hands of the workers of iniquity among Thy creatures, or to describe the vexations which have compassed me about in these days for the sake of Thy good pleasure?

Thanks be to Thee, O Thou the Lord of all names; and glory be to Thee, O Maker of the heavens, for all that I have sustained in these days at the hands of such of Thy servants as have transgressed against Thee, and of Thy people that have dealt frowardly towards Thee.

Number us, we implore Thee, with them who have stood fast in Thy Cause until their souls finally winged their flight unto the heaven of Thy grace and the atmosphere of Thy loving-kindness. Thou art, verily, the Ever-Forgiving, the Most Merciful.

—BAHÁ'U'LLÁH 19

GLORIFIED ART THOU, O MY GOD! Thou knowest that in my love for Thee I have not sought any rest, that in proclaiming Thy Cause I have denied myself every manner of tranquillity, and that in the observance of whatever Thou hast prescribed in Thy Tablets I have not delayed to do Thy bidding. I have, for this reason, suffered what no man among all the inhabitants of Thy realm hath suffered.

Thy glory beareth me witness! Nothing whatsoever can withhold me from remembering Thee, though all the tribulations of the earth were to assault me from every direction. All the limbs and members of my body proclaim their readiness to be torn asunder in Thy path and for the sake of Thy pleasure, and they yearn to be scattered in the dust before Thee. O would that they who serve Thee could taste what I have tasted of the sweetness of Thy love!

I implore Thee to supply whosoever hath sought Thee with the living waters of Thy bounty, that they may rid him of all attachment to any one but Thee.

Thou art, verily, the Omniscient, the All-Glorious, the Almighty.

—*BAHÁ'U'LLÁH 20*

GLORIFIED ART THOU, O MY LORD! Thou beholdest my tribulations and all that hath befallen me at the hands of such of Thy servants as keep company with me, who have disbelieved in Thy most resplendent signs, and turned back from Thy most effulgent Beauty. I swear by Thy glory! Such are the troubles that vex me, that no pen in the entire creation can either reckon or describe them.

I implore Thee, O Thou Who art the King of names and the Creator of earth and heaven, so to assist me by Thy strengthening grace that nothing whatsoever will have the power to hinder me from remembering Thee, or celebrating Thy praise, or to keep me back from observing what Thou hast prescribed unto me in Thy Tablets, that I may so arise to serve Thee that with bared head I will hasten forth from my habitation, cry out in Thy name amidst Thy creatures, and proclaim Thy virtues among Thy servants. Having accomplished what Thou hadst decreed, and delivered the thing Thou hadst written down, the wicked doers among Thy people would, then, compass me about and would do with me in Thy path as would please them.

In the love I bear to Thee, O my Lord, my heart longeth for Thee with a longing such as no heart hath known. Here am I with my body between Thy hands, and my spirit before Thy face. Do with them as it may please Thee, for the exaltation of Thy word, and the revelation of what hath been enshrined within the treasuries of Thy knowledge.

Potent art Thou to do what Thou willest, and able to ordain what Thou pleasest.

—BAHÁ'U'LLÁH 21

LAUDED BE THY NAME, O LORD MY GOD! How great is Thy might and Thy sovereignty; how vast Thy strength and Thy dominion! Thou hast called into being Him Who speaketh in Thy name before all who are in Thy heaven and on Thy earth, and hast bidden Him cry out amongst Thy creatures.

No sooner had a word gone forth from His lips, however, than the divines among Thy people turned back from Him, and the learned among Thy servants caviled at His signs. Thereby the fire of oppression was kindled in Thy land, until the kings themselves rose up to put out Thy light, O Thou Who art the King of kings!

Hostility waxed so intense that my kindred and my loved ones were made captives in Thy land, and they that are dear to Thee were hindered from gazing on Thy beauty and from turning in the direction of Thy mercy. This hostility failed to cause the fire that burned within them to subside. The enemy finally carried away as captive Him Who is the Manifestation of Thy beauty and the Revealer of Thy signs, and confined Him in the fortress-town of 'Akká, and sought to hinder Him from remembering Thee and from magnifying Thy name. Thy servant, however, could not be restrained from carrying out what Thou hadst bidden Him fulfill.

Above the horizon of tribulation He hath lifted up His voice and He crieth out, summoning all the inmates of heaven and all the inhabitants of the earth to the immensity of Thy mercy and the court of Thy grace. Day and night He sendeth down the signs of Thine omnipotent power and revealeth the clear tokens of Thy majesty, so that the souls of Thy creatures may be drawn towards Thee, that they may forsake themselves and turn unto Thee, and may flee from their misery and seek the tabernacle of Thy riches, and may haste away from their wretchedness into the court of Thy majesty and glory.

This is the Lamp which the light of Thine own Essence hath lit, and whose radiance the winds of discord can never extinguish. This is the Ocean that moveth by the power of Thy sovereign might, and whose waves the influence of the infidels that have disbelieved in the Judgment Day can never still. This is the Sun that shineth in the heaven of Thy will and the splendor of which the veils of the workers of iniquity and the doubts of the evil doers can never cloud.

I yield Thee thanks, O my God, for that Thou hast offered me up as a sacrifice in Thy path, and made me a target for the arrows of afflictions as a token of Thy love for Thy servants, and singled me out for all manner of tribulation for the regeneration of Thy people.

How sweet to my taste is the savor of woes sent by Thee, and how dear to my heart the dispositions of Thy providence! Perish the soul that fleeth from the threats of kings in its attempt to save itself in Thy days! I swear by Thy glory! Whoso hath quaffed the living waters of Thy favors can fear no trouble in Thy path, neither can he be deterred by any tribulation from remembering Thee or from celebrating Thy praise.

I beseech Thee, O Thou Who art my Governor and the Possessor of all names, to protect them that have branched out from me [Afnán], whom Thou hast caused to be related to Thyself, and to whom Thou hast, in this Revelation, shown Thy special favor, and whom Thou hast summoned to draw nigh unto Thee and to turn towards the horizon of Thy Revelation. Withhold not from them, O my Lord, the outpourings of Thy mercy or the effulgence of the Day-Star of Thy grace. Enable them to distinguish themselves amongst Thy people, that they may exalt Thy word and promote Thy Cause. Aid them, O my God, to do Thy will and pleasure.

No God is there but Thee, the All-Powerful, the Most Exalted, the Most High.

—BAHÁ'U'LLÁH 22

Divine Justice

In Bahá'u'lláh's later years signs of the triumph of His Cause became increasingly evident. One such sign was the spread of the Faith by 1892 beyond the borders of Persia and 'Iráq to Ádhirbáyján, Armenia, Georgia, Palestine, Turkmenistan, Lebanon, Syria, Turkey, Egypt, Sudan, Pakistan, India, and Burma. Another sign of triumph was the fulfillment of prophecies concerning the fate of Bahá'u'lláh's adversaries. Foremost among such prophecies were those regarding the demise of Sulṭán 'Abdu'l-'Azíz of Turkey and his ministers Fu'ád Páshá and 'Álí Páshá.

In 1863 Fu'ád Pá<u>sh</u>á and 'Álí Pá<u>sh</u>á had acquiesced to the demands of the Persian government, removing Bahá'u'lláh from Ba<u>gh</u>dád to Constantinople and securing His banishment to Adrianople a few months later. In 1869, only six years later, Fu'ád Pá<u>sh</u>á died prematurely of a heart condition in France. In 1871 'Álí Pá<u>sh</u>á fell ill and died within three months. In 1876 Sulṭán 'Abdu'l-'Azíz was deposed and assassinated. Bahá'u'lláh had prophesied the downfall of all three men in several Tablets, one of which, written after Fu'ád Pá<u>sh</u>á's death, states, "Soon will We dismiss the one *['Álí Pá<u>sh</u>á]* who was like unto him *[Fu'ád Pá<u>sh</u>á]* and will lay hold on their chief *[Sulṭán 'Abdu'l-'Azíz]* who ruleth the land, and I, verily, am the Almighty, the All-Compelling." *The fulfillment of these and other prophecies concerning the Ottoman Empire's collapse caused much comment throughout Persia and led many people to accept the Bahá'í Faith, among them Mírzá Abu'l-Faḍl, the Faith's greatest scholar.*

THE OTTOMAN SULṬÁN, without any justification, or reason, arose to oppress Us, and sent Us to the fortress of 'Akká. His imperial farmán decreed that none should associate with Us, and that We should become the object of the hatred of every one. The Hand of Divine power, therefore, swiftly avenged Us. It first loosed the winds of destruction upon his two irreplaceable ministers and confidants, 'Alí and Fu'ád, after which that Hand was stretched out to roll up the panoply of 'Azíz himself, and to seize him, as He only can seize, Who is the Mighty, the Strong.

—BAHÁ'U'LLÁH 23

EVERY UNBIASED OBSERVER will readily admit that, ever since the dawn of His Revelation, this wronged One hath invited all mankind to turn their faces towards the Day Spring of Glory, and hath forbidden corruption, hatred, oppression, and wickedness. And yet, behold what the hand of the oppressor hath wrought! No pen dare describe his tyranny. Though the purpose of Him Who is the Eternal Truth hath been to confer everlasting life upon all men, and ensure their security and peace, yet witness how they have arisen to shed the blood of His loved ones, and have pronounced on Him the sentence of death.

The instigators of this oppression are those very persons who, though so foolish, are reputed the wisest of the wise. Such is their blindness that, with unfeigned severity, they have cast into this fortified and afflictive Prison Him, for the servants of Whose Threshold the world hath been created. The Almighty, however, in spite of them and those that have repudiated the truth of this "Great Announcement," hath transformed this Prison House into the Most Exalted Paradise, the Heaven of Heavens.

—BAHÁ'U'LLÁH 24

NOW, PRAISE BE TO GOD, it has reached the point when all the people of these regions are manifesting their submissiveness unto Us.

—BAHÁ'U'LLÁH 25

Part 5 / COVENANT

Chapter 11 / THE COVENANT OF BAHÁ'U'LLÁH

The Kitáb-i-'Ahd— The Book of the Covenant

In the concluding years of Bahá'u'lláh's life, Tablets continued to stream from His pen, foremost among them being the Most Holy Tablet (Lawḥ-i-Aqdas), the Tablet of the World (Lawḥ-i-Dunyá), the Tablet of Maqṣúd, and Epistle to the Son of the Wolf. *Moreover, while visiting Haifa circa 1890, Bahá'u'lláh pitched His tent,* "'the Tabernacle of Glory,'" *on Mount Carmel; pointed out to 'Abdu'l-Bahá where the remains of the Báb were to be interred; and revealed the Tablet of Carmel, the Charter of the World Center of His Faith.*

Bahá'u'lláh also made provision, in the last Tablet He revealed, for the continuation of divine authority over the affairs of His Faith through the appointment of His eldest Son, 'Abdu'l-Bahá, as His successor and interpreter of His writings. This appointment marked the inauguration of the institution of the Covenant, which directs and canalizes the revolutionary forces that Bahá'u'lláh and the Báb have set in motion through their successive revelations, and ensures their harmonious and continuous operation, guarding against schism and sectarianism. It is an institution that, Shoghi Effendi explains, Bahá'u'lláh "anticipated in His Kitáb-i-Aqdas" and alluded to "as He bade His last farewell to the members of His family, who had been summoned to His bed-side, in the days immediately preceding His ascension." Entrusted to 'Abdu'l-Bahá by Bahá'u'lláh during His last illness, the document formally establishing this most mighty institution without parallel in religious history is designated by Bahá'u'lláh as the Kitáb-i-'Ahd, the Book of the Covenant. The complete text of the Tablet in English follows.

ALTHOUGH THE REALM OF GLORY hath none of the vanities of the world, yet within the treasury of trust and resignation We have bequeathed to Our heirs an excellent and priceless heritage. Earthly treasures We have not bequeathed, nor have We added such cares as they entail. By God! In earthly riches fear is hidden and peril is concealed. Consider ye and call to mind that which the All-Merciful hath revealed in the Qur'án: "Woe betide every slanderer and defamer, him that layeth up riches and counteth them."[1] Fleeting are the riches of the world; all that perisheth and changeth is not, and hath never been, worthy of attention, except to a recognized measure.

The aim of this Wronged One in sustaining woes and tribulations, in revealing the Holy Verses and in demonstrating proofs hath been naught but to quench the flame of hate and enmity, that the horizon of the hearts of men may be illumined with the light of concord and attain real peace and tranquillity. From the dawning-place of the divine Tablet the day-star of this utterance shineth resplendent, and it behoveth everyone to fix his gaze upon it: We exhort you, O peoples of the world, to

1. Qur'án 104:1–2.

observe that which will elevate your station. Hold fast to the fear of God and firmly adhere to what is right. Verily I say, the tongue is for mentioning what is good, defile it not with unseemly talk. God hath forgiven what is past. Henceforward everyone should utter that which is meet and seemly, and should refrain from slander, abuse and whatever causeth sadness in men. Lofty is the station of man! Not long ago this exalted Word streamed forth from the treasury of Our Pen of Glory: Great and blessed is this Day—the Day in which all that lay latent in man hath been and will be made manifest. Lofty is the station of man, were he to hold fast to righteousness and truth and to remain firm and steadfast in the Cause. In the eyes of the All-Merciful a true man appeareth even as a firmament; its sun and moon are his sight and hearing, and his shining and resplendent character its stars. His is the loftiest station, and his influence educateth the world of being.

Every receptive soul who hath in this Day inhaled the fragrance of His garment and hath, with a pure heart, set his face towards the all-glorious Horizon is reckoned among the people of Bahá in the Crimson Book. Grasp ye, in My Name, the chalice of My loving-kindness, drink then your fill in My glorious and wondrous remembrance.

O ye that dwell on earth! The religion of God is for love and unity; make it not the cause of enmity or dissension. In the eyes of men of insight and the beholders of the Most Sublime Vision, whatsoever are the effective means for safeguarding and promoting the happiness and welfare of the children of men have already been revealed by the Pen of Glory. But the foolish ones of the earth, being nurtured in evil passions and desires, have remained heedless of the consummate wisdom of Him Who is, in truth, the All-Wise, while their words and deeds are prompted by idle fancies and vain imaginings.

O ye the loved ones and the trustees of God! Kings are the manifestations of the power, and the daysprings of the might and riches, of God. Pray ye on their behalf. He hath invested them with the rulership of the earth and hath singled out the hearts of men as His Own domain.

Conflict and contention are categorically forbidden in His Book. This is a decree of God in this Most Great Revelation. It is divinely preserved from annulment and is invested by Him with the splendour of His confirmation. Verily He is the All-Knowing, the All-Wise.

It is incumbent upon everyone to aid those daysprings of authority and sources of command who are adorned with the ornament of equity and justice. Blessed are the rulers and the learned among the people of Bahá.[2] They are My trustees among My servants and the manifestations of My commandments amidst My people. Upon them rest My glory, My blessings and My grace which have

2. The term "learned" refers to the Hands of the Cause of God and those who attain an eminent position in the teaching work, while "rulers" refers to the members of local, national, and international Houses of Justice.

pervaded the world of being. In this connection the utterances revealed in the *Kitáb-i-Aqdas* are such that from the horizon of their words the light of divine grace shineth luminous and resplendent.

O ye My Branches! A mighty force, a consummate power lieth concealed in the world of being. Fix your gaze upon it and upon its unifying influence, and not upon the differences which appear from it.

The Will of the divine Testator is this: It is incumbent upon the Aghṣán,[3] the Afnán[4] and My Kindred to turn, one and all, their faces towards the Most Mighty Branch. Consider that which We have revealed in Our Most Holy Book: "When the ocean of My presence hath ebbed and the Book of My Revelation is ended, turn your faces toward Him Whom God hath purposed, Who hath branched from this Ancient Root." The object of this sacred verse is none other except the Most Mighty Branch ['Abdu'l-Bahá]. Thus have We graciously revealed unto you our potent Will, and I am verily the Gracious, the All-Powerful. Verily God hath ordained the station of the Greater Branch [Muḥammad 'Alí[5]] to be beneath that of the Most Great Branch ['Abdu'l-Bahá]. He is in truth the Ordainer, the All-Wise. We have chosen "the

---

3. The descendants of Bahá'u'lláh.

4. The relatives of the Báb.

5. A younger half-brother of 'Abdu'l-Bahá who opposed Him after Bahá'u'lláh's ascension and became the Arch-breaker of Bahá'u'lláh's Covenant.

Greater" after "the Most Great," as decreed by Him Who is the All-Knowing, the All-Informed.

It is enjoined upon everyone to manifest love towards the Aghṣán, but God hath not granted them any right to the property of others.

O ye My Aghṣán, My Afnán and My Kindred! We exhort you to fear God, to perform praiseworthy deeds and to do that which is meet and seemly and serveth to exalt your station. Verily I say, fear of God is the greatest commander that can render the Cause of God victorious, and the hosts which best befit this commander have ever been and are an upright character and pure and goodly deeds.

Say: O servants! Let not the means of order be made the cause of confusion and the instrument of union an occasion for discord. We fain would hope that the people of Bahá may be guided by the blessed words: "Say: all things are of God." This exalted utterance is like unto water for quenching the fire of hate and enmity which smouldereth within the hearts and breasts of men. By this single utterance contending peoples and kindreds will attain the light of true unity. Verily He speaketh the truth and leadeth the way. He is the All-Powerful, the Exalted, the Gracious.

It is incumbent upon everyone to show courtesy to, and have regard for the Aghṣán, that thereby the Cause of God may be glorified and His Word exalted. This injunction hath time and again been mentioned and recorded in the Holy Writ. Well is it with him who is enabled to achieve that which the Ordainer, the Ancient of Days hath prescribed for him. Ye are bidden moreover to respect the members of the Holy Household, the Afnán and the kindred. We further admonish you to serve all nations and to strive for the betterment of the world.

That which is conducive to the regeneration of the world and the salvation of the peoples and kindreds of the earth hath been sent down from the heaven of the utterance of Him Who is the Desire of the World. Give ye a hearing ear to the counsels of the Pen of Glory. Better is this for you than all that is on the earth. Unto this beareth witness My glorious and wondrous Book.

—*BAHÁ'U'LLÁH 1*

'Abdu'l-Bahá, the Center of Bahá'u'lláh's Covenant

The appointment of 'Abdu'l-Bahá as the Center of Bahá'u'lláh's Covenant came as no surprise to the members of Bahá'u'lláh's family, to the Bahá'ís living in the Holy Land and the Middle East, and to the officials and religious leaders in Palestine and Turkey. Born on the night that the Báb communicated His mission to Mullá Ḥusayn, 'Abdu'l-Bahá had since childhood shared in Bahá'u'lláh's sufferings and tribulations. As a boy of nine on a visit to the Síyáh-Chál, He had the soul-searing experience of seeing His beloved Father "haggard, dishevelled, freighted with chains." Soon after Bahá'u'lláh's release, 'Abdu'l-Bahá shared with Him the rigors of His banishment from their homeland.

In Baghdád, while still a child, it was 'Abdu'l-Bahá's unique distinction to recognize His Father's true station, a recognition that Shoghi Effendi says impelled Him to throw Himself at Bahá'u'lláh's feet "and to spontaneously implore the privilege of laying down His life for His sake."

During His youth in Baghdád, 'Abdu'l-Bahá served as His Father's amanuensis and won the admiration of erudite and accomplished elders with His lucid discourses and commentaries. Later, in Adrianople and then in 'Akká, He served as His Father's deputy, shielding Bahá'u'lláh from enemies, looking after the welfare of the Holy Family and their companions, meeting with government officials and religious dignitaries, making detailed arrangements for visiting pilgrims, carrying out manifold philanthropic activities to ease the plight of the people of 'Akká, and securing accommodations for Bahá'u'lláh outside the walls of the prison-city, thereby enabling Him to enjoy a measure of peace and tranquility that had long been denied.

Known throughout His life as 'Abbas Effendi ('Abbas being His given name and Effendi a Turkish title meaning "sir" or "mister") and as "'the Master'*" 'Abdu'l-Bahá was surnamed by Bahá'u'lláh the "'Most Great Branch'" and referred to in the Kitáb-i-Aqdas as the One* "Whom God hath purposed, Who hath branched from this Ancient Root." *After Bahá'u'lláh's passing, He chose to be known as 'Abdu'l-Bahá (the Servant of Bahá).*

'Abdu'l-Bahá was, Shoghi Effendi explains, "the unerring Interpreter" of Bahá'u'lláh's writings, "the perfect Exemplar" of Bahá'u'lláh's teachings, "the embodiment of every Bahá'í ideal," and "the incarnation of every Bahá'í virtue." His reality is best described by the title "Mystery of God" *given to Him by Bahá'u'lláh—a title signifying that, although 'Abdu'l-Bahá is not a Prophet, He combines, blends, and harmonizes the seemingly incompatible characteristics of human nature and superhuman knowledge and perfection.*

Having been elevated by Bahá'u'lláh to the office of Center of His Covenant, 'Abdu'l-Bahá was empowered, Shoghi Effendi says, "to impart an extraordinary impetus to the international expansion of His Father's Faith, to amplify its doctrine, to beat down every barrier that would obstruct its march, and to call into being, and delineate the features of, its Administrative Order, the Child of the Covenant, and the Harbinger of that World Order whose establishment must needs signalize the advent of the Golden Age of the Bahá'í Dispensation."

THERE HATH BRANCHED FROM the Sadratu'l-Muntahá[6] this sacred and glorious Being, this Branch of Holiness; well is it with him that hath sought His shelter and abideth beneath His shadow. Verily the Limb of the Law of God hath sprung forth from this Root which God hath firmly implanted in the Ground of His Will, and Whose Branch hath been so uplifted as to encompass the whole of creation. Magnified be He, therefore, for this sublime, this blessed, this mighty, this exalted Handiwork! . . . A Word hath, as a token of Our grace, gone forth from the Most Great Tablet[7]—a Word which God hath adorned with the ornament of His own Self, and made it sovereign over the earth and all that is therein, and a sign of His greatness and power among its people . . . Render thanks unto God, O people, for His appearance; for verily He is the most great Favor unto you, the most perfect bounty upon you; and through Him every mouldering bone is quickened. Whoso turneth towards Him hath turned towards God, and whoso turneth away from Him hath turned away from My Beauty, hath repudiated My Proof, and transgressed against Me.

6. The "Tree beyond which there is no passing"; in ancient times a tree Arabs planted to mark the end of a road. In the Bahá'í writings the term symbolizes the Manifestation of God; here it refers to Bahá'u'lláh.

7. The Kitáb-i-'Ahd, the Book of Bahá'u'lláh's Covenant.

He is the Trust of God amongst you, His charge within you, His manifestation unto you and His appearance among His favored servants . . . We have sent Him down in the form of a human temple. Blest and sanctified be God Who createth whatsoever He willeth through His inviolable, His infallible decree. They who deprive themselves of the shadow of the Branch, are lost in the wilderness of error, are consumed by the heat of worldly desires, and are of those who will assuredly perish.

—BAHÁ'U'LLÁH 2

BLESSED, DOUBLY BLESSED, IS THE GROUND which His footsteps have trodden, the eye that hath been cheered by the beauty of His countenance, the ear that hath been honored by hearkening to His call, the heart that hath tasted the sweetness of His love, the breast that hath dilated through His remembrance, the pen that hath voiced His praise, the scroll that hath borne the testimony of His writings.

—BAHÁ'U'LLÁH 3

O THOU WHO ART THE APPLE OF MINE EYE! My glory, the ocean of My loving-kindness, the sun of My bounty, the heaven of My mercy rest upon Thee. We pray God to illumine the world through Thy knowledge and wisdom, to ordain for Thee that which will gladden Thine heart and impart consolation to Thine eyes.

—BAHÁ'U'LLÁH 4

THE GLORY OF GOD REST UPON THEE and upon whosoever serveth Thee and circleth around Thee. Woe, great woe, betide him that opposeth and injureth Thee. Well is it with him that sweareth fealty to Thee; the fire of hell torment him who is Thine enemy.

—BAHÁ'U'LLÁH 5

WE HAVE MADE THEE A SHELTER for all mankind, a shield unto all who are in heaven and on earth, a stronghold for whosoever hath believed in God, the Incomparable, the All-Knowing. God grant that through Thee He may protect them, may enrich and sustain them, that He may inspire Thee with that which shall be a wellspring of wealth unto all created things, an ocean of bounty unto all men, and the dayspring of mercy unto all peoples.

—BAHÁ'U'LLÁH 6

THOU KNOWEST, O MY GOD, that I desire for Him naught except that which Thou didst desire, and have chosen Him for no purpose save that which Thou hadst intended for Him. Render Him victorious, therefore, through Thy hosts of earth and heaven . . . Ordain, I beseech Thee, by the ardor of My love for Thee and My yearning to manifest Thy Cause, for Him, as well as for them that love Him, that which Thou hadst destined for Thy Messengers and the Trustees of Thy Revelation. Verily, Thou art the Almighty, the All-Powerful.

—BAHÁ'U'LLÁH 7

WHEN THE MYSTIC DOVE WILL HAVE WINGED its flight from its Sanctuary of Praise and sought its far-off goal, its hidden habitation, refer ye whatsoever ye understand not in the Book to Him Who hath branched from this mighty Stock.

—*BAHÁ'U'LLÁH* 8

The Ascension of Bahá'u'lláh

Nine months before His ascension Bahá'u'lláh, as attested by 'Abdu'l-Bahá, had voiced His desire to depart from this world. From that time onward it became increasingly evident, from the tone of His remarks to those who attained His presence, that the close of His earthly life was approaching, though He refrained from mentioning it openly to any one. On the night preceding the eleventh of Shavvál 1309 A.H. *(May 8, 1892) He contracted a slight fever which, though it mounted the following day, soon after subsided. He continued to grant interviews to certain of the friends and pilgrims, but it soon became evident that He was not well. His fever returned in a more acute form than before, His general condition grew steadily worse, complications ensued which at last culminated in His ascension, at the hour of dawn, on the 2nd of Dhi'l-Qa'dih 1309* A.H. *(May 29, 1892), eight hours after sunset, in the 75th year of His age. His spirit, at long last released from the toils of a life crowned with tribulations, had winged its flight to His* "other dominions," *dominions* "whereon the eyes of the people of names have never fallen," *and to which the* "Luminous Maid," "clad in white," *had bidden Him hasten, as described by Himself in the Lawḥ-i-Ru'yá (Tablet of the Vision), revealed nineteen years previously, on the anniversary of the birth of His Forerunner.*

. . . .

With the ascension of Bahá'u'lláh draws to a close a period which, in many ways, is unparalleled in the world's religious his-

tory. The first century of the Bahá'í Era had by now run half its course. An epoch, unsurpassed in its sublimity, its fecundity and duration by any previous Dispensation, and characterized, except for a short interval of three years, by half a century of continuous and progressive Revelation, had terminated. The Message proclaimed by the Báb had yielded its golden fruit. The most momentous, though not the most spectacular phase of the Heroic Age had ended. The Sun of Truth, the world's greatest Luminary, had risen in the Síyáh-Chál of Ṭihrán, had broken through the clouds which enveloped it in Baghdád, had suffered a momentary eclipse whilst mounting to its zenith in Adrianople and had set finally in 'Akká, never to reappear ere the lapse of a full millennium. God's new-born Faith, the cynosure of all past Dispensations, had been fully and unreservedly proclaimed. The prophecies announcing its advent had been remarkably fulfilled. Its fundamental laws and cardinal principles, the warp and woof of the fabric of its future World Order, had been clearly enunciated. Its organic relation to, and its attitude towards, the religious systems which preceded it had been unmistakably defined. The primary institutions, within which an embryonic World Order was destined to mature, had been unassailably established. The Covenant designed to safeguard the unity and integrity of its world-embracing system had been irrevocably bequeathed to posterity. The promise of the unification of the whole human race, of the inauguration of the Most Great Peace, of the unfoldment of a world civilization, had been incontestably given. The dire warnings, foreshadowing catastrophes destined to befall kings, ecclesiastics, governments and peoples, as a prelude to so glorious a consummation, had been repeatedly uttered. The significant summons to the Chief Magistrates of the New World, forerunner of the Mission with which the North American continent was to be later invested,[8] had been issued. The initial contact with

8. The mission referred to is the Divine Plan of 'Abdu'l-Bahá for the promulgation of the Bahá'í Faith throughout the world.

a nation, a descendant of whose royal house was to espouse its Cause ere the expiry of the first Bahá'í century, had been established.[9] *The original impulse which, in the course of successive decades, has conferred, and will continue to confer, in the years to come, inestimable benefits of both spiritual and institutional significance upon God's holy mountain, overlooking the Most Great Prison, had been imparted. And finally, the first banners of a spiritual conquest which, ere the termination of that century, was to embrace no less than sixty countries in both the Eastern and Western hemispheres had been triumphantly planted.*[10]

In the vastness and diversity of its Holy Writ; in the number of its martyrs; in the valor of its champions; in the example set by its followers; in the condign punishment suffered by its adversaries; in the pervasiveness of its influence; in the incomparable heroism of its Herald; in the dazzling greatness of its Author; in the mysterious operation of its irresistible spirit; the Faith of Bahá'u'lláh, now standing at the threshold of the sixth decade of its existence, had amply demonstrated its capacity to forge ahead, indivisible and incorruptible, along the course traced for it by its Founder, and to display, before the gaze of successive generations, the signs and tokens of that celestial potency with which He Himself had so richly endowed it.[11]

—*SHOGHI EFFENDI*

BE NOT DISMAYED, O PEOPLES OF THE WORLD, when the day star of My beauty is set, and the heaven of My tabernacle is concealed from your eyes. Arise to

9. The descendant referred to is Queen Marie of Romania.

10. Shoghi Effendi wrote these words in 1944. By 1992 the Bahá'í Faith had spread to 116,000 localities in 173 countries and 45 significant territories and islands and stood behind Christianity as the second most widespread religion in the world.

11. *God Passes By,* pp. 221, 223–24.

further My Cause, and to exalt My Word amongst men. We are with you at all times, and shall strengthen you through the power of truth. We are truly almighty. Whoso hath recognized Me, will arise and serve Me with such determination that the powers of earth and heaven shall be unable to defeat his purpose.

—BAHÁ'U'LLÁH 9

LET NOT YOUR HEARTS BE PERTURBED, O people, when the glory of My Presence is withdrawn, and the ocean of My utterance is stilled. In My presence amongst you there is a wisdom, and in My absence there is yet another, inscrutable to all but God, the Incomparable, the All-Knowing. Verily, We behold you from Our realm of glory, and shall aid whosoever will arise for the triumph of Our Cause with the hosts of the Concourse on high and a company of Our favored angels.

O peoples of the earth! God, the Eternal Truth, is My witness that streams of fresh and soft-flowing waters have gushed from the rocks, through the sweetness of the words uttered by your Lord, the Unconstrained; and still ye slumber. Cast away that which ye possess, and, on the wings of detachment, soar beyond all created things. Thus biddeth you the Lord of creation, the movement of Whose Pen hath revolutionized the soul of mankind.

Know ye from what heights your Lord, the All-Glorious is calling? Think ye that ye have recognized the Pen wherewith your Lord, the Lord of all names, commandeth you? Nay, by My life! Did ye but know it, ye would renounce the world, and would hasten with your whole hearts to the presence of the Well-Beloved. Your spirits would be so transported by His Word as to throw into commotion the Greater World—how much more this small and petty one! Thus have the showers of My bounty been poured down from the heaven of My loving-kindness, as a token of My grace; that ye may be of the thankful. . . .

Beware lest the desires of the flesh and of a corrupt inclination provoke divisions among you. Be ye as the fingers of one hand, the members of one body. Thus counselleth you the Pen of Revelation, if ye be of them that believe.

Consider the mercy of God and His gifts. He enjoineth upon you that which shall profit you, though He Himself can well dispense with all creatures. Your evil doings can never harm Us, neither can your good works profit Us. We summon you wholly for the sake of God. To this every man of understanding and insight will testify.

—*BAHÁ'U'LLÁH 10*

WE REMEMBER EVERY ONE OF YOU, men and women, and from this Spot—the Scene of incomparable glory—regard you all as one soul and send you the joyous tidings of divine blessings which have preceded all created things, and of My remembrance that pervadeth everyone, whether young or old. The glory of God rest upon you, O people of Bahá. Rejoice with exceeding gladness through My remembrance, for He is indeed with you at all times.

—*BAHÁ'U'LLÁH 11*

THE TABLET OF VISITATION

THE TABLET OF VISITATION

Shortly after Bahá'u'lláh's ascension the Tablet of Visitation was compiled by Nabíl-i-A'ẓam at 'Abdu'l-Bahá's request from the writings of Bahá'u'lláh. Today it is most often read at the Shrines of Bahá'u'lláh and the Báb and in commemoration of the anniversaries of Their passing.

THE PRAISE WHICH HATH DAWNED from Thy most august Self, and the glory which hath shone forth from Thy most effulgent Beauty, rest upon Thee, O Thou Who art the Manifestation of Grandeur, and the King of Eternity, and the Lord of all who are in heaven and on earth! I testify that through Thee the sovereignty of God and His dominion, and the majesty of God and His grandeur, were revealed, and the Daystars of ancient splendor have shed their radiance in the heaven of Thine irrevocable decree, and the Beauty of the Unseen hath shone forth above the horizon of creation. I testify, moreover, that with but a movement of Thy Pen Thine injunction "Be Thou" hath been enforced, and God's hidden Secret hath been divulged, and all created things have been called into being, and all the Revelations have been sent down.

I bear witness, moreover, that through Thy

beauty the beauty of the Adored One hath been unveiled, and through Thy face the face of the Desired One hath shone forth, and that through a word from Thee Thou hast decided between all created things, causing them who are devoted to Thee to ascend unto the summit of glory, and the infidels to fall into the lowest abyss.

I bear witness that he who hath known Thee hath known God, and he who hath attained unto Thy presence hath attained unto the presence of God. Great, therefore, is the blessedness of him who hath believed in Thee, and in Thy signs, and hath humbled himself before Thy sovereignty, and hath been honored with meeting Thee, and hath attained the good pleasure of Thy will, and circled around Thee, and stood before Thy throne. Woe betide him that hath transgressed against Thee, and hath denied Thee, and repudiated Thy signs, and gainsaid Thy sovereignty, and risen up against Thee, and waxed proud before Thy face, and hath disputed Thy testimonies, and fled from Thy rule and Thy dominion, and been numbered with the infidels whose names have been inscribed by the fingers of Thy behest upon Thy holy Tablets.

Waft, then, unto me, O my God and my Beloved, from the right hand of Thy mercy and Thy loving-kindness, the holy breaths of Thy favors, that they may draw me away from myself and from the world unto the courts of Thy nearness and Thy presence. Potent art Thou to do what pleaseth Thee. Thou, truly, hast been supreme over all things.

The remembrance of God and His praise, and the glory of God and His splendor, rest upon Thee,

O Thou Who art His Beauty! I bear witness that the eye of creation hath never gazed upon one wronged like Thee. Thou wast immersed all the days of Thy life beneath an ocean of tribulations. At one time Thou wast in chains and fetters; at another Thou wast threatened by the sword of Thine enemies. Yet, despite all this, Thou didst enjoin upon all men to observe what had been prescribed unto Thee by Him Who is the All-Knowing, the All-Wise.

May my spirit be a sacrifice to the wrongs Thou didst suffer, and my soul be a ransom for the adversities Thou didst sustain. I beseech God, by Thee and by them whose faces have been illumined with the splendors of the light of Thy countenance, and who, for love of Thee, have observed all whereunto they were bidden, to remove the veils that have come in between Thee and Thy creatures, and to supply me with the good of this world and the world to come. Thou art, in truth, the Almighty, the Most Exalted, the All-Glorious, the Ever-Forgiving, the Most Compassionate.

Bless Thou, O Lord my God, the Divine Lote-Tree and its leaves, and its boughs, and its branches, and its stems, and its offshoots, as long as Thy most excellent titles will endure and Thy most august attributes will last. Protect it, then, from the mischief of the aggressor and the hosts of tyranny. Thou art, in truth, the Almighty, the Most Powerful. Bless Thou, also, O Lord my God, Thy servants and Thy handmaidens who have attained unto Thee. Thou, truly, art the All-Bountiful, Whose grace is infinite. No God is there save Thee, the Ever-Forgiving, the Most Generous.

—BAHÁ'U'LLÁH 1

REFERENCES

REFERENCES

Abbreviations Used

BHP	*Bahá'í Holy Places*
BK	*Bahíyyih Khánum*
BKG	*Bahá'u'lláh: The King of Glory*
BNE	*Bahá'u'lláh and the New Era*
DB	*The Dawn-Breakers*
DH	*Door of Hope*
ESW	*Epistle to the Son of the Wolf*
GPB	*God Passes By*
GWB	*Gleanings from the Writings of Bahá'u'lláh*
KI	*The Kitáb-i-Íqán*
MA	*Messages to America*
PB	*The Proclamation of Bahá'u'lláh*
PDIC	*The Promised Day Is Come*
PM	*Prayers and Meditations*
PUP	*The Promulgation of Universal Peace*
SC	*A Synopsis and Codification of the Kitáb-i-Aqdas*
TB	*Tablets of Bahá'u'lláh Revealed after the Kitáb-i-Aqdas*
TN	*A Traveler's Narrative*
WOB	*The World Order of Bahá'u'lláh*

PART 1 / A NOBLE YOUTH

Chapter 1 / Childhood

1 DB 12–13
2 GPB 94
3 DB 119–20
4 BNE 23–24

Chapter 2 / Youth

1 TN 34–35
2 BNE 24
3 PUP 25–26
4 DB 120–22

PART 2 / DISCIPLESHIP

Chapter 3 / Recognition of the Báb's Prophetic Mission

1 GWB 73–74
2 PM 84–86
3 PM 300

Chapter 4 / In the Service of the Cause of the Báb

1 DB 459–62
2 DB 299
3 DB 583–84
4 ESW 76–77
5 DB 461–62
6 DB 584
7 DB 375
8 KI 233–34
9 GWB 145–46
10 ESW 119–20
11 KI 234–36
12 KI 222–24
13 KI 225–27

PART 3 / PROMISED DAWN

Chapter 5 / Ṭihrán

1 DB 584–85
2 ESW 20–21
3 ESW 76–77
4 KI 190
5 DB 631–34
6 ESW 22
7 GPB 101–02
8 ESW 21
9 PB 57
10 GWB 103–04
11 WOB 124
12 PM 278–79
13 PM 20–21
14 PM 306–08
15 PM 301–02
16 PM 46–47
17 GPB 106
18 GPB 109

PART 4 / UNFOLDING REVELATION

Chapter 6 / Baghdád

1 ESW 21–22
2 GWB 228–29
3 TB 131
4 ESW 166
5 ESW 168
6 KI 249–50
7 GPB 115
8 PM 308–10
9 GPB 118
10 GPB 118
11 PM 234
12 BKG 117; GPB 118
13 DB 585
14 KI 250–51
15 GPB 119
16 GWB 88–90
17 GPB 126
18 KI 251–52
19 GPB 125
20 DB 585
21 PDIC 85
22 GPB 144
23 GWB 131–32
24 GWB 229–30
25 GPB 147
26 GPB 145
27 GPB 149
28 GWB 27–35

Chapter 7 / Constantinople

1 GWB 37
2 ESW 167–68
3 ESW 52
4 GWB 126–27
5 ESW 68–70
6 GWB 122–23
7 ESW 137–38
8 GWB 125
9 GPB 160–61
10 GPB 161
11 PDIC 40

Chapter 8 / Adrianople

1 ESW 157
2 ESW 70–71
3 ESW 164
4 GWB 146–48
5 TB 111–12
6 GPB 169
7 GPB 169–70
8 GPB 169
9 GPB 169
10 TB 75–76
11 GPB 170
12 GPB 171
13 GPB 171
14 GPB 171
15 GPB 171
16 PDIC 21–24
17 PB 47, 48–49, 50–54
18 GWB 219–20, 225–26, 230
19 PB 102–03
20 PDIC 24–25
21 GPB 180
22 GPB 181
23 GPB 179–80
24 PDIC 45–46

25 PDIC 46
26 GWB 129–30
27 WOB 178
28 PDIC 73–74
29 DB 585–86

Chapter 9 / 'Akká

1 GPB 184
2 GPB 185
3 GPB 186
4 GPB 187
5 GPB 187
6 ESW 52
7 GWB 99–100
8 ESW 56
9 GWB 115–16
10 PM 17–18
11 PM 103–06
12 PM 111–12
13 TB 233–34
14 PM 34–35
15 MA 33–34
16 MA 34
17 MA 34
18 GPB 189–90
19 ESW 23
20 GPB 190
21 GWB 100–01
22 BHP 65–66
23 BK 4
24 GPB 206
25 DB 586
26 PB 5–7
27 PB 17, 19–21
28 PB 27–29
29 PB 33–35
30 PB 83, 84–85
31 TB 262
32 TB 200
33 SC 7
34 SC 7
35 SC 7
36 GPB 216
37 GPB 216
38 GPB 216
39 PM 70–71
40 PM 200–01

Chapter 10 / Mazra'ih and Bahjí

1 DH 99
2 ESW 136–37
3 MA 34
4 MA 34–35
5 MA 35
6 MA 35
7 ESW 122–24
8 ESW 71–74
9 ESW 33–36
10 ESW 105–07
11 TB 40
12 ESW 125
13 TB 94–95
14 TB 59–60
15 ESW 86–88
16 TB 42–44
17 ESW 52–53
18 ESW 94–95
19 PM 230
20 PM 151–52
21 PM 242–43
22 PM 152–55
23 GPB 196
24 GWB 115–16
25 GPB 195–96

PART 5 / COVENANT

Chapter 11 / The Covenant of Bahá'u'lláh

1 TB 219–23
2 WOB 135
3 WOB 136
4 WOB 135
5 WOB 135
6 WOB 135–36
7 WOB 136
8 SC 27
9 GWB 137
10 GWB 139–40
11 TB 264

THE TABLET OF VISITATION

1 PM 310–13

EVENTS IN
THE LIFE OF
BAHÁ'U'LLÁH

EVENTS IN THE LIFE OF BAHÁ'U'LLÁH

Chapters 1 and 2 / CHILDHOOD AND YOUTH		**WORKS REVEALED BY BAHÁ'U'LLÁH DURING THIS PERIOD**
Birth of Bahá'u'lláh	12 November 1817	*(Because the precise dates of revelation are not available for many of Bahá'u'lláh's works, the titles are listed in alphabetical order. When specific information is known, it appears in parentheses after the title.)*
Birth of the Báb	20 October 1819	
Chapter 3 / RECOGNITION OF THE BÁB'S PROPHETIC MISSION		
Declaration of the mission of the Báb in Shíráz	23 May 1844	
Birth of 'Abdu'l-Bahá	23 May 1844	
Chapter 4 / IN THE SERVICE OF THE CAUSE OF THE BÁB		
Conference of Badasht	June 1848	
Death of Muḥammad Sháh; Accession of Náṣiri'd-Dín Sháh	4 September 1848	
Beginning of the Mázindarán upheaval at Shaykh Ṭabarsí	10 October 1848	
Imprisonment in Ámul	December 1848	

End of the upheaval at Shaykh Ṭabarsí	10 May 1849	
Martyrdom of the Báb	9 July 1850	
Chapter 5 / ṬIHRÁN		
Attempt on the life of Náṣiri'd-Dín Sháh	15 August 1852	
Imprisonment in the Síyáh-Chál of Ṭihrán	August 1852	Rashḥ-i-'Amá (Revealed in the Síyáh-Chál)
Chapter 6 / BAGHDÁD		
Banishment of Bahá'u'lláh to Baghdád	12 January 1853	Az-Bágh-i-Iláhí Báz-Áv-u-Bidih-Jámí Chihár-Vádí (The Four Valleys) Ghulámu'l-Khuld (The Youth of Paradise) Haft-Vádí (The Seven Valleys) Halih-Halih-Yá Bishárat Ḥúr-i-'Ujáb (The Wondrous Maiden) Ḥurúfát-i-Állín (The Exalted Letters) Javáhiru'l-Asrár (The Essence of Mysteries) Kalimát-i-Maknúnih (The Hidden Words) (circa 1858) The Kitáb-i-Íqán (The Book of Certitude) (1862) Lawḥ-i-Kullu'ṭ-Ṭa'ám (Tablet of All Food) Lawḥ-i-Bulbulu'l-Firáq (Tablet of the Nightingale of Bereavement) Lawḥ-i-Fitnih (Tablet of the Test)
Withdrawal of Bahá'u'lláh to Kurdistán	10 April 1854	
Return of Bahá'u'lláh from Kurdistán	19 March 1856	
Public declaration of the mission of Bahá'u'lláh in the Garden of Riḍván in Baghdád	22 April 1863	

EVENTS IN THE LIFE OF BAHÁ'U'LLÁH—*Continued*

Chapter 6 / BAG<u>H</u>DÁD *(cont.)*		**WORKS REVEALED BY BAHÁ'U'LLÁH DURING THIS PERIOD**
Departure from Garden of Riḍván for Constantinople	3 May 1863	Lawḥ-i-Hawdaj (Tablet of the Howdah) (Revealed on the journey to Constantinople) Lawḥ-i-Ḥúríyyih (Tablet of the Maiden) Lawḥ-i-Malláḥu'l-Quds (Tablet of the Holy Mariner) (Naw-Rúz 1863) Lawḥ-i-Maryam Madínat'ur-Riḍá (The City of Radiant Acquiescence) Madínatu't-Tawḥíd (The City of Unity) Munáját-i-Húríyyih (Prayer of the Maid of Heaven) Prayers (Revealed in Kurdistán) Qaṣídiy-i-Varqá'íyyih (Revealed in Kurdistán) Ṣaḥífiy-i-<u>Sh</u>aṭṭíyyih (Book of the River) Sáqí-Az-<u>Gh</u>ayb-i-Baqá (Revealed in Kurdistán) <u>Sh</u>ikkar-<u>Sh</u>ikan-<u>Sh</u>avand Subḥána-Rabbíya'l-A'lá Súratu'lláh (Súrih of God) Súriy-i-Nuṣḥ Súriy-i-Qadír (Súrih of the Omnipotent) Súriy-i-Ṣabr (Súrih of Patience, also known as Lawḥ-i-Ayyúb, Tablet of Job) (First day of Riḍván, 1863) Tafsír-i-Hú Tafsír-i-Ḥurúfát-i-Muqaṭṭa'ih (Interpretation of the Isolated Letters, also known as Lawḥ-i-Áyiy-i-Núr, Tablet of the Verse of Light)

Chapter 7 / CONSTANTINOPLE

Arrival of Bahá'u'lláh in Constantinople	16 August 1863	Lawḥ-i-'Abdu'l-'Azíz Va-Vukalá (Tablet to Sulṭán 'Abdu'l-'Azíz) Mathnavíy-i-Mubárák Subḥánáka-Yá-Hú (also known as Lawḥ-i-Náqús, Tablet of the Bell) (19 October 1863)

Chapter 8 / ADRIANOPLE

Arrival of Bahá'u'lláh in Adrianople	12 December 1863	Alváḥ-i-Laylatu'l-Quds Kitáb-i-Badí' Lawḥ-i-Aḥmad-i-'Arabí (Tablet of Aḥmad, Arabic) (circa 1865) Lawḥ-i-Aḥmad-i-Fársí (Tablet of Aḥmad, Persian) Lawḥ-i-Ashraf (Tablet of Ashraf) Lawḥ-i-Bahá (Tablet of Bahá) Lawḥ-i-Khalíl Lawḥ-i-Nápulyún I (First Tablet to Napoleon III) Lawḥ-i-Naṣír Lawḥ-i-Nuqṭih (Tablet of the Point) Lawḥ-i-Qamíṣ (Tablet of the Shirt or Robe) Lawḥ-i-Riḍván Lawḥ-i-Rúḥ (Tablet of the Spirit) Lawḥ-i-Salmán I (Tablet of Salmán) Lawḥ-i-Sayyáḥ (Tablet of Sayyáḥ) Lawḥ-i-Siráj Lawḥ-i-Sulṭán (Tablet to the Sháh of Persia, Náṣiri'd-Dín Sháh) Lawḥ-i-Tuqá (Tablet of Piety or the Fear of God) Munájátháy-i-Ṣiyám (Prayers for Fasting)
Departure of Bahá'u'lláh from Adrianople	12 August 1868	

EVENTS IN THE LIFE OF BAHÁ'U'LLÁH—*Continued*

Chapter 8 / ADRIANOPLE *(cont.)*		WORKS REVEALED BY BAHÁ'U'LLÁH DURING THIS PERIOD
		Riḍvánu'l-Iqrár Súriy-i-Aḥzán Súriy-i-Amr (Súrih of the Command) Súriy-i-Aṣḥáb (Súrih of the Companions) Súriy-i-Bayán Súriy-i-Damm (Tablet of Blood) Súriy-i-Ghuṣn (Tablet of the Branch) Súriy-i-Ḥajj I (Tablet of Pilgrimage for House of the Báb) Súriy-i-Ḥajj II (Tablet of Pilgrimage for House of Bahá'u'lláh) Súriy-i-Hijr Súriy-i-'Ibád (Súrih of the Servants) Súriy-i-Mulúk (Tablet of the Kings) Súriy-i-Qalam Súriy-i-Qamís Súriy-i-Ra'ís (Revealed on the journey to 'Akká) Súriy-i-Vidád
Chapter 9 / 'AKKÁ		
Arrival of Bahá'u'lláh in 'Akká	31 August 1868	Lawḥ-i-'Abdu'l-Vahháb Lawḥ-i-Aḥbáb (Tablet of the Friends) Lawḥ-i-Fu'ád
Death of Mírzá Mihdí, the Purest Branch	23 June 1870	Lawḥ-i-Haft Pursish (Tablet of Seven Questions) Lawḥ-i-Ḥikmat (Tablet of Wisdom)
Release from prison barracks to house within 'Akká	4 November 1870	Lawḥ-i-Hirtík Lawḥ-i-Ittiḥád (Tablet of Unity)

Murder of Siyyid Muḥammad and two of his companion Covenant-breakers in 'Akká	23 January 1872	Lawḥ-i-Malik-i-Rús (Tablet to the Czar) Lawḥ-i-Malikih (Tablet to Queen Victoria) Lawḥ-i-Mánikchí Ṣáḥib Lawḥ-i-Nápulyún II (Second Tablet to Napoleon III) Lawḥ-i-Páp (Tablet to the Pope) Lawḥ-i-Pisar-'Amm (Tablet to the Cousin) Lawḥ-i-Qad Iḥtaraqa'l-Mukhliṣún (The Fire Tablet) (circa 1871) Lawḥ-i-Ra'ís Lawḥ-i-Ru'yá (Tablet of Vision) (1 March 1873) Lawḥ-i-Salmán II (Tablet of Salmán) Lawḥ-i-Tibb (Tablet of Medicine) Súriy-i-Haykal (Súrih of the Temple)
Marriage of 'Abdu'l-Bahá and Munírih Khánum	August–September 1872	
Revelation of the Kitáb-i-Aqdas	1873	Kitáb-i-Aqdas (The Most Holy Book) (1873)

Chapter 10 / MAZRA'IH AND BAHJÍ

Bahá'u'lláh's departure from 'Akká for the Mansion of Mazra'ih and His first visits to the Riḍván Garden	early June 1877	Bishárát (Glad-Tidings) Ishráqát (Splendors) Kalimát-i-Firdawsíyyih (Words of Paradise) Lawḥ-i-Aqdas (The Most Holy Tablet) Lawḥ-i-Arḍ-i-Bá (Tablet of the Land of Bá) (1879) Lawḥ-i-Burhán (Tablet of the Proof) Lawḥ-i-Dunyá (Tablet of the World) Lawḥ-i-Maqṣúd (Tablet of Maqṣúd)
Bahá'u'lláh's occupation of the Mansion of Bahjí	September 1879	
Visit by Bahá'u'lláh to Haifa	1883	

EVENTS IN THE LIFE OF BAHÁ'U'LLÁH—*Continued*

Chapter 10 / MAZRA'IH AND BAHJÍ *(cont.)*		**WORKS REVEALED BY BAHÁ'U'LLÁH DURING THIS PERIOD**
Death of Navváb in 'Akká	1886	Lawḥ-i-Siyyid Mihdíy-i-Dahají Súriy-i-Vafá (Tablet to Vafá) Tablet of Trustworthiness (circa 1879) Tablet revealed in the house in the Garden of Riḍván Tablet to *The Times* of London (1891) Tajallíyát (Effulgences) (1885–86) Ṭarázát (Ornaments)
Two visits by Bahá'u'lláh to Haifa; revelation of the Tablet of Carmel; and Bahá'u'lláh's identification of the site of the future Shrine of the Báb	Spring 1890 and Summer 1891	Lawḥ-i-Karmil (Tablet of Carmel) (1891)
Bahá'u'lláh's revelation of *Epistle to the Son of the Wolf*	1891	Epistle to the Son of the Wolf (1891)
Chapter 11 / THE COVENANT OF BAHÁ'U'LLÁH		
Revelation of the Kitáb-i-'Ahd, Bahá'u'lláh's Book of the Covenant, the last Tablet revealed before His death	1892	Kitáb-i-'Ahd (The Book of the Covenant) (1892)

Ascension of Bahá'u'lláh	29 May 1892
Unsealing and reading of Bahá'u'lláh's Kitáb-i-'Ahd, the Book of the Covenant, at Bahjí	7 June 1892

GLOSSARY

GLOSSARY

Abá-Baṣír (Áqá Naqd-'Alí) Son of a Bábí martyr of the 1850–51 Zanján upheaval, he became one of Bahá'u'lláh's most steadfast followers in that city and was beheaded circa 1870 for refusing to recant his faith before a gathering of Muslim divines.

'Abdu'l-'Azíz, Sulṭán (1830–76) The Sulṭán of Turkey from 1861 to 1876. He was responsible for Bahá'u'lláh's banishments from Ba<u>gh</u>dád to **Constantinople**, from Constantinople to **Adrianople**, and from Adrianople to the prison-fortress of 'Akká. Willful and headstrong, he was known for his lavish expenditures and is stigmatized by Bahá'u'lláh in the Kitáb-i-Aqdas as occupying the "throne of tyranny." Bahá'u'lláh prophesied his downfall in a Tablet addressed to **Fu'ád Pá<u>sh</u>á**, the Ottoman foreign minister during Bahá'u'lláh's imprisonment in 'Akká. As a result of public discontent, which was heightened by a crop failure in 1873 and a mounting public debt, Sulṭán 'Abdu'l-'Azíz was deposed by his ministers in 1876. He died within a few days.

Adamic Cycle The cycle of religious history that began with Adam and ended with the Dispensation of the Báb. The present cycle, called the Bahá'í Cycle, or Cycle of Fulfillment, began with Bahá'u'lláh and is to last for five hundred thousand years.

Adrianople (Edirne) A city in northwest Turkey about 130 miles northwest of **Constantinople** (Istanbul) to which Bahá'u'lláh was exiled from 12 December 1863 to 12 August 1868. During the exile He suffered an attempt on His life by **Mírzá Yaḥyá** that, together with subsequent acts of treachery, forced Him to sever ties with His half-brother. After this *"most great separation"* Bahá'u'lláh's ministry reached its zenith with the revelation of the **Súriy-i-Mulúk**

(Tablet of the Kings) and Tablets to individual kings and leaders. In August 1868 **Sulṭán 'Abdu'l-'Azíz** banished Bahá'u'lláh from Adrianople to 'Akká.

Afnán Literally, twigs. Descendants of the Báb's three maternal uncles and His wife's two brothers.

Aghṣán Literally, branches. Sons and male descendants of Bahá'u'lláh.

Aḥmad, Shaykh (Shaykh Aḥmad-i-Aḥsá'í; 1743–1826) Founder of the Shaykhí school of Islám, the teachings of which prepared the way for the Báb. A respected interpreter of Islamic doctrine in the **Shí'ah** holy cities of Najaf and Karbilá, he attracted many followers even though his teachings departed from accepted Shí'ah doctrine. The primary theme of his teachings was the near advent of the long-awaited Promised One of Islám. He also taught that scriptural references to resurrection, to Muḥammad's night journey to heaven, and to the signs expected to accompany the advent of the Promised One should be interpreted as spiritual metaphors rather than as actual physical events. While traveling in Persia near the end of his life, he chose as his successor a disciple named **Siyyid Káẓim**, who eventually attained the presence of the Báb.

Aḥmad, Tablet of (Arabic) A Tablet revealed by Bahá'u'lláh around 1865 for a faithful believer from Yazd. Often read in times of trouble, it contains the remarkable promise, "Should one who is in affliction or grief read this Tablet with absolute sincerity, God will dispel his sadness, solve his difficulties and remove his afflictions." Another Tablet of the same name was revealed in Adrianople in Persian for Ḥájí Mírzá Aḥmad of Káshán, who later sided with **Mírzá Yaḥyá**.

Aḥmad-i-Azghandí, Mírzá (Mírzá Aḥmad) An erudite and ardent teacher of the Bahá'í Faith, formerly one of the most outstanding Muslim divines of Khurásán. Before the Báb's declaration of His mission in 1844, Mírzá Aḥmad-i-Azghandí compiled all of the Islamic prophecies and traditions pertaining to the advent of the long-awaited Promised One, an immense work containing almost twelve thousand traditions.

'Alí-Ján, Mullá A Bahá'í from Mázindarán who was executed in Ṭihrán in 1883.

'Alí-Muḥammad The Báb's given name.

'Álí Páshá (Muḥammad Amín 'Álí Páshá; 1815–71) One of the chief ministers of **Sulṭán 'Abdu'l-'Azíz**. As a close associate of **Fu'ád Páshá**, he shared responsibility for Bahá'u'lláh's successive banishments from Baghdád to **Constantinople**, from Constantinople to **Adrianople**, and from Adrianople to 'Akká. Bahá'u'lláh rebukes 'Álí Páshá in the Súriy-i-Ra'ís and the Lawḥ-i-Ra'ís, which are addressed to him.

Áqá Ján, Mírzá Bahá'u'lláh's amanuensis, attendant, and companion for forty years from the beginning of His exile in Baghdád until His ascension in 1892. Mírzá Áqá Ján is regarded as the first to have recognized Bahá'u'lláh's station as a Manifestation of God and was honored by Him with the title Khádimu'lláh (Servant of God). He broke Bahá'u'lláh's Covenant by turning against 'Abdu'l-Bahá after Bahá'u'lláh's passing.

Áqá Ján-i-Kaj-Kuláh (known as Kaj-Kuláh, or "Skew-Cap") An accomplice of **Siyyid Muḥammad** and a follower of **Mírzá Yaḥyá** who created many troubles for Bahá'u'lláh and His companions in Adrianople and 'Akká.

Áqá Khán-i-Núrí, Mírzá (I'timádu'd-Dawlih) Prime minister of Persia under **Náṣiri'd-Dín Sháh** during Bahá'u'lláh's imprisonment in the **Síyáh-Chál** (Black Pit) of Ṭihrán in August 1852.

Áqásí, Ḥájí Mírzá The bigoted, cruel, and treacherous prime minister of Persia under **Muḥammad Sháh**. Termed by **Shoghi Effendi** the "Antichrist of the Bábí Dispensation," he was "the chief instigator of the outrages perpetrated against the Báb." Eighteen months after blocking an interview between the Báb and the Sháh he fell from power and died, abandoned and impoverished.

Áqáy-i-Kalím See **Músá, Mírzá**.

Ashraf (Mírzá Ashraf-i-Ábádí) A great teacher of the Bahá'í Faith who was arrested and hanged in 1888 in Iṣfahán when Ẓillu's-

Sulṭán (eldest surviving son of **Náṣiri'd-Dín Sh// áh** and virtual ruler of two-fifths of Persia) discovered that one of his secretaries was learning about the Faith through him.

Ashraf-i-Zanjání A Bahá'í from Zanján who was martyred in 1870. Bahá'u'lláh often praised his steadfastness and that of his mother, who, when summoned to the scene of his execution in an effort to induce him to recant his faith, promised to disown him if he compromised his beliefs. Remaining faithful to the end, he was led to his death moments after his friend **Abá-Baṣír** was beheaded. He died with Abá-Baṣír's body in his arms.

Azal Literally, eternity. Refers to **Mírzá Yaḥyá**, who was also known as Ṣubḥ-i-Azal (Morning of Eternity).

Azalís Followers of Ṣubḥ-i-Azal, or **Mírzá Yaḥyá**.

Bahá, People of Followers of Bahá'u'lláh; Bahá'ís.

Bayán, The In general terms, the revelation of the Báb as set down in His writings. The term can also refer to two of His writings in particular—one in Persian, the other in Arabic.

Caravansary In eastern countries, an inn for caravans where they rest at night—usually a large, bare building surrounding a court.

Constantinople (Istanbul) The largest city and seaport in northwest Turkey to which Bahá'u'lláh was exiled for about four months from August through December of 1863. While in Constantinople Bahá'u'lláh refused to engage in the custom of visiting government officials to ask for favors. The Persian ambassador alleged that Bahá'u'lláh opposed governmental authority, resulting in an edict from **Sulṭán 'Abdu'l-'Azíz** banishing Him to **Adrianople**.

Farmán An order, command, or royal decree.

Fatḥ-'Alí Sháh Sháh of Persia from 1798 to 1834 who was notorious for his enormous number of wives and concubines, his incalculable progeny, and the disasters that his rule brought upon his country. Bahá'u'lláh's father, Mírzá Buzurg, was a minister of Fatḥ-'Alí Sháh.

Fu'ád Páshá (Keçeci-Zádih Muḥammad; 1815–69) One of the

chief ministers of **Sulṭán 'Abdu'l-'Aziz**. He shared responsibility with **'Álí Pa<u>sh</u>á** for Bahá'u'lláh's successive banishments from Ba<u>gh</u>dád to **Constantinople**, from Constantinople to **Adrianople**, and from Adrianople to 'Akká.

Heroic Age The period of Bahá'í history encompassing the ministries of the Báb, Bahá'u'lláh, and 'Abdu'l-Bahá. It began on 22 May 1844 with the Báb's declaration of His mission and ended in 1921 with the ascension of 'Abdu'l-Bahá or, more specifically, in 1932 with the passing of His sister, Bahíyyih <u>Kh</u>ánum, the Greatest Holy Leaf. It is also referred to as the Apostolic, or Primitive, Age.

Ḥijáz (also Hejaz, Hedjaz, or Al-Hijaz) A region in southwestern Arabia that is considered the holy land of the Muslims because it contains many places connected with the life of Muḥammad, including the sacred cities of Medina and Mecca.

Howdah A covered seat or pavilion carried by a mule, camel, horse, or other animal.

Ḥujjat (Mullá Muḥammad-'Alí of Zanján) Literally, the Proof. A title given by the Báb to an erudite Muslim cleric and Bábí convert who, from the pulpit, directed his disciples to embrace the Báb's Cause. He became the leader of the Bábís in Zanján and died in 1851 during the Zanján upheaval.

Ḥusayn <u>Kh</u>án, Ḥájí Mírzá (1827–81) Also known as **Mu<u>sh</u>íru'd-Dawlih**. The Persian ambassador to **Constantinople** who pressured the Ottoman authorities on behalf of the Persian government to banish Bahá'u'lláh from Ba<u>gh</u>dád to Constantinople, from Constantinople to **Adrianople,** and from Adrianople to 'Akká. Despite his plottings, he was favored with kindly and respectful words from Bahá'u'lláh testifying to the faithfulness and honesty with which he carried out his duties. In his later years Ḥájí Mírzá Ḥusayn <u>Kh</u>án came to regret his actions against Bahá'u'lláh. He sought forgiveness from 'Abdu'l-Bahá, used his influence to protect the Bahá'ís from persecution, and recognized that it was a mistake to have banished Bahá'u'lláh from Persia because he believed that one day people from all over the world would make pilgrimage to Bahá'u'lláh's shrine, just as Muslims visit Mecca.

Ḥusayn, Mullá (Mullá Ḥusayn-i-Bus͟hrú'í) The one to whom the Báb first declared His mission on 22 May 1844 and the first to believe in Him. Designated by the Báb as the Bábu'l-Báb (Gate of the Gate), he was known for his profundity of learning, tenacity of faith, courage, singleness of purpose, high sense of justice, and unswerving devotion. He became the first of eighteen **Letters of the Living.** In 1849 he died a martyr at the fort at S͟hayk͟h Tabarsí.

Ka'bih The cube-like stone building in Mecca that contains the Black Stone. It is the Muslim Qiblih, or point to which the faithful turn in prayer, and the goal of pilgrimage for Muslims.

Kamál Pás͟há (Yúsuf Kamál Pás͟há; 1808–76) A minister in the Court of **Sulṭán 'Abdu'l-'Azíz** who visited Bahá'u'lláh at the time of His exile in **Constantinople**. In 1861 he was appointed deputy to **Fu'ád Pás͟há**, the prime minister, and replaced him when Fu'ád Pás͟há resigned.

Kamálu'd-Dín, Ḥájí Mírzá A Bábí who went to Bag͟hdád seeking enlightenment from **Mírzá Yaḥyá**, whom he knew had been chosen by the Báb to be the nominal head of the Faith after His passing and until the Promised One appeared. After becoming disillusioned by Mírzá Yaḥyá's superficial response to his request for a commentary on a verse from Qur'án 3:93, he put the question to Bahá'u'lláh, Who revealed a Tablet known as the Lawḥ-i-Kullu'ṭ-Ṭa'ám (Tablet of All Food). Ḥájí Mírzá Kamálu'd-Dín recognized the author of the Tablet as the Promised One. Bahá'u'lláh cautioned him not to divulge his discovery and directed him to return to his home in Naráq, Persia, to share the Tablet with the Bábís there.

Káẓim (Mullá Káẓim) A learned Persian divine who became a Bahá'í in the early 1870s and was forced to leave his hometown when his conversion became known. His activities in spreading the Faith eventually brought him to the attention of S͟hayk͟h Muḥammad-Báqir (the Wolf), who ordered his death in Iṣfahán in 1877 and, after the execution, had his body hung from a pole in the public square, where it was subjected for three days to gross indignities.

Káẓim, Siyyid (Siyyid Káẓim-i-Ras͟htí; 1793–1843) Disciple and appointed successor of **S͟hayk͟h Aḥmad**. He continued the work of preparing other <u>Sh</u>ay<u>kh</u>í disciples to recognize the long-awaited Promised One of Islám and suffered many attacks and denunciations from the orthodox divines. Not long before his death he charged his disciples to scatter and search in earnest for the Promised One. One of those who responded was **Mullá Ḥusayn**, who became the first to find and recognize the Báb.

Letters of the Living The first eighteen people who independently sought out, found, and recognized the Báb. Included among them are **Mullá Ḥusayn**, the first to believe in Him; **Ṭáhirih**, the first woman to believe in Him; and **Quddús**, the eighteenth Letter of the Living and the most eminent among them.

Lote-Tree, Divine or **Sacred** One of Bahá'u'lláh's titles. The English translation stems from the Arabic term *Sadratu'l-Muntahá,* meaning, literally, "the tree beyond which there is no passing"—a reference to the tree that, in ancient Arabia, was planted to mark the end of a road.

Mázindarán The native province of Bahá'u'lláh in northern Persia that borders the Caspian Sea.

Mírzá A contraction of *amír-zádih* meaning "son of a prince, ruler, commander, or governor." When used after a name, it means "prince." When used before a name, it denotes a clerk, scribe, or scholar or conveys the honorific sense of "Mister."

Most Great Branch A title given by Bahá'u'lláh to 'Abdu'l-Bahá emphasizing 'Abdu'l-Bahá's station in relation to Bahá'u'lláh's.

Muezzin A Muslim crier who summons the faithful to prayer five times daily, usually from a minaret.

Muftí An expounder of Muslim law who gives a sentence or judgment on a point of religious jurisprudence.

Muḥammad-'Alí, Mírzá A son of Bahá'u'lláh and younger half-brother of 'Abdu'l-Bahá who opposed Him after Bahá'u'lláh's ascension and became the Arch-Breaker of Bahá'u'lláh's Covenant.

Muḥammad, Siyyid (Siyyid Muḥammad of Iṣfahán; Siyyid of Iṣfahán) Designated by **Shoghi Effendi** as "the Antichrist of the

Bahá'í Revelation" and described as a "black-hearted scoundrel" and the "living embodiment of wickedness, cupidity and deceit." Bahá'u'lláh refers to him in the Kitáb-i-Aqdas as the one who led **Mírzá Yaḥyá** astray.

Muḥammad-Qulí, Mírzá A faithful younger half-brother of Bahá'u'lláh who, reared in Persia under His care, later shared His exiles.

Muḥammad Sháh Sháh of Persia from 1834 to 1848. During his reign he left much of the affairs of his office in the hands of his prime minister and former tutor, **Ḥájí Mírzá Áqásí**, to the country's extreme detriment. At one point he sent an emissary named Siyyid Yaḥyáy-i-Dárábí (later known as **Vaḥíd**) to investigate the claims of the Báb. As a result of his investigation Siyyid Yaḥyá became a fervent Bábí, arousing Muḥammad Sháh's own interest in meeting the Báb. The Sháh summoned the Báb to Ṭihrán but then allowed Ḥájí Mírzá Áqasí—who feared the loss of his power and position—to order instead that the Báb be imprisoned in Máh-Kú, thus preventing the meeting. Muḥammad Sháh died in 1848.

Muḥsin Khán, Mírzá (Mu'inu'l-Mulk) Persian ambassador to Constantinople in the 1880s when the **Azalís** were plotting against the Bahá'ís.

Mullá Muslim priest, theologian, judge.

Músá, Mírzá (Áqáy-i-Kalím or Jináb-i-Kalím; d. 1887) A younger brother of Bahá'u'lláh who recognized the station of the Báb about the same time that Bahá'u'lláh did and who recognized Bahá'u'lláh's station and faithfully served Him throughout His exiles. Mírzá Músá often served as Bahá'u'lláh's deputy in meeting with government officials and religious leaders until 'Abdu'l-Bahá took on that function.

Mushír An honorific title bestowed by the Sháh or Sulṭán on a very high-ranking official. In civil circles it refers to someone of higher office than a minister; in military use, to a field or fleet marshal.

Mushíru'd-Dawlih Literally, advisor of the government. An honorific title bestowed on the Persian ambassador to **Constantinople**. See **Ḥájí Mírzá Ḥusayn Khán**.

Muṣṭafá, Mírzá A devoted Bahá'í who was martyred in Tabríz circa 1866/67 after his teaching activities aroused the Muslim clergy's anger. One of the early Bábís, he recognized Bahá'u'lláh's station upon attaining His presence in Baghdád before Bahá'u'lláh's public declaration of His mission.

Nabíl-i-A'ẓam A title of Mullá Muḥammad-i-Zarandí meaning "The Most Great Nabíl." He is the author of *The Dawn-Breakers,* a history of the early years of the Bahá'í Faith, and is often called Bahá'u'lláh's poet laureate.

Najaf-'Alí A Bahá'í who was martyred in Ṭihrán circa 1886/87. A survivor of the 1850–51 Zanján upheaval and one of the few to recognize Bahá'u'lláh's station during His exile to Baghdád, he bore Tablets of Bahá'u'lláh from **Adrianople** to Ṭihrán, in consequence of which he was brutally tortured and beheaded.

Naṣír, Ḥájí (Ḥájí Muḥammad-Naṣír) One of the few Bábís to survive the 1848–49 massacre at the fort at Shaykh Ṭabarsí, he was persecuted repeatedly for the rest of his life. After attaining Bahá'u'lláh's presence in 'Akká, he returned to Persia and settled in Rasht, where he taught the Faith continuously. There, although advanced in age, he was cast into prison, where he died as a martyr in 1888.

Náṣiri'd-Dín Sháh (1831–96) Successor to the Persian throne after **Muḥammad Sháh** and one of Persia's most notorious rulers, he reigned from 1848 to 1896. During his reign and by his orders the Báb was executed and Bahá'u'lláh was imprisoned in the **Síyáh-Chál** of Ṭihrán and, upon His release, banished from Persia. Bahá'u'lláh stigmatizes him as the "Prince of Oppressors."

Núr Literally, light. A district of the northern Iranian province of Mázindarán, where Bahá'u'lláh's ancestral home was located.

Primal Point A title of the Báb. According to Persian mystical tradition, all writing is said to originate from a point or dot.

Qayyúmu'l-Asmá' (Arabic) The Báb's commentary on the

Súrih of Joseph (Qur'án 12). Regarded by the Bábís as their Qur'án, it was revealed on the night of the Báb's declaration of His mission to **Mullá Ḥusayn**. The basic purpose of the book was to forecast what the true Joseph (Bahá'u'lláh) would, in a succeeding Dispensation, suffer at the hands of one who was at once His archenemy and blood brother.

Quddús Literally, the Most Holy. The title bestowed by the Báb on Ḥájí Muḥammad-'Alíy-i-Bárfurú<u>sh</u>í, the last **Letter of the Living**, who was second only to the Báb in rank. He accompanied the Báb on a pilgrimage to Mecca and attended the Conference of Bada<u>sh</u>t in June 1848. He joined the Bábís in the fort at <u>Sh</u>ay<u>kh</u> Ṭabarsí later that year and from there was taken to his native town of Bárfurú<u>sh</u>, where in 1849 he was martyred.

Riḍá-Qulí-i-Tafri<u>sh</u>í, Mírzá A follower of **Mírzá Yaḥyá** and an accomplice of **Siyyid Muḥammad** who publicly disgraced the Bahá'í Faith in 'Akká and whom Bahá'u'lláh expelled from the community of believers. He also participated with Siyyid Muḥammad in interpolating some Tablets of Bahá'u'lláh with passages intended to anger the local populace and distributed the falsified texts widely.

Riḍván Literally, paradise. The name given by Bahá'u'lláh to the Najíbíyyih Garden of Ba<u>gh</u>dád, to the Garden of Na'mayn near 'Akká, and to the annual twelve-day festival commemorating Bahá'u'lláh's declaration of His mission to His companions in 1863.

Sadratu'l-Muntahá See **Lote-Tree, Divine** or **Sacred**.

Ṣafá, Ḥájí Mírzá (Ḥájí Mírzá Ḥasan-i-Ṣafá) A man of learning and a leading figure among the Ṣúfís of **Constantinople** who was very respected in government circles. He had traveled widely in Africa and Asia and lived in Constantinople during Bahá'u'lláh's exile there. He visited Bahá'u'lláh more than once and, aware of Bahá'u'lláh's innate knowledge, evinced respect and humility. However, he collaborated with the Persian ambassador **Ḥájí Mírzá Ḥusayn <u>Kh</u>án** in spreading within influential circles false accusations about Bahá'u'lláh that the ambassador used to win the Sulṭán's order banishing Bahá'u'lláh to **Adrianople.**

Shaykh A title of respect given especially to a revered teacher or head of a Ṣúfí order.

Shaykhu'l-Islám A leading Shí'ah divine appointed by the Sháh in every large city to be head of the religious court.

Shí'ah Islám (Shí'ih) One of two major branches of Islám. Shiite Muslims regard the heirs of 'Alí as Muḥammad's legitimate successors and reject the other caliphs and **Sunní** legal and political institutions. Many Shiites await the appearance of the Twelfth, or Hidden, Imám. The Báb and Bahá'u'lláh considered Shí'ah Muslims followers of the true sect of Islám.

Shimírán, Gate of A northern district of Ṭihrán. In the 1850s it was on the edge of the city, close to a moat that was filled in during the reign of **Náṣiri'd-Dín Sháh**.

Shíráz The city in Iran that is the capital of the province of Fárs and the birthplace of the Báb. It was the scene of the Báb's declaration of His mission on 22 May 1844.

Shoghi Effendi The title by which Shoghi Rabbaní (1 March 1897–4 November 1957), great-grandson of Bahá'u'lláh, is generally known to Bahá'ís. (Shoghi is an Arabic name meaning "yearning" or "zeal"; Effendi is a Turkish equivalent for "sir" or "master.") He is the Guardian of the Bahá'í Faith, the position to which he was appointed in 'Abdu'l-Bahá's Will and Testament and which he assumed upon 'Abdu'l-Bahá's passing in 1921. Born to Ḍíyá'iyyih Khánum, 'Abdu'l-Bahá's eldest daughter, Shoghi Effendi is a descendant of the Báb through his father, Mírzá Hádí Shírází Afnán, and was raised in 'Abdu'l-Bahá's household under His tutelage.

Shujá'u'd-Dawlih, Prince A son of 'Alí-Sháh, the Ẓillu's-Sulṭán (Shadow of the King) during **Muḥammad Sháh's** reign from 1834 to 1848, and a grandson of **Fatḥ-'Alí-Sháh**. Prince Shujá'u'd-Dawlih visited Bahá'u'lláh's home in Baghdád and was prominent in the circle of **Ḥájí Mírzá Ḥusayn Khán**, the Persian ambassador in **Constantinople** who sent the prince to visit Bahá'u'lláh as his representative upon His arrival in Baghdád.

Síyáh-Chál The Black Pit. The subterranean dungeon in Ṭihrán in which Bahá'u'lláh and many Bábís were imprisoned from August through December 1852, following the attempted assassination of **Náṣiri'd-Dín Sháh** by a small group of misguided Bábís who sought to avenge the Báb's execution. Bahá'u'lláh received the intimation of His prophetic mission in the Síyáh-Chál, which is regarded by Bahá'ís as the holiest place in Ṭihrán.

Sublime Porte A reference to the Imperial Gate (or *Báb-i-Hümayun,* mistranslated by Westerners as "Sublime Porte") of the Sulṭán's palace in **Constantinople**, through which foreign ambassadors were admitted.

Sunní Islám The largest sect of Islám, it accepts the caliphs as Muḥammad's legitimate successors and as heads of Islám, denying the hereditary Imáms' claim to succession.

Súriy-i-Mulúk Bahá'u'lláh's Tablet of the Kings, revealed in **Adrianople**. Referred to by **Shoghi Effendi** as "the most momentous Tablet revealed by Bahá'u'lláh," it addresses collectively, and unequivocally and forcefully proclaims Bahá'u'lláh's station to, the monarchs of East and West, the Sulṭán of Turkey, the kings of Christendom, the French and Persian ambassadors to the Ottoman Empire, the Muslim clergy in **Constantinople,** the people of Persia, and the philosophers of the world. Passages from the Tablet that have been translated into English can be found in *Gleanings from the Writings of Bahá'u'lláh,* LXV, LXVI, CXIII, CXIV, CXVI, and CXVII and in *The Promised Day Is Come,* pp. 20–21 and 89–90.

Ṭáhirih Literally, the Pure One. The title given by the Báb to Fáṭimih Umm-Salamih (1817/18–1852)—also known by the titles Qurratu'l-'Ayn (Solace of the Eyes) and Zarrín-Táj (Crown of Gold)—the only woman among the **Letters of the Living**. She is remembered by Bahá'ís as the noblest member of her sex in, and the greatest heroine of, the Bábí Dispensation and the first martyr for the emancipation of women.

Taqí Khán, Mírzá (Mírzá Taqí Khán-i-Faráhání; Amír Kabír, "the Great Emir") Prime minister of Persia during the reign of **Náṣiri'd-Dín Sháh** and a bitter enemy of the Bábí Faith, he was involved in the persecution of Bábís at Shaykh Ṭabarsí, Nayríz, and Zanján and was responsible for the execution of the Báb. Eventually the Sháh dismissed him and, envious of his power, had him murdered.

Taqíy-i-Qazvíní, Mullá (Mullá Taqíy-i-Baraghání) The uncle and father-in-law of **Ṭáhirih,** he was extremely hostile to the teachings of **Shaykh Aḥmad** and **Siyyid Káẓim,** the heralds of the Báb. Because of his abusive tirades against their teachings, he was stabbed to death in his mosque in Qazvín in 1847 by one of their admirers. After His relatives went to Ṭihrán to accuse Bahá'u'lláh of helping the assassin to escape, Bahá'u'lláh was arrested and imprisoned. But the accusations were soon found to be baseless, and He was freed after a short time.

Túmán A Persian unit of currency.

'Ulamás The Muslim religious hierarchy.

Vaḥíd (Siyyid Yaḥyá; Siyyid Yaḥyáy-i-Dárábí) An erudite, eloquent, and influential emissary of **Muḥammad Sháh** who was sent by him to interrogate the Báb but was instead converted and became the most learned and influential of the Báb's followers. He was martyred in the Bábí upheaval at Nayríz in 1850.

Vazír (vizír, vizier) In Persia and the Ottoman Empire, the prime minister or minister of state.

Yaḥyá, Mírzá Also known as Ṣubḥ-i-Azal (Morning of Eternity), a younger half-brother of Bahá'u'lláh. The majority of Mírzá Yaḥyá's life was dominated by jealousy of Bahá'u'lláh to such a degree that he sought to undermine and eventually murder Him. A few months before the Báb's martyrdom, the Báb designated Mírzá Yaḥyá, in a Tablet addressed to Bahá'u'lláh, as His appointed nominee until such time as the Promised One would appear. This deflected attention from Bahá'u'lláh and left Him free to direct in His quiet but effective manner the activities of the Báb's disciples. When Bahá'u'lláh and His family were exiled from **Adrianople** to 'Akká, Mírzá Yaḥyá was sent to Cyprus, where he died in 1912 alone, dishonored, and forgotten.

BIBLIOGRAPHY

BIBLIOGRAPHY

The following works are those from which extracts were taken or from which material was used to prepare the explanatory passages. Readers seeking more information about the life of Bahá'u'lláh may wish to consult *Bahá'u'lláh; Bahá'u'lláh: The King of Glory; Bahá'u'lláh, The Prince of Peace: A Portrait; The Covenant of Bahá'u'lláh; God Passes By;* and *The Revelation of Bahá'u'lláh,* volumes 1–4.

'Abdu'l-Bahá. *Memorials of the Faithful.* Translated by Marzieh Gail. Wilmette, Ill.: Bahá'í Publishing Trust, 1971.

______. *The Promulgation of Universal Peace: Talks Delivered by 'Abdu'l-Bahá during His Visit to the United States and Canada in 1912.* Compiled by Howard MacNutt. 2d ed. Wilmette, Ill.: Bahá'í Publishing Trust, 1982.

______. *A Traveler's Narrative Written to Illustrate the Episode of the Báb.* Translated by Edward G. Browne. New and corrected ed. Wilmette, Ill.: Bahá'í Publishing Trust, 1980.

[Bahá'í International Community, Office of Public Information, New York]. *Bahá'u'lláh.* Wilmette, Ill.: Bahá'í Publishing Trust, 1991.

Bahá'u'lláh. *Epistle to the Son of the Wolf.* 1st pocket-size ed. Translated by Shoghi Effendi. Wilmette, Ill.: Bahá'í Publishing Trust, 1988.

______. *Gleanings from the Writings of Bahá'u'lláh.* 1st pocket-size ed. Translated by Shoghi Effendi. Wilmette, Ill.: Bahá'í Publishing Trust, 1983.

______. *The Kitáb-i-Íqán: The Book of Certitude.* 1st pocket-size ed. Translated by Shoghi Effendi. Wilmette, Ill.: Bahá'í Publishing Trust, 1983.

———. *Prayers and Meditations.* 1st pocket-size ed. Translated by Shoghi Effendi. Wilmette, Ill.: Bahá'í Publishing Trust, 1987.

———. *The Proclamation of Bahá'u'lláh to the Kings and Leaders of the World.* Haifa: Bahá'í World Centre, 1967.

———. *A Synopsis and Codification of the Kitáb-i-Aqdas: The Most Holy Book of Bahá'u'lláh.* [Compiled by the Universal House of Justice.] Haifa: Bahá'í World Centre, 1973.

———. *Tablets of Bahá'u'lláh Revealed after the Kitáb-i-Aqdas.* 1st pocket-size ed. Compiled by the Research Department of the Universal House of Justice. Translated by Habib Taherzadeh et al. Wilmette, Ill.: Bahá'í Publishing Trust, 1988.

Bahá'u'lláh, 'Abdu'l-Bahá, Shoghi Effendi, and Bahíyyih Khánum. *Bahíyyih Khánum: The Greatest Holy Leaf.* Compiled by the Research Department at the Bahá'í World Centre. Haifa: Bahá'í World Centre, 1982.

Bahá'u'lláh, the Báb, and 'Abdu'l-Bahá. *Bahá'í Prayers: A Selection of Prayers Revealed* by *Bahá'u'lláh, the Báb, and 'Abdu'l-Bahá.* New ed. Wilmette, Ill.: Bahá'í Publishing Trust, 1991.

Balyuzi, H. M. *'Abdu'l-Bahá: The Centre of the Covenant of Bahá'u'lláh.* London: George Ronald, 1971.

———. *The Báb: The Herald of the Day of Days.* Oxford: George Ronald, 1973.

———. *Bahá'u'lláh: The King of Glory.* Oxford: George Ronald, 1980.

———. *Eminent Bahá'ís in the Time of Bahá'u'lláh with Some Historical Background.* Oxford: George Ronald, 1985.

Blomfield, Lady (Sitárih Khánum). *The Chosen Highway.* Wilmette, Ill.: Bahá'í Publishing Trust, n.d.; repr. 1975.

Esslemont, J. E. *Bahá'u'lláh and the New Era: An Introduction to the*

Bahá'í Faith. 5th rev. ed. Wilmette, Ill.: Bahá'í Publishing Trust, 1980.

Gail, Marzieh. *Bahá'í Glossary.* Wilmette, Ill.: Bahá'í Publishing Trust, 1955.

Ḥaydar-'Alí, Ḥájí Mírzá. *Stories from the Delight of Hearts: The Memoirs of Ḥájí Mírzá Ḥaydar-'Alí.* Translated and abridged by A. Q. Faizi. Los Angeles: Kalimát, 1980.

Hofman, David. *Bahá'u'lláh, the Prince of Peace: A Portrait.* Oxford: George Ronald, 1992.

Momen, Moojan, ed. *The Bábí and Bahá'í Religions, 1844–1944: Some Contemporary Western Accounts.* Oxford: George Ronald, 1981.

Momen, Wendi, ed. *A Basic Bahá'í Dictionary.* Oxford: George Ronald, 1989.

Nabíl-i-A'ẓam [Muḥammad-i-Zarandí]. *The Dawn-Breakers: Nabíl's Narrative of the Early Days of the Bahá'í Revelation.* Translated and edited by Shoghi Effendi. Wilmette, Ill.: Bahá'í Publishing Trust, 1932.

Perkins, Mary. *Hour of the Dawn: The Life of the Báb.* Oxford: George Ronald, 1987.

Ruhe, David S. *Door of Hope: A Century of the Bahá'í Faith in the Holy Land.* Oxford: George Ronald, 1983.

Shoghi Effendi, comp. *The Bahá'í Faith 1844–1952.* Wilmette, Ill.: Bahá'í Publishing Committee, 1953.

[———]. *Directives from the Guardian.* New Delhi: Bahá'í Publishing Trust, n.d.

———. *God Passes By.* Rev. ed. Wilmette, Ill.: Bahá'í Publishing Trust, 1974.

———. *Messages to America: Selected Letters and Cablegrams Addressed to the Bahá'ís of North America, 1932–1946.* Wilmette, Ill.: Bahá'í Publishing Committee, 1947.

———. *The Promised Day Is Come.* 3d ed. Wilmette, Ill.: Bahá'í Publishing Trust, 1980.

———. *The World Order of Bahá'u'lláh: Selected Letters.* New ed. Wilmette, Ill.: Bahá'í Publishing Trust, 1991.

Taherzadeh, Adib. *The Covenant of Bahá'u'lláh.* Oxford: George Ronald, 1992.

———. *The Revelation of Bahá'u'lláh: Adrianople 1863–68.* Oxford: George Ronald, 1977.

———. *The Revelation of Bahá'u'lláh: 'Akká, The Early Years 1868–77.* Oxford: George Ronald, 1983.

———. *The Revelation of Bahá'u'lláh: Baghdád 1853–63.* Rev. ed. Oxford: George Ronald, 1976.

———. *The Revelation of Bahá'u'lláh: Mazra'ih & Bahjí 1877–92.* Oxford: George Ronald, 1987.

[The Universal House of Justice, comp.] *Bahá'í Holy Places at the World Centre.* Haifa: Bahá'í World Centre, 1968.

———. *Messages from the Universal House of Justice: 1963–86.* Wilmette, Ill.: Bahá'í Publishing Trust, Forthcoming.

———. *Wellspring of Guidance: Messages, 1963–68.* 2d ed. Wilmette, Ill.: Bahá'í Publishing Trust, 1976.